ECUMENISM, MEMORY, & GERMAN NATIONALISM, 1817–1917

RELIGION AND POLITICS
Michael Barkun, *Series Editor*

Other titles in Religion and Politics

Contemporary Muslim Apocalyptic Literature
David Cook

From Slogans to Mantras: Social Protest and Religious Conversion in the Late Vietnam Era
Stephen A. Kent

Islamist Opposition in Authoritarian Regimes: The Party of Justice and Development in Morocco
Eva Wegner

Localizing Islam in Europe: Turkish Islamic Communities in Germany and the Netherlands
Ahmet Yükleyen

Millennialism, Persecution, and Violence: Historical Cases
Catherine Wessinger, ed.

Missionary Politics in Contemporary Europe
José Pedro Zúquete

Priest-Indian Conflict in Upper Peru: The Generation of Rebellion, 1750–1780
Nicholas A. Robins

Religion and the Rise of Nationalism: A Profile of an East-Central European City
Robert E. Alvis

Tabernacle of Hate: Seduction into Right-Wing Extremism, Second Edition
Kerry Noble

ECUMENISM, MEMORY, & GERMAN NATIONALISM, 1817–1917

STAN M. LANDRY

SYRACUSE UNIVERSITY PRESS

First Edition 2014
14 15 16 17 18 19 6 5 4 3 2 1

An abridged version of Chapter 4 appeared as "That All May Be One? Church Unity and the German National Idea, 1866–1883," Stan M. Landry, *Church History* 80, no. 2 (June 2011): 281–301. Copyright © 2011 American Society of Church History. Reprinted with the permission of Cambridge University Press.

∞ The paper used in this publication meets the minimum requirements of the American National Standard for Information Sciences—Permanence of Paper for Printed Library Materials, ANSI Z39.48-1992.

For a listing of books published and distributed by Syracuse University Press, visit our website at www.SyracuseUniversityPress.syr.edu.

ISBN: 978-0-8156-3336-5 (cloth) 978-0-8156-5250-2 (e-book)

Library of Congress Cataloging-in-Publication Data

Landry, Stan M.
Ecumenism, memory, and German nationalism, 1817–1917 / Stan M. Landry. — First Edition.
pages cm. — (Religion and politics)
Includes bibliographical references and index.
ISBN 978-0-8156-3336-5 (cloth : alk. paper) — ISBN 978-0-8156-5250-2 (e-book) 1. Christianity and politics—Germany—History—19th century. 2. Nationalism—Germany—History—19th century. 3. Nationalism—Religious aspects—Christianity. 4. Germany—Church history—19th century. I. Title.
BR115.P7L273 2014
322'.1094309034—dc23 2013040789

Manufactured in the United States of America

For Jen

Stan M. Landry was born and raised in New Orleans, Louisiana. He studied history and philosophy at the University of New Orleans and modern German cultural history at the University of Arizona, where he earned the PhD in May 2010. He has been awarded several internationally competitive prizes, including grants from the German Academic Exchange Service (DAAD) and a Fulbright Fellowship from the Institute for International Education. Research for *Ecumenism, Memory, and German Nationalism, 1817–1917* was conducted at churches, archives, and libraries in Germany and the United States. He is published in *Church History*, the *Journal of Religion and Society*, and the *Lutheran Quarterly*. He currently serves as Lecturer in History at Arizona State University.

CONTENTS

ACKNOWLEDGMENTS

I OWE ENORMOUS debts of gratitude to Susan A. Crane, Susan Karant-Nunn, Peter W. Foley, Fabio Lanza, Suzanne L. Marchand, George S. Williamson, and Anthony J. Steinhoff. They have all read early, piecemeal, and final drafts of this manuscript and offered innumerable comments, criticisms, and insights. Nietzsche quipped that a student repays a teacher poorly if one always remains a student. My own evolution from student to scholar at the University of Arizona is a testament to Susan A. Crane's excellence as an advisor. In our many conversations, Susan Karant-Nunn made the sixteenth century present, while Peter W. Foley kept me firmly grounded in nineteenth-century German religion and theology. Fabio Lanza has been a careful reader of this manuscript, but more importantly, a good friend. And Sue Marchand, George Williamson, and Tony Steinhoff have all been extraordinarily generous with their time. Their wise counsel has improved this manuscript immeasurably.

I must also thank Manfred P. Fleischer for his advice in researching the histories of German ecumenism and for generously sharing his notes with me at the beginning of this process. In addition, I owe thanks to Thomas A. Brady for his suggestions in conceptualizing this project in its early stages. Attendees of meetings of the American Society of Church History, the German Studies Association, the Sixteenth-Century Conference, and an informal works in progress seminar at the University of Arizona also offered invaluable comments on my research. Indeed, a single perceptive question from Jesse A. Spohnholz at the Sixteenth-Century Conference in Montreal in 2010 helped me to structure the narrative of this manuscript. Finally, the editors and anonymous readers of Syracuse University Press offered thoughtful and detailed suggestions for revising the manuscript that made it much stronger overall. *Ecumenism, Memory, and German Nationalism, 1817–1917*, would not have been possible without the input and insights of the aforementioned. Any imperfections that remain in the manuscript are a result of my own oversight.

I should also thank the library staffs at the University of Arizona and the University of Arizona Special Collections, the Pitts Theology Library at Emory University, the Eberhard-Karls University of Tübingen, the Bavarian State Library, and archivists and librarians at the German Evangelical Church (EKD) archives in Stuttgart, Düsseldorf, and Karlsruhe for their tireless help. Research was made possible by the generous financial support of a University of Arizona Barbara Payne Robinson Fellowship; a University of Arizona Social and Behavioral Sciences Research Institute dissertation research grant; and most of all, a German Academic Exchange Service (DAAD) dissertation research grant. An abridged version of chapter 4 appeared in the journal *Church History: Studies in Christianity and Culture* 80, no. 2 (June 2011). In addition to the anonymous reviewers of the article, I must thank the editors of *Church History* and Cambridge University Journals for permission to reproduce here material from my writings.

I will always remember Anke, Leo, and Veit for their wonderful hospitality in Tübingen and for lessons in preparing Swabian food. Their warmth and companionship made it much more bearable to be away from family, friends, and home for so long. Finally, I must thank my wife Jennifer and my family and friends for their extraordinary patience with me on those many days in which I would work from the time I awoke until it was time for bed. Their encouragement and support made this manuscript possible. It is dedicated to them.

INTRODUCTION

THIS ALTERNATIVE HISTORY of German national unification had its origins, oddly enough, in a conference room in Montreal, Quebec. In October 2010, I delivered a paper to the Society for Reformation Research on the topic of the 1883 anniversaries of Martin Luther's birth. With tongue planted firmly in cheek, I thanked the audience for allowing an historian of nineteenth-century Germany to crash their sixteenth-century conference. After the panel, one of the audience members graciously approached me to assure that I would always be welcome at their meetings. After all, he remarked, historians of the sixteenth century are quite dedicated to liberating the histories of the Protestant Reformation from the staid and standard narratives that were produced by German historians writing during the nineteenth century.[1] Contemporary historians of nineteenth-century Germany who were willing to revisit the master narratives of modern German history might only contribute to this process.

While it had not occurred to me at the conference, over time I began to recognize that I, too, was working to emancipate German histories from German historians who had written during the nineteenth century. But instead of the Reformation, I was concerned with how the master narratives of nineteenth-century German nationalism might have been colored by nineteenth-century nationalist historians. Writing during the late nineteenth century and looking back in time for foundational myths upon which to anchor what was in fact a disparate and discontinuous history of German national unification, these historians massaged German history in order to justify Otto von Bismarck's *kleindeutsch* unification of Germany under

Prussian leadership and to suggest that the German Reich established in 1871 represented the culmination of previous centuries of German history and the only possible outcome of popular German nationalism.[2] But this reading of German history—rife with Prussian bias and teleological blind spots—tended to obscure other voices and parallel movements that espoused competing conceptions of the German national idea. This manuscript seeks to restore to view a nationalist movement that has so far occupied the historical blind spots and the shadows of German national unification—German Christian ecumenism.

When the German lands liberated themselves from Napoleonic France in 1814, a century of debate ensued about how best to define and construct the new German nation. But nineteenth-century German nationalists who sought to realize a unified German nation-state were faced with two overwhelming barriers: the political fragmentation of the German lands and the confessional divide between German Catholics and Protestants. Indeed, during the early nineteenth century, the confessional divide increasingly became not only a religious but a national-political problem in the German lands. After the Napoleonic Wars, the German Wars of Liberation, and the redrawing of the map of Europe at the 1815 Congress of Vienna, religious and political boundaries no longer coincided.[3] This led to a reconfessionalization of European Christianity and corresponding increases in religious conflict.[4] Coupled with the emergence of European nationalism and the modern political nation-state, this meant that from the early nineteenth century forward, the confessional divide and the German National Question—or how to define and construct a German nation—would be inextricably linked.

Even after 1871, when the German nation was unified politically, the confessional divide persisted as a national-political problem. And because the confessional divide touched nearly every social, cultural, and political question in the German lands, any solution to the German National Question that failed to bridge the gap between Catholics and Protestants was necessarily incomplete. But in fact there was a nationalist movement that attempted to negotiate the political and religious diversity of the German lands—the Christian ecumenical movement. Arguing that interconfessional peace was a precondition for any unified German nation-state, German proponents of church unity suggested how to address the national question and the confessional question all at once.

This volume argues that Christian ecumenism points to an alternative path of German nationalism and that nineteenth-century German ecumenists contributed to uniting the German people across profound social, political, and cultural divisions that had existed since the Reformation. In a nation deeply split by religious difference, ecumenism was essential to the unification of the German nation as a whole. The efforts of these ecumenists were not on behalf of a secular or political religion that worshipped the nation as a god. Instead, German ecumenists included bona fide Christians who believed that bridging the confessional divide would best serve the interests of national unity. Indeed, I hope this book will restore what has so far been obscured in the conventional narratives of German national unification and show that the unification of Germany under the auspices of iron and blood was neither inevitable nor uncontested. Ideas of the German nation were constructed not only through the marginalization and exclusion of minorities, but also by promoting unity across long-standing internal divides.

Two Master Narratives of German History: The Course of National Unification and the Confessional Divide between Catholics and Protestants

The standard narratives of German national unification suggest that a modern national consciousness among Germans first developed as a result of German involvement in the Napoleonic Wars. After the liberation of the German lands from the French Empire, the conventional histories of German national unification suggest that the paramount issue facing midcentury German nationalists was whether the nation would take a "greater German" (*großdeutsch*) or "smaller German" (*kleindeutsch*) complexion. Advocates of the "greater German" position sought the establishment of a German nation under the auspices of the Austrian Empire, while supporters of the "smaller German" solution wished to exclude Austria and proposed a unified nation of north German states to be led by Prussia.

Beginning in the early nineteenth century and proceeding through the Revolutions of 1848, German nationalism seemed as if it would proceed on an inexorable march toward realization in a liberal German nation-state. However, the ascendance of Prussia, the decline of the Austrian Empire, and the political and military machinations of Otto von Bismarck resulted in a "revolution from above" and the establishment of a Prussian-led German Empire. Thus the master narratives of German unification typically begin with Germany's liberation from Napoleonic France, proceed through the European revolutions, and find resolution in the establishment of the empire.

But alongside each of these developments—all of which are considered the bellwethers of German nationalism and German national unification—were Christian ecumenists and ecumenical groups who warned that the German National Question could never be properly resolved until the confessional divide between Catholics and Protestants was overcome. In each of these instances, German ecumenism represented a competing and popular expression of German nationalism. Indeed, whenever and wherever the German Question was most fiercely debated, ecumenists were there to proffer their own vision of the German national idea. While not part of the master narratives of German nationalism and national unification, this ecumenical impulse persisted, and expressions of ecumenical nationalism were articulated at the same sites of German nationalism that the old narratives recognize.

This suggests that rather than being marginal to German nationalism, "ecumenical nationalism" was intrinsic to the process of German national unification. The recurrence of the impulse to heal the confessional divide for the sake of German national unity has its own history—one that parallels the master narratives of German unification and complements recent revisionist scholarship on nineteenth-century German nationalism. This revisionist scholarship has challenged the master narrative by pointing to how local and regional concerns; dynastic loyalties; and gender, social, and cultural status all informed the construction of the German national idea.[5] This manuscript is indebted to that scholarship, but it goes a step further to ask how confessional identity and difference colored the construction of the nineteenth-century German national idea.

To be sure, many nineteenth-century nationalists routinely exploited differences among German Catholics, Protestants, and Jews to construct confessionally and racially exclusive notions of German national identity. And historians of German religion have conducted a great deal of valuable research into what is called the "confessionalization of the national idea," or how Germans appealed to religious identities and differences to define confessionally exclusive ideas of the German nation.[6] So the relationship between German nationalism and the confessional divide has been well covered. But the relationship between German nationalism and those efforts to bridge the confessional divide has so far been ignored. If nationalists used confessional identity and difference to construct racially and confessionally exclusive ideas of the German nation, the question is begged: how might have proponents of church unity imagined the German nation and German national identity? Historians of the confessionalization of the national idea have only considered how confessional antagonism contributed to ideas of the German nation. They have not asked how interconfessional cooperation and those efforts to overcome intra-Protestant and interconfessional divides might have also colored ideas of the German nation and German national identity. This leaves open a historiographical niche—the "interconfessionalization," or "ecumenization," of the national idea—into which I envision this manuscript fitting. Nineteenth-century German ecumenists imagined a confessionally unified German nation in a union of the separated churches that was inclusive of both Catholics and Protestants. *Ecumenism, Memory, and German Nationalism, 1817–1917*, acknowledges that the confessional divide is critical to understanding nineteenth-century German nationalism. But instead of focusing on how confessional antagonism and conflict informed German nationalism, it explains how ecumenical efforts to overcome religious difference and heal the confessional divide shaped the German national idea.

The term *ecumenism* comes from the Greek *oikoumene*, meaning "universal" or "the entire world." It was first used in its contemporary sense to describe the desire for Christian unity during the nineteenth century.[7] The terms *irenic* and *irenical* were also widely used during the nineteenth century.[8] Irenicism refers to the desire for rapprochement, mutual understanding, and interconfessional peace between separated Christian confessions. It may or may not imply a desire for church unity but carries a stronger connotation than "toleration." Ecumenism refers to the desire for all those ideas encapsulated by irenicism, but also for an eventual union of separated churches and confessions, usually in a manner that accommodates the distinctive beliefs and practices of both. This might include a formal union of the separated churches or an association of separated congregations and religious communities. It could manifest itself as a lay or a clerical movement. Ecumenism does not necessarily entail a synthesis of confessionally divided congregations or a conversion of one church to another; it could also entail a broader understanding of the church universal that included formerly separated confessions. In the case of nineteenth-century German ecumenism, it might be useful to imagine an "ecumenical continuum" whose simplest desiderata were mutual understanding, accommodation, and interconfessional peace and whose ultimate ideal was ecclesiastical union.[9] In a nation so heavily encumbered by the confessional divide between Catholics and Protestants, any act from rapprochement to reunion that can be mapped onto this continuum represented a unifying force in the lives of the German people and the German nation.

The ecumenization of the national idea had been obscured by nineteenth-century German nationalist historians and by another master narrative of German history—the ostensible strength of the confessional divide. Still a historiographical article of faith amongst present-day German historians, the religious divide between nineteenth-century Catholics and Protestants inflected much of German society, culture, and politics. But it was not absolute.

Nineteenth-century German Catholics, Protestants, and in fact Jews lived in shared social and cultural spaces. Their communities engaged each another both in conflict and coexistence, and their interests and experiences often overlapped.[10]

Recent works by Helmut Walser Smith, as well as Konrad Jarausch and Michael Geyer, suggest how historians might acknowledge the strength of the German confessional divide while still recognizing those interconfessional encounters and overlapping experiences.[11] Smith's *The Continuities of German History* (2008) is especially helpful as a model for integrating continuities over the *longue durée* of German history, such as the confessional divide, while challenging teleological views like those of the nineteenth-century nationalist historians. Smith himself was responding to the work of Konrad Jarausch and Michael Geyer in *Shattered Past* (2003), which argued that German history has been characterized by rupture and conflict rather than continuity but at the same time stressed the need to recognize multiple subjects and multiple histories rather than a single, teleological narrative of German history. I see *Ecumenism, Memory, and German Nationalism* occupying a space between these two important works—restoring the forgotten subjects and histories of German ecumenical nationalism to historical consciousness but still acknowledging the depth of the German confessional divide over the long run.

In addition to elucidating coexistence and cooperation across the confessional divide, *Ecumenism, Memory, and German Nationalism* complicates the very idea of the German confessional divide. Originally referring to the social, cultural, and political differences that existed between Roman Catholics and Lutherans in the Holy Roman Empire, the confessional divide later included Reformed Christians with the Westphalian Peace of 1648. The legal recognition of Reformed Christians created an intra-Protestant divide between Lutherans and Reformed, in addition to the general Catholic-Protestant divide that included Catholic-Lutheran and Catholic-Reformed subdivisions. This is to say nothing of the Christian-Jewish divide in the German lands; the status of Christian dissenters, nonconformists, and nonbelievers; and the divides within a confession between orthodox and heterodox members.

But multiple confessional divides meant multiple ideas of church unity and expressions of ecumenism. Indeed, at times there seemed to be as many ecumenisms as ecumenists in nineteenth-century Germany, each of whom sought to heal intra-Protestant, Catholic-Evangelical, and Christian-Jewish divides. And to be sure, the precise meaning of the terms ecumenical and irenical could be loose and fluid in such cases. But despite the nature of the confessional divide in question and the proposed ecumenical solution, peace, mutual understanding, cooperation, solidarity, and community were almost always the common goals among German ecumenists.

As the confessional divide was conceived to permeate every aspect of German society, culture, and politics, by healing that divide ecumenists imagined that they might solve every problem that proceeded from it—most notably the German National Question. More than a begrudging religious toleration for the sake of national solidarity, church unity constituted a panacea for not only the national question, but for every problem that resulted from the division between German Catholics and Protestants. This in itself should be enough to compel us to consider the as yet unacknowledged relationship between ecumenism and German nationalism.

This is precisely why *Ecumenism, Memory, and German Nationalism* examines the histories of German nationalism and German national unification from an interconfessional perspective—one that underlines the interaction and overlapping histories of German Catholics and Protestants rather than treating each group in isolation. Histories of nineteenth-century German society, culture, and politics have been predicated on the ostensible strength of the confessional divide. These same histories have assumed a close relationship between Protestantism and German nationalism. This manuscript complicates that relationship by revealing how Catholics, Protestants, and Christian ecumenists alike participated in the formation of the German national idea—pointing to an interconfessional history of

German nationalism. As such, it occupies a space among revisionist accounts of German unification and within the historiography of the confessionalization of the national idea. But *Ecumenism, Memory, and German Nationalism* departs from both to explore how German national identity was imagined across the confessional divide and conceived as a confessionally unified political community.

In addition to reviving a forgotten and parallel vision of German nationalism, I hope this book will reveal that it was ecumenical nationalists who were instrumental in uniting the German people and the German nation. Their campaigns to heal the confessional divide and to foster mutual understanding, peace, and cooperation between German Catholics and Protestants were as effective as any law or decree from Berlin at bridging deep divisions within German society and culture. The confessionally inclusive German national idea to which they were dedicated helped to complete what was until then Germany's unfinished national unification.

Indeed, in a 2006 essay, the historian George S. Williamson remarked that "any analysis of modern German religious history must start from the fact of Germany's confessional divide."[12] And to be sure, there is much religious conflict in nineteenth-century German history. But we may ask: is it necessary that any analysis of modern German religious history must end with the confessional divide? Historians of Germany are naturally concerned with confessionalism because since the Reformation, confession had served as the most salient expression of German social identity and difference. But that is precisely why the history of ecumenism in nineteenth-century Germany is noteworthy. It represents efforts to bridge the confessional and social divides that had for so long separated the German people. After all, to imagine a reunion of the separated confessions was to imagine a notion of German unity. Indeed, the history of ecumenism suggests that issues of paramount importance in nineteenth-century Germany, issues of unity and diversity, identity and difference, need not have been settled through conflict or decided by iron and blood; they could also have been resolved in an ecumenical manner, through dialogue, mutual understanding, and cooperation. This is why the history of ecumenism in nineteenth-century Germany points to a parallel history of German nationalism—one that flourished and competed with the conventional narratives of German national unification, but also one whose ecumenical campaigns, be they wholly, partly, or only moderately successful, were essential in helping Germans negotiate the confessional divide.

Ecumenism, Memory, and National Identity

The ecumenism and the nationalism of nineteenth-century proponents of church unity recounted in this manuscript was heavily informed by German collective memories of religion. Indeed, images and memories of Martin Luther and the Protestant Reformation were instrumental to how ecumenical nationalists imagined religious union and German national unity. German ecumenists sought to unite Catholics and Protestants by appropriating two of the most authoritative and foundational sites of memory in nineteenth-century Germany: Martin Luther and the Protestant Reformation. Memories of Luther and the Reformation provided a useable past for Germans that could be used and abused in order to shape the present. But memories of Luther and the Reformation were rarely neutral or uncontested. German Catholics and Protestants, orthodox Christians and ecumenists, political radicals and reactionaries all claimed to best represent the memories and legacies of Luther and the Reformation. As with so many national heroes, the invocation of Martin Luther could divide as well as unite a community.

The German collective memory of religion informed how one approached the German confessional divide. In turn, one's relationship to the confessional divide colored one's attitude toward the German National Question. Thus Luther and the Reformation functioned as mnemonic tools that nationalists used in the construction of the German national idea. But memories of Luther and the Reformation had historically been confessional—the exclusive purview of German Protestants. Refashioning them from icons of religious separation into symbols of national unity accessible to all Germans, proponents of church unity deployed ecumenical memories of Luther and the Reformation to ground their inclusive ideas of the German nation.

The historian Thomas Nipperdey began his magisterial history of nineteenth-century Germany with the quip, "In the beginning was Napoleon." By this he meant that the paramount issues of nineteenth-century German history, those issues of national unity and diversity, German identity and difference, had their origins in the Napoleonic Wars, the dissolution of the Holy Roman Empire, and the German Wars of Liberation.[13] But Nipperdey could, and perhaps should, have opened *Germany from Napoleon to Bismarck, 1800–1866* (1996) with this observation: "In the beginning was Luther." Napoleon may have been the short-term cause of nineteenth-century Germany's political, social, and cultural situation. But contemporaries who sought to rebuild and redefine Germany after liberating themselves from Napoleonic France located the origins of so many of those contested issues of German unity and diversity and identity and difference with Martin Luther and the German Reformation. The effects of the schism between the churches, the politicization of the Reformation by secular princes, the separation of the confessions, and the eventual process of confessionalization[14] were still manifest well into the nineteenth century, when the German national question came to the fore. From then on the national question was inseparable from the German confessional question. And one could not address the confessional question, or how German Catholics and Protestants should best coexist and cooperate in a multiconfessional Germany, without directly confronting, or at least thinking around, memories of Luther and the Reformation.

The theoretical framework for the memory angle of this manuscript owes its debts to Maurice Halbwachs's notion of collective memory and Pierre Nora's concept of sites of memory. Halbwachs distinguished between personal memories and collective memories, or those memories that we frame in terms of their relation to some group to which we belong.[15] Whereas one might assume that personal memories and collective memories oppose one another, Halbwachs noted that every personal memory must be mediated by some social or collective framework. According to Halbwachs, "We often replace our remembrances within a space and time whose demarcations we share with others [and] situate them within dates that have meaning only in relation to a group to which we belong".[16] Thus we remember the past through the context or viewpoint of the social groups to which we belong. For Halbwachs, these collectives are "confined in space and time," that is, historical, and keep alive memories that are important to the collective.[17]

Collectives may include nations, cultures, locales, religious communities, and social organizations—essentially any social group with which an individual identifies. Collectives may also exist within collectives, such as the orthodox, liberal, and ecumenical religious collectives that existed within their wider churches in nineteenth-century Germany. Collective memories and the shared commemoration of common sites of memory lend cohesion to and define a community.[18] Indeed, collectives construct their identities as distinct and cohesive groups by appealing to their shared memories of the past.[19] But memory can be selective. What a collective chooses to remember and forget defines that group's collective identity. Memory is selective in another way, as it can be invoked to support a group's interests and ideologies. Memory is present-oriented and recall is context-dependent. That is, collective memory relates itself to contemporary events and situations, so that memories become meaningful within the context in which they are being recalled.[20]

Each collective that I consider in this manuscript remembered Luther and the Reformation in such ways as to reinforce their own interconfessional identities and their distinctive notions of German confessional and national unity. Their collective memories of Luther and the Reformation were not always populated by specific references to Luther's works, teachings, or episodes from his life. They were also informed by popular traditions, folk memories, and nineteenth-century accounts of Luther and the Reformation, all of which were mediated by one's collective identities. These memories of Luther and the Reformation colored how nineteenth-century ecumenists imagined church unity and the German nation, and their ideas of church unity and the German nation colored the memories they invoked. Thus their collective memories and identities existed in a dialectic relationship, each mutually reinforcing one another.

The French historian Pierre Nora referred to those spaces around which a collective's memories and identities crystallize as sites of memory. According to Nora, a site of memory is "any significant entity, whether material or nonmaterial in nature, which by dint of human will or the work of time has become a symbolic element of the memorial heritage of any community."[21] That is, sites of memory are places, people, customs, objects, and ideas, including museums, archives, cemeteries, collections, festivals, anniversaries, treaties, depositions, monuments, sanctuaries, and private associations that have been invested with some mnemonic significance that intentionally evokes or triggers memories.[22] The purpose of these sites is to remind the community of the presence of its past: to stop time and thus stop forgetting and to buttress the collective memory and identity of a community.[23] In nineteenth-century Germany, Luther and the Reformation were sites of memory that functioned as "foundational events, multifaceted usable historical realities and conflict-afflicted sites of memory."[24] Some German nationalists invoked these memories on behalf of a confessionally exclusive notion of German identity, but ecumenists deployed memories of Luther and the Reformation to bridge the confessional divide for the sake of German unity.

Each chapter of this volume corresponds to an episode from nineteenth-century German history that underlines the close relationships between the confessional divide, the collective memory of religion, and German nationalism. Indeed, nineteenth-century German ecumenism was most prevalent during those moments when the idea of the German nation and the meaning of German national identity were hotly contested and highly ambiguous. And in every instance, memories of Luther and the Reformation were deployed to ground these competing notions of the German national idea.

The ecumenical impulse within German nationalism first appeared after the German emancipation from Napoleonic France, when German nationalism was in its nascent stages. It emerged again during the 1840s, when popular frustration with secular and ecclesiastical authorities erupted into a revolution that sought to reimagine the German nation. It recurred in the 1860s, when atheism, liberalism, and revolution were perceived to threaten traditional notions of German identity and unity. And it arose yet again after Germany's formal unification in 1871, when minority religious communities were marginalized by the German state in order to realize cultural uniformity. Its culmination came at the 1917 anniversaries of the Reformation, where German Catholics and Protestants invoked postconfessional memories of Luther to affirm their shared national identities.

Nineteenth-century German ecumenism was not just a means to reunite the separated confessions. It was also a way of imagining German national unity and a response to the ostensible limitations of parallel nationalist movements that failed to take the confessional divide into account. This points to the connections among each ecumenical group recounted in this book and suggests why the ecumenical impulse continued to recur and to garner popular support despite its lack of formal success at uniting the churches: namely, because the ecumenical efforts in each of these cases represented differing reactions to the same root cause—the confessional divide and its hindrance of German national unity. Indeed, nineteenth-century German ecumenism represented an attempt to address the German confessional and national questions all at once, questions that nineteenth-century proponents of church unity saw as inextricably linked. The above episodes in German history are lenses through which we may view a panorama of debates about interconfessional relations and discover the significance of these debates for ideas of German confessional and national unity and identity. Each moment represents a site at which religion, memory, and political culture intersected and new ideas of German confessional and national unity were imagined.

The first of these moments begins in 1817 and in Prussia. After the dissolution of the Holy Roman Empire in 1806, German nationalists became consumed with how to build a German nation-state. In this nascent period of the German Question, religious affiliation was still a primary signifier of German identity. As such, the Reformation anniversaries of 1817 provided a useable past for German nationalists to ground their notions of German national identity. German ecumenists celebrated the anniversaries in common with Catholics, Protestants, and in some cases, even Jews, suggesting a way of being German that cut across the confessional divide. The interconfessional commemoration of Luther and the Reformation at these anniversaries underscores the close relationship among German collective memories of religion, Christian ecumenism, and nascent ideas of the German nation. Although obscured by teleological narratives of German nationalism, the Reformation anniversaries of 1817 represented the first example of a recurring ecumenical cum nationalist impulse that sought to repair the confessional divide for the sake of German national solidarity.

The second chapter recounts the "revolutionary ecumenism" of two dissident religious communities. The Revolutions of 1848 were the loci of mid-nineteenth-century German nationalism. And support for a revolutionary solution to the German Question came from both sides of the confessional divide. Theology served as an ersatz politics in revolutionary Germany, and the efforts of the ecumenical "German Catholic" movement and Protestant Friends to unite the confessions were easily translated into national-political terms. These groups invoked Luther as a revolutionary figure upon which to ground their "Reformation of the nineteenth century" and to justify their dissent from the established Catholic and Protestant churches. Their wildly popular campaigns were undertaken on behalf of a revolutionary ecumenism—a model of religious and national unity dedicated to the establishment of a general Christian communion consisting of Catholics and Protestants united in their subversion of ecclesiastical and secular authorities for the cause of freedom of religion, conscience, and German unity. While the ecumenical and nationalist movements of the "German Catholics" and Protestant Friends perished with the failure of the Revolutions of 1848, the ecumenical impulse to unite the separated confessions for the sake of German national unity persisted.

Although the Revolutions of 1848 had failed, conservatives worried as liberal nationalist movements continued to threaten traditional Europe. This led a group of prominent German conservatives to meet in Erfurt in 1860 to propose that a nation might be conceived in the confessionally reunited subjects of a German Christian state to be led by a holy alliance of Austria and Prussia. Chapter 3 examines these reactionary ecumenists and their conception of the Austro-Prussian holy alliance as an inclusive form of German political unity and a buttress against atheism, liberalism, nationalism, and the kleindeutsch unification of the German lands. Invoking Luther as a bulwark against revolution and espousing a sacralized vision of Großdeutschland that acknowledged Prussian's increasing hegemony over the German lands, this conception of unity sought to mediate between a simple kleindeutsch or groß vision of the German nation by appealing to the shared Christian histories and traditions of Catholic and Protestant Germans. Their model of unification not only accounted for the confessional divide, but also acknowledged the political realities of a conservative and multicultural Austria and an increasingly powerful Prussia. And their eschewal of liberal nationalism for a union of Austria and Prussia was consistent with the contemporary political structure of the German Confederation. While their ecumenical dreams were deferred upon the outbreak of the Austro-Prussian War of 1866, the Erfurt Group anticipated the tensions later caused by Germany's incomplete unification and heavily influenced the next generation of German Christian ecumenists.

Despite the political unification of the German Empire in 1871, the long-standing confessional divide between German Catholics and Protestants persisted. Proving that previous generations of ecumenists had been right all along, the new German government sought to address the persistence of this divide. But instead of the inclusive solution proposed by generations of German ecumenists, the new German imperial government sought to address the confessional divide by creating and enforcing religious homogeneity, most famously through the *Kulturkampf* legislation. Indeed, the establishment of a kleindeutsch German Empire under Prussian-Protestant hegemony, the anti-Catholic policies of the Kulturkampf and the 1883 Luther anniversaries all conflated Protestantism with German national identity and facilitated the marginalization of German Catholics from contemporary society, culture, and politics. Most German Catholics withdrew into socially isolated milieux. However, as the fourth chapter illustrates, Ut Omnes Unum—an ecumenical group of German Catholics and Protestants—challenged the conflation of Protestantism and German national identity. As the center of German nationalism's weight shifted from making Germany to making Germans, Ut Omnes Unum proposed an interconfessional notion of German national identity inclusive of both Catholics and Protestants. As such, the group represented a biconfessional and ecumenical opposition to Bismarck and the Kulturkampf, and thus a Catholic third way between withdrawal into an isolated Catholic milieu and the Protestant marginalization of German Catholicism.

The final chapter considers how the confessional divide as a national-political issue was overcome. The outbreak of the First World War compelled German Catholics and Protestants to close ranks and declare a cessation in confessional hostilities in response to a shared external threat. The Reformation anniversary festivals of 1917, which were celebrated in spite of the war, functioned as sites of memory at which Catholics and Protestants mutually invoked Luther as a universally accessible German hero, and thus a touchstone for an interconfessional German identity. Those anniversaries pointed to the "deconfessionalization" of the relationship between the national question and the confessional question and the culmination of a century of ecumenical efforts to fashion an interconfessional German national idea. After 1917, confessional antagonism rarely gained traction as a determinant of German national identity, and Protestant and exclusivist historical narratives that posited straight lines between Luther and Bismarck or 1517 and 1871 were mostly rejected. To be sure, the confessional truce between German Catholics and Protestants would not result in a formal union of the separated churches or eliminate all instance of confessional antagonism. But one lasting effect of this truce was the acceptance of a notion of being German that included both Catholics and Protestants.

ECUMENISM, MEMORY, & GERMAN NATIONALISM, 1817–1917

1

FOR THE SAKE OF THE GERMAN FATHERLAND

Church Unity and the German National Idea at the 1817 Reformation Anniversaries

ON OCTOBER 14, 1806, Napoleon Bonaparte passed through the university town of Jena after crushing the vaunted Prussian army at the battles of Jena and Auerstedt. A witness—the young philosophy professor G. W. F. Hegel—remarked that Napoleon represented a world-historical soul who seemed to dominate the entire world from horseback, and Hegel confessed that it was impossible not to admire the French emperor. Hegel's would prove to be a minority opinion among Germans. In that same fateful year, the Holy Roman Empire would be dissolved; Napoleon would march triumphantly through Berlin; and French troops would be garrisoned throughout the Prussian Kingdom, which became a client state of the French Empire.

Hegel's admiring views of the emperor notwithstanding, the disastrous events of 1806 unleashed a wave of anti-French sentiment and German patriotism throughout the Old Reich. In his *Speeches to the German Nation* (1808), the philosopher J. G. Fichte roused his fellow Germans—which he defined in terms of a shared language and culture—in defense of their fatherland. The fitness guru Friedrich Ludwig Jahn founded social clubs that combined physical education, patriotic song, and moral education in order to foster a Prusso-German patriotism in which Prussia took pride of place among the German lands. And the writer Erntz Mortiz Arndt—who exclaimed that he hated all the French without exception, in the name of God and his people—envisioned the lesser German polities dissolving into an Austro-Prussian German state. These combined sentiments later manifested themselves as a nascent German nationalism.[1] Anti-French and protonationalist feelings were stoked even more when Prussia rejected French rule and joined an alliance including Austria, Russia, the United Kingdom, Sweden, and Spain that would help to defeat Napoleon in a series of conflicts known in Prussia as the Wars of Liberation (1813–1815). After the allied victories and the emancipation of Prussia and other German client states from French rule, demands for social and political reform, nostalgia for the old Reich, and the desire for a unified German nation-state became more prominent.

In response to these demands, the Prussian statesmen Karl vom Stein and Karl August von Hardenberg pursued a course of reforms that was intended to convert Germans from compliant subjects into active citizens.[2] Popularly known as a revolution from above and undertaken during the Napoleonic occupation while the Prussian king Friedrich Wilhelm III (r. 1797–1840) was weak, these policies sought to modernize the Prussian state and its administration and to unite the Prussian people against the French revolutionary threat. The Stein-Hardenberg era was inaugurated with meritocratic reforms of the Prussian military that were designed to address the defeats at Jena and Auerstedt.[3] In addition to the overhaul of the Prussian army, serfdom was abolished, restrictions on the sale of land to non-nobles were lifted, taxes were made uniform between town and country, and some political liberties were extended to Jews. The Stein-Hardenberg reforms had begun during the Napoleonic occupation and proceeded through the Wars of Liberation. But by the fall of 1817, the process of reform had begun to stall. The restored Prussian king had failed to make good on some promises—most notably a Prussian constitution—and the competing interests of the monarchy, aristocracy, and bureaucracy limited additional reforms. This led reformers within the Prussian Kingdom to grow ever more impatient.

Thus on October 18, 1817 a group of German university students with liberal and nationalist tendencies, many of whom were veterans of the Wars of Liberation, assembled at the Wartburg Castle in Eisenach. United under the mantra of "Honor, Freedom, Fatherland" (*Ehre, Freiheit, Vaterland*) the students agitated for a reform of German colleges, demanded the liberal constitution that King Friedrich Wilhelm had promised, and envisaged a unification of the German states. The occasion for the Wartburg Festival itself was heavy with nationalist sentiments. October 18, 1817 was in fact the fourth anniversary of the Battle of Leipzig, a decisive Prussian victory over Napoleon. Moreover, the year 1817 was the tercentennial of the Protestant Reformation, and the students' demands and the Wartburg Castle itself were steeped in memories of Martin Luther and the Reformation.[4] The Wartburg Castle was the place where Saxon duke Friedrich the Wise (1463–1525) had given refuge to Martin Luther after the latter's excommunication from the Roman Catholic Church. Here Luther had translated the New Testament from Greek into German, creating a standardized German language that nationalists such as Fichte would later identify as the defining characteristic of the German nation.

Luther himself seemed present among the students, who celebrated the reformer as a German citizen and patriot who had embodied the liberal characteristics of reason, virtue, and freedom. The celebrants of the festival sang the Lutheran hymn "A Mighty Fortress"—which Heinrich Heine would later call the German Marseillaise—along with other patriotic songs. And in a ritual that recalled Luther's ostentatious burning of the papal bull that excommunicated him, they burned books written by conservative and anti-democratic authors. As such, the celebrants of the Wartburgfest identified the Reformation as the first salvo of a long process of German national liberation and unification. Indeed, claimed the students, just as Luther had freed the German people from the spiritual bondage of the Roman Catholic Church, the Wartburger, celebrants of the Wartburg Festival, would advocate for the political liberation of the

German states from the conservative princes. This use and abuse of religious icons was not accidental. The appeal to images and memories of religion permeated the histories of nineteenth-century German nationalism.

The year 1817 would in fact prove to be a watershed year for German nationalism. Wartburg seemed to represent a defining moment in the nascent German nationalist movement. And, indeed, conventional narratives of German national unification point to the 1817 Wartburgfest as one of the earliest instances of a nationalism that culminated in the unification of the German Empire in 1871. But in fact, early German nationalism was a diffuse phenomenon. It represented neither a single coherent ideology nor an orientation to a consistent vision of the German nation. Thus the Wartburgfest represented only one strain of early German nationalism—one whose contemporary significance and relationship to the fait accompli of 1871 was exaggerated by later German nationalists searching for a foundational myth upon which to ground their current ideologies.

But just two weeks after the Wartburgfest, a quite different idea of what it meant to be German—and what a unified German nation might look like—was expressed by celebrants of the three hundredth anniversaries of the Protestant Reformation. Though not as overtly political as the Wartburgfest, these anniversaries—which were celebrated throughout Protestant Germany and represented as much of a pan-German event as the assembly of several hundred students in Eisenach—functioned as a platform for an alternate vision of a unified German nation. Less concerned with constitutions or forms of government, the celebrants of these anniversaries envisioned a unified German nation that was based on a shared Christian religion.

In the German lands, where religious affiliation was still a primary signifier of identity and difference and the confessional divide between Catholics and Protestants was so deeply entrenched, to imagine a union of the separated churches—or at least a shared Christian religion—was perhaps the most obvious and immediate means of imagining a unified German nation. To this end, and on the occasion of the Reformation anniversaries, unions of the Reformed and Lutheran Churches were effected with royal and popular support, first in Prussia and then throughout the German lands. First conceived as a Prussian royal initiative with the intention of consolidating political and ecclesiastical authority, these unions attracted widespread support but also provoked raucous opposition from orthodox Lutherans. This impulse toward intra-Protestant unity was accompanied by expression of interconfessional Christian unity. The festivities surrounding the anniversaries were attended by German Catholics, Protestants, and in some cases, Jews, all of whom sought peaceful coexistence and cooperation with one another for the sake of German solidarity. In some cases, the possibility of formal reunions of the separated Catholic and Protestant Churches were floated in the interests of German unity.

As with the Wartburger, celebrants of the Reformation anniversaries appealed to a distinct memory of Luther and the Reformation that gave credence to their visions of German unity. But rather than invoking the enlightened and bourgeois Luther as the students at Wartburg did, celebrants of the 1817 anniversaries recalled a Luther who eschewed sectarianism and who might serve as a German national hero accessible to all Germans. During this uncertain and nascent period of German nationalism, it was only natural to appeal to foundational and authoritative German icons. Indeed, memories of Luther and the Reformation provided a useable past for nineteenth-century Germans that could be deployed in order to shape the present. And in fact, the presence of the past—especially memories of Martin Luther and the Protestant Reformation—ran through the subsequent histories of German nationalism like a black, gold, and red thread. The issues of religion and nationalism were in fact inextricably linked. How one approached Luther and the Reformation colored how one approached the contemporary confessional divide. And one's orientation to the confessional question inflected how one thought of the national question. The significance of this relationship between memory, religion, and nationalism endured throughout the long nineteenth century and was part and parcel of this strain of "ecumenical" German nationalism.

It is the task of this chapter to uncover the origins of what has been erased in the standard narratives of German nationalism. The foundational myths of the master narratives—most notably the Wartburgfest—have tended to obscure competing forms of German nationalism such as the intra-Protestant and interconfessional ecumenism of the 1817 Reformation anniversaries. But rather than being marginal to the national question, religious identity and difference were intrinsic to what it meant to be German. Thus I intend to chart the Reformation anniversaries of 1817 as the start of a recurring impulse in the histories of German nationalism. This impulse was dedicated to the same ends as the Wartburger—a unified German nation—but the nation of the anniversary celebrants was defined by the vision of a shared German Christian religion informed by memories of Martin Luther and the Protestant Reformation.

The 1817 Reformation Anniversaries

Anniversaries are moments at which memories are recollected, contested, and remade. Anniversaries focus the mind on the objects of their commemoration. But memory is historically conditioned. Memories of the past evoked by anniversaries are remembered in relation to contemporary concerns. The meaning of the memories and the anniversaries that commemorate them are remade in the process.[5] The memory of Luther and the Reformation had been commemorated at anniversary festivals throughout Germany every hundredth year since 1617. Individual states also celebrated anniversaries to commemorate their states' or ancestral rulers' adoption of Lutheranism or Calvinism. And each Reformation anniversary reflected changes in how Luther was remembered.

The 1617 Reformation anniversary was an orthodox affair. Celebrated like holy days such as Christmas and Easter rather than as memorial days, the centennial of the Reformation reflected the contemporary concern with Lutheran confession building and the establishment of a Lutheran orthodoxy. Indeed, from 1550 to 1700, Luther was the subject of dogmatic theology and confessional polemics, and contemporary representations and memories of the reformer concentrated on his doctrine rather than his person.[6] The 1717 Reformation anniversary was celebrated in the spirit of German Pietism. Pietism was associated with a renewal of individual spirituality, and Luther's eighteenth-century biographers, increasingly laymen rather than clerics, emphasized the reformer's pious zeal and individual personality.[7] Despite the different inflections of their commemorations—one orthodox and the other Pietist—the 1617 and 1717 Reformation anniversary celebrations were both strictly Lutheran affairs. Neither German Calvinists, Catholics, nor Jews participated in either anniversary celebration.[8] But the 1817 Reformation anniversaries were celebrated in an irenical and ecumenical fashion, with German Catholics, Reformed Christians, and in some cases Jews attending and participating in the festivities for the first time.

Changing ecclesiastical and political conditions in the late eighteenth and early nineteenth centuries pointed to the viability of both intra-Protestant and interconfessional unity. By the early nineteenth century, confessional relations had improved in Germany and Austria. Dogmatic differences between denominations were blunted by enlightened opposition to the religious enthusiasm of the seventeenth century and by 150 years of respite from religious war.[9] From 1750 to 1790, the sense of Protestant solidarity waned and confessional tensions decreased as Roman Catholicism became less of a threat to Protestantism and it became clear that no great power was any longer dedicated to abolishing any particular confession.[10] During the French Revolution, Protestant governments found an unlikely ally in the papacy to condemn the regicidal and republican French state. And during the Wars of Liberation, German Catholics and Protestants united in opposition to Napoleon.[11] Napoleon's dissolution of the German ecclesiastical states—sovereign territories within the German lands that were ruled by bishops—maintained the trend of increasing confessional integration even after the Wars of Liberation. These developments were also consistent with the irenical character of the contemporary German Awakening Movement. Leaders of the Awakening Movement, including the cleric Nikolaus von Zinzendorf (1700–1760), the Jesuit Johann M. Sailer (1751–1832), and the Lutheran theologian Gottfried Thomasius (1802–1875), de-emphasized confessional difference, making a pan-Christian spirituality possible.

In addition to structural factors, subjective motives contributed to increasing confessional integration and cooperation. Historians have noted the existence of a postrevolutionary renewal of piety among intellectuals in the figures of the German Catholic theologian and mystic Franz von Baader (1765–1841), who proposed a "holy alliance" of Christian states and a reunion of the Roman and Orthodox Churches, and Ignaz Lindl (1774–1846), a south German Catholic priest who preached an apocalyptic and ecumenical message to Catholics and Protestants in Bavaria.[12] The figures of von Baader and Lindl, although marginal, reflected the desire among Romantic intellectuals for the renewal of a unified, pre-Reformation Catholic Church.

Early-nineteenth-century German Protestant clerics also expressed a desire for church unity. The Lutheran Church historian Jacob Gottlieb Planck (1751–1833) advocated an unhurried, voluntary, and formal union of the Reformed and Lutheran churches that would reconcile what he saw as their minor external differences.[13] And in an 1812 pamphlet, the Reformed theologian Friedrich Samuel Gottfried Sack (1738–1817), the presiding cleric at young Friedrich Wilhelm III's confirmation, noted improving confessional relations as a sign that now was the appropriate time to attempt a reunion of the Reformed and Lutheran Churches.[14]

The Prussian annexation of Catholic Silesia in 1742 and the Bavarian acquisition of the heavily Protestant Palatinate in 1816 made these states confessionally heterogeneous. The annexation of regions heavily populated by confessional Others provided the state with a stake in maintaining and encouraging confessional peace. Indeed, this religious heterogeneity, coupled with the post-Napoleonic revival of Christian piety, would lead to increasing confessional tensions later in the century.[15] Nevertheless, state officials in confessionally mixed regions encouraged confessional integration for the purpose of de-emphasizing confessional difference and the social discord that sometimes resulted.[16] Indeed, both Prussia and the Bavarian Palatinate were at the vanguard of campaigns for intra-Protestant church unions.

The Prussian Union

It was within this context of increasing confessional integration and popular demands for interconfessional peace that King Friedrich Wilhelm III called for a unification of the Reformed and Lutheran Churches in Prussia. The Prussian Union would be inaugurated on October 31, 1817, and celebrated at the Reformation anniversary festivals of the same weekend. The king proclaimed the Prussian Union on the occasion of the Reformation anniversary festival in order to legitimize the union by associating it with the memory of Luther, thus underlining the new Evangelical Church's continuity with the Reformation. In order to establish a union of the Reformed and Lutheran Churches on the occasion of an anniversary traditionally identified with Luther, Friedrich Wilhelm III and other pro-union figures would have to remake the memory of Luther from one that evoked the confessional divide to one that suggested intra-Protestant unity. The king's proposal for a Prussian Union elicited both accolades and opposition that were articulated in the sermons, speeches, and pamphlets delivered and distributed at the Reformation anniversary festivals.

Friedrich Wilhelm himself was among the most outspoken supporters of a union of the Reformed and Lutheran Churches. The king was a devoted Calvinist whose spirituality was influenced by Pietism. He desired to be known as a righteous ruler of a strong Christian state and believed that a strong and unified church was essential to the well-being of state and society. The king sought a unification of the separated Protestant churches because he believed it would ensure the strength of both the Prussian church and state by dissolving an internal divide that had traditionally separated his subjects. The king's interfaith marriages might also have informed his ecclesiastical policies. Friedrich's first wife, the immensely popular Queen Louise (d. 1810), was devoutly Lutheran. His second wife, Princess Auguste von Harrach, was Catholic. But in fact, Friedrich had desired a union of the Prussian Reformed and Lutheran Churches as early as the 1790s. The king had envisioned that such a union might serve as the kernel for a German national church that would welcome other Protestant state churches and even Catholic congregations.[17] Thus Friedrich imagined that a reunion of Germany's separated confessions might inspire a renewed bond and increased solidarity among German Christians. And as the 1817 anniversary approached, the king's ministers advised him to pursue a union of Reformed and Lutheran Churches. They assured him that it would broaden and strengthen the Prussian state church, that it would represent an enlightened form of religious tolerance, and that it might address the growing problems of confessionally mixed marriages and confessional discord within his confessionally heterogeneous kingdom.[18] Moreover, they said that because the union would be effected not only in Prussia proper, but also in Prussia's newly acquired territories in the Rhineland and Westphalia, it would have the effect of establishing an institution that transcended regional boundaries and thus facilitate a national or pan-German sense of Evangelical identity in its members. To be sure, King Friedrich Wilhelm III was no German nationalist. But he did envision his expanding Prussian kingdom unencumbered by the intra-Protestant confessional divide, and he would use the occasion of the 1817 Reformation anniversaries to realize that vision.

On September 27, 1817, the king issued an order summoning representatives of the Lutheran and Reformed Churches to attendance at an intra-Protestant service and celebration of the Eucharist on October 30 in Berlin. This service had two purposes: to celebrate the memory of the Reformation and to inaugurate the Prussian Union of the Reformed and Lutheran Churches into a unified Evangelical Church.[19] Friedrich Wilhelm III proposed a shared celebration of the Eucharist between Reformed and Lutheran churchgoers at the services to inaugurate the Prussian Union. Sidestepping the potentially thorny issue of the Real Presence—Lutherans believe in the physical presence of Jesus with the host, while Reformed Christians recognize that presence as symbolic—each communicant would be allowed to interpret the meaning of the Eucharist for oneself. Friedrich believed that this shared celebration of Communion could have a unifying effect on his Reformed and Lutheran subjects. He identified the shared celebration of Communion as evidence of adoption of the Prussian Union, seeing that celebration as a performative act that would denote a congregation's membership into the new Evangelical Church.

Ecclesiastical and Popular Support for the Prussian Union

The king found overwhelming support for the union from the Berlin Synod, the governing body of the Prussian Lutheran Church. Friedrich Schleiermacher (1768–1834), the presiding officer of the synod of Berlin and a supporter of the Evangelical Union, published an official declaration on behalf of the synod that expressed support for the king's order of September 27. The declaration acknowledged that the Eucharist might be a site of contestation between Reformed and Lutheran Christians during the 1817 debates about union. But it also suggested that a common celebration of Communion between Reformed and Lutheran congregations might assuage tensions between the confessions and serve as an example for other congregations. Indeed, the synod's declaration noted that throughout the early nineteenth century, Reformed had attended Lutheran services and sermons, that Lutherans had their children baptized and catechized by Reformed pastors, and that Reformed and Lutheran clergy and laity had blessed interconfessional marriages. Schleiermacher and the synod envisioned the common celebration of Communion as a progression of these irenical practices and the consummating act of unification of the separated confessions.[20]

Although the Berlin Synod advocated a union of the Reformed and Lutheran Churches, it condemned both fanaticism and indifference on the matter of the Prussian Union. The synod's goal was neither to foment theological strife nor to eliminate every distinction between the Reformed and Lutheran confessions, but instead to encourage an ecumenical celebration of the Eucharist that would facilitate unification. No Evangelical congregations would be expected to give up key doctrinal questions or to casually overlook the differences and sometimes nasty polemics that accompanied theological debate. However, for the sake of confessional peace, the synod did advise prospective Evangelical congregations to acknowledge their principal points of agreement—of which there were many—and to omit controversial points of disagreement from their discussions. On the question of the Real Presence, the congregations should reflect on the words of Christ at the Last Supper rather than squabble over the different interpretations of those words offered by Reformed and Lutheran theologians over the years.[21]

Based on Friedrich's September 27 order, Reformed and Lutheran ministers met at the Church of St. Nicholas in Berlin and celebrated the anniversary of the Reformation on Saturday, October 30, 1817, by taking Communion in common. The king attended the service but did not accept Communion, preferring to wait until the Sunday service to accept the sacrament. On the morning of Sunday, October 31, 1817, Friedrich introduced the first unified Evangelical Christian congregation at the royal chapel in Potsdam by announcing a union of the chapel's Reformed and Lutheran congregations. The Berlin Synod composed a tentative union liturgy for this service. The royal court was in attendance, along with sixty important Reformed and Lutheran ministers. The king hoped that the unification of the Potsdam chapel would serve as an ecumenical model for all Protestant communities in Prussia. On the evening of Sunday, October 31, Friedrich traveled from Potsdam to Wittenberg. There, he attended the festival service at the Wittenberg Schloßkirche, where Luther had posted his Ninety-Five Theses. Then the king attended the groundbreaking ceremonies of the city's new Luther memorial.[22]

Friedrich sought popular support for the union after formally establishing the Evangelical Church in Potsdam. In order to legitimize the new church, the king had identified himself and the proposed union not only with Luther and the Reformation, but with a long-standing Hohenzollern policy of religious toleration and a line of Prussian rulers who had persistently tried to unify the separated confessions:

> My enlightened ancestors, the elector Johann Sigismund, the elector Georg Wilhelm, the great elector Friedrich Wilhelm, King Friedrich I, and King Friedrich Wilhelm I, as the history of their reign and their lives prove, had already attempted with pious solemnity, to unite both separated Protestant churches, the Reformed and the Lutheran into an Evangelical-Christian Church in their lands.[23]

Friedrich sought to position himself and to ground his ecclesiastical policies within this Hohenzollern tradition of religious toleration and intra-Protestant irenicism. Johann Sigismund (1572–1619), elector of Brandenburg, had converted to Calvinism on December 25, 1613, but never insisted that his Lutheran subjects convert to Calvinism.[24] The Great Elector Friedrich Wilhelm (1620–1688) protected the religious freedom of his Catholic subjects. He had also invited French Protestants expelled by the 1685 revocation of the Edict of Nantes to resettle in Brandenburg-Prussia, allowed them to retain their religious practices, and paid for their relocation. Over one hundred thousand French Protestants accepted his offer.[25] King Friedrich I (r. 1701–1713) administered several churches at which both Lutherans and Reformed were appointed to preach. At the 1705 consecration of the French Cathedral in Berlin, Friedrich I had copies of the Augsburg Confession and the Heidelberg Catechism laid side by side on the altar as a symbol of Prussian confessional unity.[26] King Friedrich Wilhelm I (r. 1713–1740) saw little difference between the Reformed and Lutheran religions; he regarded their differences as little more than a squabble among theologians. Thus, he favored unification of the separated confessions and encouraged the construction of union churches for Reformed and Lutheran use.[27]

Following in this tradition, Friedrich Wilhelm III argued that the Reformed and Lutheran Churches were "two slightly divergent confessions" separated only by external differences and thus should be united.[28] The Prussian Union was in accordance with the ultimate purposes of Christian unity and corresponded with the original intentions of the reformers, who had not desired a separation of Protestantism into Lutheran and Reformed confessions. The king also claimed the union was enthusiastically demanded by his Reformed and Lutheran subjects.[29] Anticipating reservations about a state-sponsored, compulsory union of the Reformed and Lutheran Churches, Friedrich argued that the union would not constitute a conversion of Reformed to Lutheranism or Lutherans to the Reformed Church, but, rather, a revitalized Evangelical Church in the spirit of the Reformation and the reformers. The union would not only revitalize German Protestantism but also contribute to the renewal of domestic piety and alleviate the social discord that accompanied the intra-Protestant confessional divide.[30]

The king strongly endorsed the Prussian Union, and he was not alone. It also enjoyed significant clerical and popular support. Entry into the union was optional for each congregation, but by May 1825 almost 70 percent of Prussian congregations had adopted it. Some union congregations received copies of the Evangelical liturgy that were signed by the king and included his personal blessing. Others received silver medallions designed by the Prussian architect Karl Friedrich Schinkel (1781–1841), depicting a mother church embracing her two Protestant sons.[31] In the majority-Catholic states of the Rhineland and Westphalia, relations between the minority populations of Reformed and Lutherans had grown increasingly close. This contributed to the popularity of an Evangelical union in those regions.[32] For example, a pro-union community in the Rhenish Prussian city of Wuppertal expressed its support for the Evangelical Church in documents codifying the union. The community members imagined their congregation as an embodiment of Friedrich's promise that the union would not entail a conversion of Reformed to Lutheranism or Lutherans to Reformed. The Wuppertal community avowed that union would not dilute the confessional identities of their Evangelical congregation. The symbolic books of the Lutheran and Reformed Churches, the Augsburg Confession and the Lutheran and Heidelberg Catechisms, would retain their existence and value in the community insofar as they corresponded with each other. In cases where they did not correspond, the matter would be left to the conscience of the congregant.[33]

Advocates of union in regions outside Prussia used the occasion of the Reformation anniversary to call for a reunion of local Reformed and Lutheran congregations in their own communities. Supporters of union in Nassau did not wish to be known as Lutherans or Calvinists because the reformers themselves had eschewed sectarianism and did not want Protestant Christians to refer to themselves as separate denominations. The different names were a reflection of confessional separation and divide. Accordingly, advocates of union in Nassau desired the name of Evangelical Christian Church to underline their unity.[34] Indeed, the use of the word *evangelical* to describe the newly unified congregations evoked memories of the Reformation. Ecumenists appropriated this designation, which Lutherans had originally used to refer to themselves, in order to underline the continuity of the contemporary unions with the Reformation. Reflecting its widespread popular support, the Nassau Union proposal was composed by a local synod and voted on by Protestant heads of household.[35] The Duke of Nassau officially proclaimed the union of the Reformed and Lutheran Churches in his duchy on October 31, 1817. Further south, in Frankfurt, Reformed pastors preached in Lutheran churches, and Lutheran pastors administered communion in Reformed churches in support of a union in that city.[36] Indeed, the congregation of a local union effected in the Palatinate town of Bad Bergzabern claimed that the new Evangelical Church recalled the congregations of the apostolic age and early Reformation, before confessional distinctions and denominational differences were established.[37] For this congregation, the union evoked memories of a pre-confessional period of Christianity and the early Reformation that were representative of the intra-Protestant unity realized in the Evangelical Church.

The Berlin Synod's recommendation of an ecumenical celebration of the Evangelical Eucharist was accompanied by Schleiermacher's own ecumenical memories of the Reformation. This memory acknowledged both Luther and Zwingli's contributions to German Protestantism. In his 1817 Reformation anniversary address to the University of Berlin, Schleiermacher had noted that at the anniversary festivals, Protestants celebrated the memory of those features of the Reformation that were common to both Luther and Zwingli: the restoration of the authority of scripture, the recognition that faith alone could atone for man's sins, the defeat of superstition and ritualism, and the abolition of intermediaries between God and man.[38] Thus Schleiermacher invoked a Reformation history of shared traditions and trajectories rather than one of separation between the confessions. He sought to remake the confessional memory of the anniversary into one that evoked intra-Protestant unity in order to reconcile Reformed and Lutherans within the new Evangelical Church. Schleiermacher's support for the Prussian Union, read alongside his nationalist aspirations expressed during the Wars of Liberation—"My greatest wish after liberation is for one true German Empire, powerfully representing the entire German folk and territory"—point to the social and political import of the union in Prussia and in other German lands.[39] Much as Friedrich Wilhelm III imagined, the Prussian Union and others like it might serve as the foundations of a German national church, which in turn would unite the German people and territories across confessional boundaries.

Indeed, with royal, ecclesiastical, and popular support, unions were ultimately realized and recognized by Nassau (1817), Fulda (1818), the Rhineland-Palatinate (1818), Anhalt (1820), Baden (1821), Rhenish Hesse (1822), Hesse (1823), and Württemberg (1827). Unions were not effected in Bavaria, Saxony, Mecklenburg, or Hanover due to the negligible numbers of Reformed Christians in those states, although individual Reformed and Lutheran congregations were free to unite themselves. Apart from some orthodox Lutheran detractors, these unions enjoyed overwhelming popular support. Indeed, the most vociferous opposition to the Prussian Union church arose in the 1820s—not on the basis of the union itself, but in response to the introduction of a new liturgy. Orthodox opposition notwithstanding, these union churches represented German national institutions that were instrumental in both healing the intra-Protestant divide and uniting Germans across region and confession.

Throughout the century, German nationalists would create institutional structures—social organizations, sporting clubs, and scholarly academies—that they hoped might unite Germans in the absence of a strong state.[40] The 1817 Prussian Union Church and those that followed its model had achieved just that—establishing a pan-German social and cultural institution that unified Germans across multiple divides. These unions endured throughout the nineteenth century and helped to foster a pan-German Protestantism with which all German Protestants, Lutheran and Reformed, could identify. The unions were remarkable in light of the bitter enmity between Lutherans and Calvinists during the sixteenth century. Indeed, the 1555 Peace of Augsburg—which established a truce between the Catholic Holy Roman Empire and the Lutheran princes—did not recognize Calvinism as a legal religion in the empire. In fact, it would require a thirty years war for Reformed Christians to be recognized in the German lands. To effect a union between these two churches was not only an ecclesiastical success, but a social and political one as well—the unions seemed to erase deep divisions within German Protestantism and seemed to resolve issues that had been present since the Reformation era. While some intra-Protestant animosities persisted, these unions were, overall, effective at helping to keep the confessional peace between German Lutherans and Calvinists and represented an integral stage in the process of removing intra-Protestant religious difference as a category of German identity.

The Interconfessional Celebration of the 1817 Anniversaries

Protestants were not the only ones celebrating the contemporary Reformation anniversaries in a spirit of German unity. Across Germany, responding to the Prussian king's ecumenical efforts and to their own desire to bridge the German confessional divide, irenical Catholics, Protestants, and in limited cases even Jews, enthusiastically participated in the Reformation anniversary festivals, calling for a cessation of religious antagonism, pleading for interconfessional coexistence and cooperation, and advocating church unity. Their participation in these festivals, and their invocation of irenical memories of Luther marked a shift in German collective memories of the Reformation. Instead of evoking the German confessional divide and painful memories of separation, these irenical Catholics, Protestants, and Jews refashioned memories of Luther and the Reformation into symbols of German interconfessional unity. And by imagining notions of German unity that cut across the confessional divide—still the most salient manifestation of German identity and difference—these proponents of intra-Protestant and interconfessional unity also reflected on an idea of German national unity. Indeed, the 1817 Reformation anniversaries anticipate how confessional identity and difference, unity and diversity, would be employed throughout in the century to imagine the German nation.

German collective memories of Luther and the Reformation had traditionally been linked to painful memories of separation, religious war, and the confessional divide. By proposing solutions for overcoming this conflict in anniversary sermons, speeches, and pamphlets, and by celebrating the anniversaries in common with Catholics, Reformed, Lutherans, and in limited cases, Jews, irenical participants in the 1817 Reformation anniversaries sought to refashion the hitherto confessionally exclusive character of the anniversary festivals into celebrations of interconfessional unity. And while their desire for interconfessional peace and church unity was inspired by a sincere piety, the ecumenical celebrants of the 1817 Reformation anniversaries, by imagining a reunion of the separated confessions, were also in effect proposing a basis for German national unity.

Many of the sermons and speeches delivered at the 1817 anniversaries invoked memories of Luther and the Reformation in order to call for interconfessional peace and to explore the possibilities of church unity. In his Reformation sermon, Valentin Karl Veillodter (1769–1828), a Lutheran pastor in Nuremberg, preached that the anniversary was no occasion for bitter feelings between Lutherans,

Reformed, or their Catholic brothers.[41] Instead, Veillodter suggested that his congregation act in the "spirit of brotherly concord" toward Catholics and Reformed during the Reformation anniversary.[42] Indeed, he reminded his congregation that during the Napoleonic Wars, members of the Catholic, Lutheran, and Reformed Churches had united in their shared love of the fatherland in order to oppose external threats to German freedom. Once again, at the 1817 Reformation anniversaries, they were united in their desire for interconfessional peace. Veillodter claimed that, as with their close alliances during the Wars of Liberation, a union of the separated confessions would only serve to strengthen German national unity and solidarity.[43]

The Bamberg Lutheran pastor Ernst Anton Clarus (1776–1848) began his Reformation sermon by explicitly stating that the Reformation anniversary was not a celebration of the confessional divide.[44] Clarus called on his congregation to give thanks to everyone who was united in attendance at the service and anniversary festival, without distinction of confession.[45] He then asked his congregation to recall the centuries of religious bigotry and violence that had plagued Germany and contrasted these painful memories to the union of the Reformed and Lutheran Churches in Prussia, which he believed represented a final nullification of the animosities between the Protestant denominations.[46] Clarus concluded his sermon by reminding the congregation that the Gospel bound them and German Catholics together as brothers. He enumerated the similarities between the Evangelical and Catholic Churches, including shared histories and shared traditions that might serve as a basis for rapprochement between, and an ultimate reunion of, the separated confessions.[47] Clarus hoped that a reunion of the separated confessions could strengthen the German churches. But he also believed that by eliminating the confessional divide, a reunion of the churches would encourage feelings of unity and solidarity among German Christians throughout the fatherland.[48] For Clarus, proposing a reunion of the separated confessions was a way of imagining German national unity.

In nearby Erlangen, the Lutheran theologian Gottlieb Philipp Christian Kaiser (1781–1848) told his congregation that the Reformation was still in progress, that it must remain in progress, and that it would only be completed through a reunification of all of the Christian confessions.[49] Kaiser contrasted the expressions of tolerance and cooperation between Catholics, Reformed, and Lutherans at the 1817 anniversary with the Lutheran exclusivity of the 1617 and 1717 anniversaries. According to Kaiser, the ecumenical celebration of the 1817 anniversary pointed to the hopeful prospects of a final reunion of the separated Christian confessions.[50] The ecumenical sermons of Veillodter, Clarus, and Kaiser were representative of the general Lutheran pro-union position.

Based on reports describing the irenical celebrations of the Reformation anniversary in Bamberg and other neighboring towns, the reception of the ecumenical sentiments of Veillodter's, Clarus's, and Kaiser's sermons was positive. Esteemed members of the Bamberg Catholic Church attended Reformation Sunday services at the local Evangelical Church and participated in the festivities that followed. Catholic notables shared a common meal with local Evangelical clerics at the city museum.[51] The majority of participants in these irenical celebrations expressed the desire to commemorate their common celebration of the memories of Luther and the Reformation.[52] They sought to refashion the meaning of the anniversary from a confessionally exclusive commemoration of the confessional divide into a celebration of German interconfessional unity. Irenical celebrations of the Reformation anniversary were reproduced further afield from those of Bamberg. Lutheran, Reformed, and Catholic children attended catechism classes together in Gleusen.[53] Catholics and even some Jews attended the anniversary festivities in Mühlhausen and Trabelsdorf.[54] Also in Trabelsdorf, short books on Reformation history were donated to the poor, and money was raised for German translations of the New Testament for Christian children and the Old Testament for Jewish children.[55] Confessionally mixed families in Küps celebrated together. The Küps city pastor expressed hope that these celebrations, by their "concord, decency, and fraternal spirit," would leave an unforgettable joyful memory in his congregation of the interconfessional participation at the anniversary.[56]

To be sure, the particular inflections of local commemorations of the 1817 Reformation anniversaries might have been animated by local and regional religious concerns. But as the historian Alon Confino has shown, the German nation could be imagined as a local metaphor.[57] Nineteenth-century Germans imagined the nation as an extension of their locale. And if the nation was a local metaphor in nineteenth-century Germany, then the effort to reimagine or recast the local community in interconfessional or ecumenical terms was all at once a vision of German national unity. A nationwide reception of ecumenical nationalism need not be the condition for it making a difference—every locale that imagined an interconfessional community which had overcome the confessional divide was a kind of German nation writ large. Indeed, to assume that these ecumenists had to implement their plans on a national scale all at once is to presuppose a conception of nationalism that only works from the top down and is uninformed by local communities. That kind of presupposition is what caused German nationalist historians to lose sight of the importance of these local groups and local efforts to overcome the confessional divide. By proposing a rapprochement between the separated confessions in their own hometowns, and through their irenical participation in their local Reformation anniversary festivals, German Catholics, Protestants, and Jews imagined a German nation that was unencumbered by the confessional divide.

German Catholics noted the ecumenical possibilities of the 1817 Reformation anniversary as well. Maximilian Prechtl (1757–1832), a Benedictine priest from Bavaria who had written several ecumenical treatises and histories, noted that the Reformation anniversary had aroused the piety of German Protestants, whom he called Catholics' "separated brothers."[58] Prechtl encouraged Catholics to use the occasion of the anniversary to review those tendencies that had contributed to the persistence of the confessional divide and to try to overcome them. The key to interconfessional peace was a confrontation with those painful memories of separation.[59] To this end, many

German Catholics took a sympathetic view of the Reformation anniversary and became better acquainted with Luther, the Reformation, and their Protestant neighbors through the festival, according to an Evangelical historian of the 1817 anniversaries who had read widely among the festival reports, sermons, and speeches.[60] But, Prechtl argued, the celebrants must take care that the anniversary does not reawaken or strengthen old sectarian animosities.[61] Instead, he recommended that Catholics and Protestants celebrate the festival in the spirit of Christ. Through their irenical celebration, an anniversary that had traditionally evoked the German confessional divide might become an anniversary of confessional reunion.[62]

The ecumenical hopes expressed by Veillodter, Clarus, Kaiser, and Prechtl were evident at anniversary festivals in Thuringia, where Reformed, Catholics, and a handful of Jews marched together in the festival processions. One Thuringian Jew who had marched and contributed to the festival's poor collection claimed he had done so because Luther's work had benefited the Jews and the Reformation had blessed every religion.[63] Jewish participation in the Reformation anniversary festivals, although atypical, was all the more noteworthy given the anti-Semitic inflection of the Wartburgfest and the violent anti-Semitic Hep-Hep Riots that would sweep through Germany in 1819.[64] The German students and liberals assembled at the Wartburgfest burned Jewish books that they deemed "anti-German," and anti-Semitic rhetoric could be heard. But contemporary enlightened and Reform Jews regarded Luther as a reformer who had embodied religious toleration and emancipation.[65] In fact, Luther's anti-Jewish writings were completely unknown in early-nineteenth-century Germany.[66] This made memories of Luther and the Reformation even more accessible to contemporary German Jews. None of the primary sources from 1817 that this author has examined suggest that Jewish participants in the Reformation anniversary festivals were objects of proselytization. They were willing celebrants in those irenical commemorations of Luther and the Reformation that seemed to suggest a temporary dissolution of the German confessional divide.

The Thuringian Jew was not the only non-Protestant to acknowledge a debt to Luther. An anonymous Catholic writer in Erlangen used the occasion of the Reformation anniversary to praise Luther's contributions to German Catholicism and suggest the possibility for reconciliation between Catholics and Protestants. The writer argued that Luther had contributed a great deal to the promotion of theological studies among Catholic laypeople; that the Protestant Reformation had compelled the Catholic Church to reform itself; and that Protestant iconoclasm had contributed to the elimination of abuse of icons, relics, and other superstitions within Catholic churches.[67] The author acknowledged doctrinal differences between Catholics and Protestants but affirmed the merits of both, acknowledging Christ as the common source of their faith and the kingdom of heaven as the common goal of both confessions.[68]

At anniversary services some sermons seeking interconfessional peace between German Catholics and Protestants nevertheless stopped short of endorsing a reunion of the churches. The Munich Lutheran theologian Ludwig Friedrich von Schmidt (1764–1857) exemplified this position. Schmidt professed his wish that the 1817 Reformation anniversaries not be held. In his anniversary sermon, Schmidt argued that the festivals might reawaken the old hostilities between Catholics, Reformed, and Lutherans. Moreover, an anniversary festival should commemorate an institution or relationship, such as the founding of a state, the consecration of a church, or a marriage, not a religious-historical event such as the publication of Luther's Theses.[69] Schmidt believed that any celebration of a Reformation anniversary must be irreligious, because what he identified as the bitter consequences of the Reformation—the separation of the confessions, the Thirty Years' War, and subsequent outbreaks of hatred and religious persecution—should not be commemorated.[70] The anniversary, he believed, should certainly not be used to introduce a compulsory union of the separated Protestant confessions. Although he was neither an ecumenist nor pro-union, Schmidt applauded efforts to secure peaceful coexistence between Catholics and Protestants and recognized the significance of Luther's memory for interconfessional relations in general and church unity in particular. He recommended a proscription of those memories—neither forgetting nor transcending, but suspending them for the sake of confessional peace.

Like Schmidt, the Augsburg Lutheran pastor G. H. Kayser argued that the most appropriate way to celebrate the memories of Luther and the Reformation was in the spirit of unity with Catholics. But he stopped short of advocating reunion with Catholics. In fact, Kayser explicitly opposed it. Nevertheless, Kayser minimized the differences between Catholics and Protestants and argued that the 1817 Reformation anniversary celebration should include Catholics so long as they and others did not attempt to unify that which lay separated according to God's will, the divide between Roman Catholic and Evangelical Christianity.[71] Schmidt and Kayser reflected a variety of positions on interconfessional relations that were expressed at the 1817 Reformation anniversaries. These included both ecumenical German Christians who sought a reunion of the separated confessions and those irenical Catholics and Protestants who sincerely desired interconfessional peace and cooperation but stopped short of advocating church unity. And in nearly every case, these figures appealed to memories of Luther and the Reformation to locate themselves within the varied spectrum of debate on interconfessional relations.

The irenical tendencies of Catholic, Reformed, and Lutheran celebrants of the 1817 Reformation anniversaries pointed to a notion of German unity that transcended the confessional divide. Perhaps they were not proper nationalists like Fichte, Jahn, or Arndt. However, they did envision and espouse a religiously unified German nation. Even irenical figures such as Schmidt and Kayser, who had stopped short of endorsing a full reunion of the churches and instead encouraged mutual understanding and peaceful coexistence between German Catholics, Protestants, and Jews, recognized the interrelated histories and traditions of each group within the German lands and how they might be used to bridge the confessional divide for the sake of the German fatherland. Because the national question was inseparable from the confessional question in nineteenth-century Germany, by imagining a reunion of the separated confessions the ecumenical celebrants of the 1817 Reformation anniversaries were also reflecting on ideas of German national unity. Their notions of German unity presaged the increasingly explicit association of confessional identity and difference with ideas of the German nation.

Conclusion

The ecumenical celebration of the 1817 Reformation anniversaries represents the first instance of the ecumenical impulse within German nationalism—the desire to heal the confessional divide as a condition of German national unification. These irenical and ecumenical efforts represented a means of being German that cut across the confessional divide. And they suggested a German national idea that was inclusive rather than exclusive of one's religious Other. In a polity within which confessional identity and difference went all the way down, inflecting German politics, society, and culture, ecumenism proposed a notion of German unity that addressed some of the highest obstacles confronting the formation of a unified nation.

If Wartburg was a watershed for German nationalism, the 1817 anniversaries were a watershed for ecumenical nationalism. And to be sure, ecumenical nationalism was a form of German nationalism that endured long after the Wartburger and their sympathizers were marginalized, censored, or arrested by the German authorities. With the encouragement of the archconservative Austrian statesman Klemens von Metternich (1773–1859), Friedrich Wilhelm III cracked down on Prussian nationalists, arresting Jahn and Arndt. The year 1819 witnessed the introduction of the Karlsbad Decrees, a series of measures that institutionalized a conservative reaction that would rule for two decades.

While the irenical celebrants of the Reformation anniversaries had made great strides in overcoming the German confessional divide, confessional tensions flared again subsequently. Feuds between old Lutheran holdouts from the Union church and Evangelical Protestants defined Prussian religious life in the 1820s and 1830s. And Catholics and Protestants in the Rhineland and Bavaria were increasingly at odds over mixed marriages and the rights of religious minorities. But right on cue—when, after two decades of reaction, German liberals had once again forced the national question into public debate and at a point when confessional tensions seemed just about to boil over—two prominent groups of German ecumenists emerged who sought to reunite Catholics and Protestants in the interests of a unified German nation. Their campaigns, which contemporaries dubbed the "Reformation of the nineteenth century," were steeped in memories and images of Martin Luther.

2

THE ECUMENICAL VANGUARD

Ecumenism, Nationalism, and Luther-Worship in the German Revolutions of 1848

DORMANT FOR MOST of the 1820s and 1830s, nationalism made a dramatic return to the center of German civic life during the Revolutions of 1848. Beginning in Paris and spreading throughout Europe, the revolutions would provide the quiescent German nationalist movement with its most concrete hopes of establishing a unified German nation-state. During the height of the revolutions in the German lands, riots and bloody street fighting between German nationalists and Prussian loyalists had engulfed Berlin, compelling the Prussian king Friedrich Wilhelm IV to promise a constitution, a popular assembly, and greater integration of the Prussian kingdom into a unified German state. To these ends, nationalists from across the German lands assembled during the spring of 1848 in Frankfurt, with the purpose of drafting a constitution that would serve as the basis for a unified German nation-state. One of the most contested questions among the delegates was that of a kleindeutsch or grossdeutsch German nation—that is, would Austria be excluded or included in a unified German nation? On March 28, 1849, the German National Assembly finalized the German constitution in favor of the kleindeutsch solution and elected the Prussian king Friedrich Wilhelm IV (r. 1840–1860) emperor of Germany. In public, Friedrich graciously declined the imperial title, explaining that the Frankfurt Parliament had not the right to bestow it, although he reassured the delegates of his commitment to German national unification. Privately, however, the king remarked that he could never accept "a crown from the gutter" that had been so tainted by revolution.

Not only was Friedrich's rejection of the imperial title a death knell for the National Assembly, but it also seemed as the German nationalist movement as a whole would grind to a halt until some other opportune time. Indeed, the failures of the Frankfurt Parliament and the German revolutionaries are often pointed to as evidence of Germany's distaste for liberalism and its flawed path toward modernization, and as an episode that was ostensibly redeemed by Bismarck's realpolitker unification of the German Empire.[1] But this reading of 1848 tends to obscure contemporary forms of German nationalism that were as popular, and arguably as effective, at uniting the German people as the 48ers. Two groups in particular—the dissident religious congregations known as the Protestant Friends and German-Catholic Movement—were ecumenical cum nationalist movements at the vanguard of *Vormärz* (i.e., pre-revolutionary) and revolutionary German nationalism.

The Protestant Friends and the German-Catholic Movement were Vormärz religious communities that severed ties with the mainstream German Evangelical and Catholic churches in order to realize confessional, national, and gender harmony by promoting religious freedom, interconfessional cooperation, and confessionally mixed marriages. Both groups invoked memories of Luther as a spiritual liberator and the Reformation as an instance of religious revolution in order to justify their subversion of the ecclesiastical and secular authorities that denied their constituents freedom of religion and hindered confessional and national unity. Their "modern secession from Popery" was informed by memories of Martin Luther as a revolutionary who had liberated Germany from the spiritual bondage of the papacy. Their nineteenth-century Reformation, led by the Protestant pastor Leberecht Uhlich and the defrocked Catholic chaplain Johannes Ronge, was directed against the governing hierarchy of the Evangelical Church and the ultramontane faction within the Roman Catholic Church. Although persecuted by the authorities, these dissident religious communities found extraordinary resonance across Vormärz Germany, attracting more than one hundred thousand men and women to their religious services, rallies, and social organizations. Because they shared the same goals of religious freedom and confessional unity, the Protestant Friends and German-Catholic Movement maintained close ties and informally cooperated beginning in 1845. In 1850, both as a practical measure and a reaction to the failure of the 1848 Revolutions to unify the German nation, the Protestant Friends and German Catholics united to form the Free Congregations.

Well before the confessional politics of the Catholic-dominated Center Party and before Bismarck's Kulturkampf had proposed notions of German unity that excluded the confessional Other,[2] the dissenting congregations introduced a notion of German unity that was inclusive of both Catholics and Protestants. If theology was ersatz politics in Vormärz Germany, the Protestant Friends and German Catholics were proponents of a revolutionary ecumenism—a model of confessional unity dedicated to the establishment of a general Christian communion consisting of German Catholics and Protestants united in their subversion of ecclesiastical and secular authorities for the cause of freedom of religion and conscience. Their Vormärz campaigns on behalf of interconfessional peace and German unity represented a recurrence of the ecumenical nationalist impulse which echoed that of a previous generation of ecumenists active at the 1817 Reformation anniversaries.

During the height of the era of revolutionary German nationalism, the Protestant Friends and German Catholics rivaled better-known revolutionaries and nationalists in popular appeal. Their campaigns on behalf of religious freedom, interconfessional cooperation, and confessionally mixed marriages as a means of securing religious and national unity—dubbed a "Reformation for the nineteenth century" by contemporaries—brought together thousands of Catholics and Protestants in a spirit of German unity. More effective in uniting the German people around a shared national cause than any law or decree from the Frankfurt Parliament, many of the 48ers themselves recognized the Protestant Friends and German Catholics as the model form of German nationalism.

This chapter recognizes the ecumenical nationalism of the Protestant Friends and German-Catholic Movement as the center of the Vormärz and 1848 Revolutions rather than as a movement at the peripheries of German nationalism. While historians have predominantly treated these congregations as examples of Vormärz-era mass piety or as nascent German political movements, this chapter seeks a synthesis of previous interpretations.[3] It argues that the Protestant Friends and German Catholics were spiritual, social, and political revolutionaries whose campaigns were informed by memories of Luther as liberator of Germany from spiritual bondage and the Reformation era as one of revolution that was being replayed during the nineteenth century. The widespread popular appeal and influence of these ecumenical groups demonstrate that the desire to overcome the confessional divide and to reunite the separated churches as a condition of German national unification was a recurrent impulse within German nationalism that manifested itself whenever the German National Question was debated. For ecumenical nationalism to be at the vanguard of the most significant expression of German nationalism of the nineteenth century thus far suggests just how essential Christian ecumenism was conceived to be for the resolution of the German National Question.

Political and Ecclesiastical Tensions of the Vormärz

During the 1820s and 1830s, confessional relations had become strained between Catholics and Protestants and within Protestant churches over matters of liturgical innovation and church administration. In the political sphere, the German nationalism of the 1820s and 1830s had lain dormant but was not wholly silent. The Revolutions of 1830, along with the Greek independence movement and Polish uprisings against Russian rule, inspired German nationalists. In the wake of 1830, the democratic literary society known as Young Germany was established, a festival in Hambach drew thousands of republican and nationalist Germans and Polish refugees, and liberal Germans protested the Karlsbad Decrees.[4] But the revolutions made few lasting inroads within the German lands. Prussia was hardly affected by the revolutions at all.

Friedrich Wilhelm III's persecution of the separatist Old Lutherans and their mass emigration from Germany in 1837 strained relations between orthodox Lutherans and Evangelical Protestants in Prussia. The Old Lutherans were a group of Prussian Lutheran congregations that had consistently refused to join the Evangelical Church or adopt its controversial 1822 liturgy. Friedrich Wilhelm III had marginalized Old Lutherans in eastern Prussia and Silesia since 1817 because of their refusal to join the Prussian Union. After 1830, when the king used the tercentenary of the Augsburg Confession to compel holdout congregations to adopt the 1822 liturgy, Old Lutheran clergy and laity who dissented were routinely defrocked and arrested. Friedrich's culture minister, Karl von Altenstein, even ordered the army into some of the most recalcitrant Old Lutheran parishes to enforce Prussian religious policies. On September 2, 1837, Friedrich Wilhelm III finally permitted the Old Lutherans to legally emigrate from Prussia. Thousands left for the United States and Australia, but intra-Protestant relations, especially between orthodox and Evangelical Protestants, remained tense.[5]

Catholic and Protestant relations in the Rhineland faltered during the Cologne Troubles of 1837, massive Catholic uprisings touched off by the Prussian government's arrest of a Catholic archbishop who had forbidden mixed marriages. The Kölner Wirren, or Cologne Troubles, were massive Catholic demonstrations against the Prussian government's 1837 arrest of Archbishop Clemens August von Droste-Vischering (1773–1845). Agreements of 1825 and 1834 between the Catholic Church and Prussian state stipulated that sons of confessionally mixed marriages would be raised in the faith of the father and daughters in the faith of the mother. But Archbishop Droste-Vischering, invested in 1836, refused to honor these agreements because they contradicted the Catholic teaching that all children of mixed marriages must be raised as Catholics. The archbishop also forbade Catholic priests from performing mixed marriages unless the parents guaranteed that all of the children would be raised Catholic. For refusing to uphold the 1825 and 1834 agreements, King Friedrich Wilhelm III had Droste-Vischering arrested. The arrest provoked a raucous Catholic reaction and heightened confessional tensions between Catholics and Protestants in Rhenish Prussia.[6]

The Bavarian Genuflection Edict of 1838, which stipulated that Protestant soldiers marching in state festival processions must kneel before the Eucharist, was met by fierce opposition from Protestant subjects of the Catholic kingdom of Bavaria. In August 1838, King Ludwig I of Bavaria (r. 1825–1848) issued an edict that required both Catholic and Protestant soldiers to genuflect as the Eucharist passed their ranks during the festival of Corpus Christi and at all other religious processions. This edict provoked the so-called Kniebeugungsstreit, or Kneeling Conflict. A Catholic monarch forcibly compelling his Protestant soldiers to show reverence to the sacrament scandalized the Bavarian Protestant clergy and laity. In 1844 a Lutheran minister named Wilhelm Redenbacher (1800–1876), who advised Protestant soldiers to disobey the order, was defrocked and jailed along with other critics of the edict. Although the king finally rescinded the edict in 1845, it contributed to increasing confessional tensions between Catholics and Protestants in Bavaria.[7]

The resurgence of ultramontanism and commensurate fears about the increasing Roman influence in German ecclesiastical and social affairs created suspicion among orthodox Catholics, liberal Catholics, and Protestants. The resurgence of ultramontanism within the German Catholic Church in the 1840s strained relations between orthodox Catholics and liberal Catholics and Protestants. During the 1840s, ultramontane clerics were invested with the bishoprics of Mainz, Cologne, Munich, and Breslau. These bishops demanded that priests be trained in closed Catholic seminaries rather than in the German universities and sought to organize the clergy into a strict and obedient hierarchy that deferred to Rome rather than independent-minded German bishops.[8] But German Protestants had received Roman intervention into German political and ecclesiastical affairs with great suspicion since the Thirty Years' War.[9] Thus the resurgence of ultramontanism heightened suspicions and tensions between German Catholics and Protestants. But it also pitted ultramontane Catholics and liberal Catholics against one another and precipitated the emergence of dissident movements such as the German-Catholic Movement.[10]

The ascendancy of the Romantic and Pietist Friedrich Wilhelm IV to the Prussian throne in 1840 was met with hopeful anticipation for reform. These hopes were frustrated when the king passed reactionary policies and partnered with ultramontane Catholics and orthodox Protestants to quash religious dissent and enforce strict obedience to the hierarchy of the Evangelical Church. His policies added to increasing confessional tensions. The new king demanded the Evangelical clergy's fidelity to the Prussian state church and sought the cooperation of orthodox parties within the Catholic and Evangelical churches to counteract dissenting and revolutionary movements.[11] Friedrich's willingness to cooperate with ultramontane Catholics and orthodox Protestants strained relations both within and between the confessions and indirectly enabled the resurgence of ultramontanism within the Roman Catholic Church in Germany. The deteriorating social conditions of the Hungry 40s, caused by widespread food shortages that were intensified by recession and a banking panic, heightened these tensions and exacerbated popular dissatisfaction with authorities. The Protestant Friends and German-Catholic Movement proposed a revolutionary solution to the increasing confessional tension, state deference to orthodox religious parties, and state persecution of religious nonconformists during the Vormärz by proposing a reunion of the separated confessions that would be united in opposition to ecclesiastical and secular authorities that denied freedom of religion and conscience.

The Protestant Friends

The handling by Johann Heinrich Bernhard Dräseke (1794–1849) of the Sintenis Affair of 1840 touched off the religious dissent of the Protestant Friends. Since 1832, Bishop Dräeske had served as superintendent of the Magdeburg Consistory, which governed the local Prussian-Saxon church. But in 1840 he reprimanded pastor W. F. Sintenis (1794–1859) for his heretical views regarding the Lutheran veneration of the crucifix. While the Consistory had censured Sintenis for denying the divinity of Christ, in fact he had only condemned Lutheran veneration of the crucifix as idolatrous. Fearing a popular backlash from the local churches, Dräeske decided to merely censure Sintenis for his heresy rather than remove him from his post. But this mild admonition by Dräeske and the consistory was no more acceptable to Sintenis's supporters than his removal. Indeed, for his censure of Sintenis, Dräseke was widely accused of establishing a nineteenth-century Inquisition.[12] In response, sixteen Lutheran clergymen met in Gnadau on June 29, 1841, to discuss how to respond to the censure of Sintenis. In protest of the Sintenis Affair, the clergymen, seeking greater autonomy for their congregations and independence from consistorial oversight, agreed to withdraw from the Lutheran Church in the Prussian province of Saxony. These sixteen clerics and their congregations, led by the Pömmelte pastor Leberecht Uhlich (1799–1872), collectively became known as the Protestant Friends.

Leberecht Uhlich had been dedicated to the maintenance of intra-Protestant unity and had grave reservations about formally splitting from the Prussian-Saxon church to found the Protestant Friends. Nevertheless, Uhlich attended and endorsed a conference of the dissenting congregations held in Leipzig in May 1842 at which the Protestant Friends asserted their independence of the Prussian-Saxon church and defined the shared tenets of their communion, which encouraged popular expressions of piety, the free interpretation of scripture, support for lay control of Protestant congregations, and independence from consistorial oversight.

Because they agitated for the independence of their congregations from court and consistory, the Protestant Friends were identified by the Prussian state as politically subversive. In August 1845 the Prussian government prohibited them from meeting publicly on the grounds that the group sought to subvert the existing ecclesiastical and political order. Despite their prohibition in Prussia, the

Protestant Friends found supporters throughout Germany and were strongest in Saxony. Among the most notable Saxon congregations were those of the politically active Gustav Adolf Wislicenus (1803–1875) in Halle; Eduard Baltzer (1814–1887), founder of the German vegetarian movement, in Nordhausen; and Leberecht Uhlich in Magdeburg. There were approximately seventy congregations and twenty thousand members of the Protestant Friends throughout Germany on the eve of the 1848 revolutions.

The German-Catholic Movement

Religious dissent appeared on both sides of the confessional divide in pre-revolutionary Germany. On October 1, 1844, the Silesian Catholic priest Johannes Ronge published an open letter to Bishop Wilhelm Arnoldi of Trier. In his letter, Ronge decried recent pilgrimages to Trier cathedral and its exhibition of the Holy Coat as idolatrous, and he personally attacked the bishop for encouraging superstition and fanaticism. For his insolence, Ronge was defrocked and excommunicated from the church, but he continued to preach and attracted thousands of supporters. His followers, and other congregations inspired by Ronge's teachings to withdraw from the Roman Catholic Church, became known as the German-Catholic Movement.

The German-Catholic Movement emerged as a result of the resurgence of ultramontanism and the increasing Catholic orthodoxy that was evident at the August 1844 exhibition of the Holy Coat in Trier.[13] Bishop Wilhelm Arnoldi of Trier had been promising to stage an exhibition of the Holy Coat since his consecration in 1842. The Holy Coat was a relic that had ostensibly been worn by Christ and housed at the cathedral in Trier since the fourth century. In consultation with Metternich, and with the cooperation of the Prussian government, the exhibition of the coat began in August 1844.[14] Over one million pilgrims traveled from Germany, France, Belgium, and Holland to witness the relic. Rumors of miraculous cures of sick pilgrims spread throughout Germany. Indeed, a female relation of the archbishop at the center of the Cologne Troubles, Droste-Vischering, claimed to be cured of her disability as soon as she beheld the Holy Coat.[15]

Liberal Catholics received mass displays of piety like the pilgrimages to the Holy Coat with considerable suspicion. The Silesian Catholic chaplain Johannes Ronge (1813–1887) was particularly troubled by the pilgrimages. Accordingly, on October 1, 1844, Ronge published an open letter to Bishop Arnoldi of Trier decrying the exhibition of and pilgrimages to the Holy Coat as "festivals of idolatry and dishonorable spectacles of superstition and fanaticism," all of which Ronge believed were encouraged by the Roman hierarchy. Ronge had also claimed that Bishop Arnoldi offered indulgences to pilgrims who made contributions toward the repair of the local cathedral. For this offense, Ronge identified Arnoldi as the "Tetzel of the nineteenth century" and admonished readers of the letter not to dishonor the good work of early modern reformers such as Jan Huss, Ulrich von Hutten, and Martin Luther by participating in the pilgrimages to or veneration of the Holy Coat.[16]

For his condemnation of the pilgrimage and his attacks on Arnoldi, Ronge was duly defrocked and excommunicated by the Catholic Church in December 1844. Despite his excommunication, Ronge continued to preach, winning scores of supporters. Roman Catholic congregations in Leipzig, Dresden, Worms, and Breslau that were inspired by Ronge's letter severed themselves from the church and issued their own confessions of faith. In March 1845 a German Catholic council of fifteen of these dissenting congregations met in Leipzig to declare themselves a German-Catholic Church and define their shared beliefs, which the historian Manfred P. Fleischer recognized as a "middle way between papacy and Protestantism."[17] The shared German Catholic beliefs defined at the Leipzig conference advocated episcopalism rather than ultramontanism, asserting independence from the Roman bishop "and his hangers on."[18] The German Catholics relied on liberal Protestant dogmatics and Protestant models of church administration to oppose the authority of the Catholic ecclesiastical hierarchy, especially the Roman pontiff's claim of primacy among the bishops. In addition, the Leipzig Conference advocated freedom of religion and conscience. It recognized scripture as the basis of Christian faith and claimed the right to freely examine it according to their conscience. And the German-Catholic congregations assembled in Leipzig acknowledged two sacraments: baptism and the Lord's Supper, which they recognized as a commemorative, rather than literal, communion with Christ's body and blood. German-Catholic congregations were governed and ministers chosen according to the vote of their members, including women. They sought the abolition of priestly celibacy, indulgences, and auricular confession while eschewing the use of sacramentals, relics, and icons.[19]

Although the German-Catholic Movement was immediately banned in Austria, Bavaria, and Hessen, liberal Prussian ministers, including Crown Prince Wilhelm and Culture Minister Eichhorn, initially welcomed it as a bulwark against the increasing power of the ultramontane movement. On the eve of the 1848 revolution, the German Catholics could boast 259 congregations and approximately 70,000 followers, including tens of thousands of Protestants.[20]

According to Ronge and his supporters, the ostentatious display of and mass pilgrimages to the Holy Coat symbolized the Roman hierarchy's increasing control over the German Catholic clergy and laity and the consolidation of the ultramontane party within the church. Ronge identified the veneration of the coat and other relics as superstitions that represented the continuing mental and spiritual bondage of the German people by the Roman ecclesiastical hierarchy. He believed these abuses demanded Catholic attention and oversight; indeed, they demanded a new Reformation: "In the sixteenth century, the exaction of absolution money hastened the advent of Protestantism, for which the people had been long prepared. In the nineteenth century, the idolatrous exhibition of the Holy Coat at Treves, was the immediate cause. The aim of the hierarchy was to show its victory over Protestantism in Germany, and to get money. The like consequences must follow in the nineteenth as in the sixteenth century."[21] The sixteenth-century indulgence controversy and the nineteenth-century display of and pilgrimage to the Holy Coat of Trier were both tipping points for their respective reformations. Ronge recounted the origins and development of the German-Catholic Movement, or the "modern secession from popery," in his 1852 history, *The Reformation of the Nineteenth Century*. In it, Ronge imagined himself as a latter-day Luther, challenging the Roman hierarchy with the ultimate goal of emancipating the German people from their mental and spiritual bondage.[22]

The Reformation of the Nineteenth Century

The Protestant Friends and German Catholics both sought ecclesiastical independence from the orthodox parties in their respective churches. Emancipation from orthodoxy was a prerequisite for overcoming the bitterest consequence of the sixteenth-century Reformation: the confessional divide. Leberecht Uhlich noted that the proscription of presbyterian independence and religious freedom by ecclesiastical authorities created an environment in which powerful factions excluded weaker ones by defining them as heterodox. This of course led to "manifold schisms and disunions" within the church.[23] He also accused orthodox Protestants of working "like brothers, hand in hand" with the Pope and Jesuits against every instance of religious progress and reunification.[24]

The Protestant Friends invoked memories of Luther's rejection of the spiritual tutelage of the Catholic Church in order to justify their opposition to the consistorial control of the contemporary Evangelical Church over their own congregations.[25] In his 1845 Reformation sermon titled "Here I Stand," Uhlich preached on Acts of the Apostles 4:13–21, in which Peter and John defy the Sanhedrin and continue to proselytize in Jesus's name. Uhlich identified this episode of biblical history with Luther's famous defiance of the Roman ecclesiastical hierarchy at the 1521 Diet of Worms and with the dissenting congregation's defiance of the Magdeburg Consistory. He concluded the sermon, an act of open defiance against the established church's claims of control over individual congregations, by channeling Luther himself, exclaiming, "Here I stand, I can do no other," to justify his congregation's opposition to the consistory.[26]

According to Johannes Ronge, orthodox parties on both sides of the confessional divide opposed reconciliation between German

Catholics and Protestants despite the fact that the laity longed for peace between the confessions. The Roman Catholic clergy and the orthodox Protestant party, both of whom demanded "a blindly obedient laity," could never allow for a reunification of Catholics and Protestants into independent and enlightened congregations because such a reunion would completely undermine their ecclesiastical and secular authority.[27] The German Catholic pastor Gustav von Struve (1805–1870) echoed Ronge's sentiment by protesting the ecclesiastical and secular authority of the orthodox parties. Struve, the son of a Bavarian diplomat to Russia, had variously worked as a journalist, dramatist, lawyer, politician, and German-Catholic pastor. He was a member of the Frankfurt Parliament, participated the 1848–1849 revolutions in Baden, and was eventually exiled to the United States for his revolutionary activity. According to Struve, "The German-Catholics rise up against the stable nature and the rigid dogmatism of the Roman Catholic Church, the Friends of Light against biblical literalism, which is imposed on them by the state and the Pietists. The spirit should be free and rule over the dead letter of the Bible, Roman dogma, and the Protestant symbols."[28] The German Catholics called on Catholics and Protestants alike to resist the dogmatism and literalism of the Roman hierarchy and Evangelical state churches. Indeed, Ronge identified the politicization of the sixteenth-century Reformation with contemporary Evangelical state churches. He noted that early modern Protestant secular rulers had usurped authority in matters of faith and that Luther had finally regretted that he had sought their help in stewarding the Reformation.[29] Indeed, Ronge identified contemporary Protestant princes as "the armed bishops and popes" of the nineteenth-century churches who suppressed religious minorities and inhibited religious progress and liberty just as the Reformation-era Catholic Church had done.[30]

Members of the dissenting congregations worried that a triumphant and interventionist papacy would completely abolish Protestantism in Germany. The Prussian court of Friedrich Wilhelm IV, with its deference to ultramontane Catholics and orthodox Protestants in opposition to progressive religious communities, served as "evidence" of this plan. According to the dissenting congregations, only they could prevent the abolition of German Protestantism, doing it by completing the sixteenth-century Reformation and uniting the separated confessions.[31] The nineteenth-century Reformation would realize freedom of religion and conscience, annul ecclesiastical hierarchies, and do so as a unified German Christian church that included Catholics and Protestants.[32]

In their efforts to effect a nineteenth-century Reformation, the Protestant Friends invoked doctrines of Protestant liberty to justify their demands for religious freedom and their opposition to the state church hierarchies. The Protestant Friends framed their participation in a nineteenth-century Reformation and their opposition to, and persecution by, spiritual and secular authorities within a schema of memory that recalled Luther's opposition to the early modern papacy.[33] Uhlich underlined this point by exclaiming:

> It is, therefore, not to be tolerated, that any person, be it a temporal or spiritual lord, shall stand up and issue his mandate, and endeavor to enforce it, saying: "Ye, people of the nineteenth century, must hold yourselves implicitly bound by the forms and ordinances of the sixteenth century, must adopt the doctrines of the Augsburg Confession, the primitive conception of Martin Luther, (justification by faith alone, &c.) without change or limitation"! It is the privilege and the duty of every Christian to think for himself, to examine the records and traditions of by-gone ages for himself, to search the scriptures, and to embrace the Christian system from a free and unbiased conviction. . . . But since in this our day many persons, some of whom occupy stations of great power and influence, strive to introduce the universal authority of the old statutes and customs of Christianity, we enter our *protest* against it, this being our right as Protestants, and our duty as Christians. We pledge ourselves to that Protestant liberty which Luther defended by his undaunted courage, which Jesus Christ has purchased for us with his blood.[34]

Thus Luther was not significant for his theology or the doctrines and dogmas he defined; his memory was significant to the Protestant Friends as a revolutionary symbol of defiance of the secular and spiritual authorities who abused Luther's memory by invoking it to bolster their own authority. Luther did not represent adherence to intractable dogma or unreflective deference to spiritual authority but, rather, the revolutionary possibility of spiritual emancipation. The sixteenth-century Reformation was not about a redefinition of doctrine or a revaluation of theology; it was about the radical assertion and defense of spiritual freedom. This is what the Reformation represented to the dissenting congregations. And it was this radical memory of Luther that informed the nineteenth-century Reformation. Indeed, undue deference to Luther himself or the Lutheran doctrine could threaten this radical notion of Protestant liberty. Uhlich and the Protestant Friends rejected the sentiment that they should defer to the letter of some sixteenth-century doctrine simply because it originated with Luther. Such a sentiment would contradict the Protestant liberty that Luther had won through the Reformation.

The Protestant Friends appealed to the German Evangelical clergy to join them to defend the legacy of the Reformation—namely, the free investigation of divine truths of Christianity against the compulsory dogmas of an authoritarian church—and for recognition of their dissenting congregations. They promised the Protestant clergy that if they preached the true Christianity of tolerance and love their churches would fill up, their congregations would become the vanguard of Protestantism, and they would be carrying on the spirit of the Reformation.[35]

German Catholics were prohibited from meeting in Austria, Bavaria, and Hessen from their inception. Prussia, initially hospitable to the anti-ultramontane proclivities of the German Catholics, would soon persecute them. In 1845 the Magdeburg Consistory recommended the removal of Leberecht Uhlich from his pastoral office for leading Bible studies that the local police had identified as "subversive." An 1847 Prussian law expelled dissenting congregations from the state church, identified them as political clubs, levied heavy fines on them, and then prohibited them as popular assemblies subversive of public order. As a result, Ronge was arrested and jailed for merely celebrating the German-Catholic mass.[36]

The ideals of Protestant liberty and freedom of religion and conscience for which dissenting congregations were persecuted were not merely ends, but means to promote the ultimate goals of religion: to unite all men and all confessions in love and inspire them with mutual regard for each others' ideas.[37] To this end, the Protestant Friends and German Catholics had informally cooperated and maintained close relations since 1845. But at a May 1850 conference held in Leipzig that was attended by representatives of thirty congregations of the Protestant Friends and representatives of approximately one hundred congregations of German Catholics, a majority of the attending parties elected to unite to form the Free Congregations. Not every congregation accepted the union of the Protestant Friends and German Catholics. A handful of Saxon German-Catholic congregations rejected the union on the grounds that it might threaten the autonomy of their congregations. But a majority of congregations countenanced the alliance.[38] This union may be understood as both a practical measure that could help realize the goals of two like-minded associations and as a reaction to the failure of the 1848 revolutions to unify Germany. Both groups were committed to a liberal Christianity, decried every hierarchical and dogmatic restriction on religious freedom and self-determination, and saw Christian sentiments actualized not in confessions of faith but in thoroughgoing social and political engagement.[39] More importantly, they sought to unify the separated confessions and proposed notions of German unity and identity that included both German Catholics; Protestants; and in some limited cases, Jews.

The Free Congregations and German National Unity

The Free Congregations advocated interconfessional peace and cooperation between German Catholics and Protestants in order to heal the most bitter wound of the Reformation: the German confessional divide. Johannes Ronge ultimately desired a unification of German

Catholics and Protestants into a general Christian church. Indeed, the German-Catholic historian Georg Gervinus (1805–1871) recognized confessional unity to be "the very essence" of German Catholicism.[40] The Protestant Friends likewise sought to improve relations with Catholics and encouraged intra-Protestant unity among the sects and parties of the Evangelical Church. The dissenting congregations also acknowledged similarities among German Catholicism, the Protestant Friends, and Reform Judaism as potential bases for cooperation among German Catholics, Protestants, and Jews. And the Free Congregations' vision of confessional unity would facilitate German national unity.

Ronge claimed that the German people shared his desire for interconfessional unity. He pleaded that religion, which ought to be an institution that unites, should no longer be a cause of separation between German citizens. He implored his readers to go to their clergymen and pastors and announce that they would no longer be disunited from their countrymen: German Catholics and Protestants were fellow Christians and citizens.[41] As such there was no legitimate basis for the persistence of the confessional divide. It was only maintained by ecclesiastical and secular authorities to preserve the control of ultramontane Catholics and orthodox Protestants over the laity of their respective churches.

German liberals and republicans received the emergence of the dissenting congregations and their opposition to ecclesiastical authorities with excitement and great expectations. While not necessarily ecumenical, many of the Frankfurt MPs who supported the German Catholics and Protestant Friends were in fact religiously tolerant and politically pluralist. These German nationalists sought to establish a nation that would include Catholics, Protestants, and even Jews but would remain confessionally or ecumenically "nonaligned."[42] Indeed, liberals referred to Leberecht Uhlich as "the Saxon O'Connell," identifying him with Daniel O'Connell, the Irish nationalist and champion of Catholic emancipation.[43] The radical jurist and philosopher Arnold Ruge (1802–1880), a compatriot of Marx, Engels, and the other Left Hegelians, opined that the Protestant Friends' campaigns for religious freedom and dedication to maintaining a lay-governed "people's church," which he identified as a continuation and renewal of the German Reformation, would be more effective at realizing the 1848 revolutionaries' aspiration of German national unity than the revolutionaries themselves.[44] The historian Georg Gervinus and the radical politician Robert Blum, members of German Catholic congregations in Heidelberg and Leipzig, respectively, and elected deputies to the 1848 Frankfurt Parliament, hoped that the dissenting congregations could reconcile the separated confessions into a national church that would serve as a basis for German national unity.[45] German liberals and republicans who were sympathetic to what the dissenting congregations stood for must have also been impressed by their popular appeal.

During a missionary tour throughout Germany in 1845, Ronge delivered a series of wildly popular sermons, speeches, and letters—typically in Evangelical Churches—to thousands of supporters and interested Roman Catholics and Protestants. He attracted "thousands upon thousands" for an event in Frankfurt am Main, thirteen thousand for a service in Offenbach, fifteen thousand for a speech in Ulm, and thirty thousand in Königsberg.[46] In his sermons and speeches, Ronge announced that the time had come for German Catholics and Protestants to reach out to each other, and that every sign of the times clearly pointed toward the possibility of a reunion of the separated German states into a unified nation and the separated confessions into a general Christian church.[47] To this end, he invoked the memory of the early Reformation, a pre-confessional era that had eschewed sectarianism and envisioned the Christian church as a single body of believers. This, claimed Ronge, was precisely the kind of church the reformers had originally sought to establish before secular rulers had cynically politicized the Reformation and was the kind of national unity that Germany deserved.[48]

The German Catholics' vision of unity was inclusive. Informally attending or even joining a German Catholic congregation was voluntary and did not entail compulsory conversion or professions of dogma. Interested parties could come and go from the congregations as they pleased. This notion of unity entailed a unity in diversity; a unity among a multiplicity of religious forms without the yoke of a binding uniformity.[49] This German Catholic notion of unity in diversity (*Einheit in die Mannigfaltigkeit*) entailed an acceptance and celebration of difference without any threat of coercion or compulsion to revise one's beliefs.[50] Such inclusive notions of unity made it easy for Roman Catholics and Protestants to freely join German Catholic congregations. A group of Protestants from the Lower Saxon town of Oldenburgh left their Evangelical churches and joined the local German Catholic congregation because, according to them, Luther himself had never intended to abandon the Catholic Church altogether but only to reform its false doctrines. For them, the nineteenth-century German Catholic congregations were closer in spirit to Luther's model of a reformed catholic church than either nineteenth-century Roman Catholicism or Evangelical Protestantism.[51]

The Protestant Friends and German Catholics sought not only to unite Catholics and Protestants, but encouraged rapprochement among the various Protestant sects as well. The various Protestant sects and Protestant free churches (churches independent from, yet recognized by, the state churches) would be unable to inspire the piety and enthusiasm necessary to be socially or nationally effective if they remained separated.[52] Accordingly, the Protestant Friends worked with mainstream Protestant associations such as the Gustav-Adolf Verein to encourage tolerance and unity among the separated Protestant denominations. An early-twentieth-century historian of the Protestant Friends who was sympathetic to the Free Religious Movement compared Uhlich's reforming efforts with those of Philip Melanchthon; even after the sixteenth-century break with the papacy, Melanchthon and other irenical reformers sought rapprochement with Catholics. After withdrawing his congregation from the Saxon state church, Uhlich sought to maintain ties with mainstream Protestants and establish new ones with German Catholics.[53] At a fall 1843 meeting of the Protestant Friends, the participants attempted to define the basic tenets of Protestantism in such a way as to appeal to a wider number of Evangelicals and longed for a Protestant church that could accommodate a plurality of differing conceptions of faith.[54]

The dissenting congregations' intra-Protestant and interconfessional ecumenism extended, in limited cases, to Jews. Two contested features of the concept *nation* in the German Revolution of 1848 were whether the nation was predominately Catholic or Protestant and whether Jews could be citizens. The dissenting congregations eschewed confessional notions of the nation and argued that the "German nation" must be inclusive of Catholics and Protestants. But some members of the Free Congregations explored and promoted unity with members of the Reform Jewish communities.[55] One such figure was Carl Scholl (1807–1863), the minister of Mannheim's German Catholic congregation. Scholl, a theologian, playwright, and revolutionary who had dabbled in pantheism and Left Hegelianism as a youth and advocated a "religion of humanity" during his later years, professed that he became a German Catholic because in the movement he recognized "not only the basis of a unification of Catholicism and Protestantism, but also the possibility of a union of Protestantism and reformed Judaism."[56] In addition to Scholl's group of supporters in Mannheim, the local Hamburg Free Congregation included several Jews. And in 1847 the Königsberg congregation held its services—no other venue could be found—at the local synagogue with the blessing of the Jewish community. In 1857 an Offenbach German Catholic minister stood in for a local rabbi at a Jewish funeral.[57]

Jews were invited to attend, and several joined, congregations of the Protestant Friends and German Catholics in Frankfurt. Michael A. Meyer has identified a relationship, in the form of shared interests and agendas, among the Protestant Friends, German Catholics, and the Reformed Jewish community in Frankfurt.[58] Leberecht Uhlich identified his position as minister and pastoral duties with those of the local Magdeburg reform rabbi.[59] Scholl himself noted the similarities between liberal Protestantism and Reform Judaism. He even imagined a unification of the two groups on this basis and frequently spoke of Jesus as an enlightened Jewish reformer.[60] Like Scholl, most

German liberals supported Jewish emancipation. But German liberal support for Jewish emancipation was usually motivated by the liberals' desire to position themselves against German conservatives rather than by pure altruism.[61] Indeed, several federal states passed laws granting Jews full civic rights at the very outset of the March revolutions. But while German liberals countenanced emancipation, a religious union with the Jews remained another matter.

Scholl's notion of a union of Protestants and reformed Jews did not receive widespread support among either German Jews or German Christians. Indeed, the Jewish response to the dissenting congregations was divided. While contemporary Jewish radicals were sympathetic to revolutionary Christian communities, most German Jews remained at arms length from the Protestant Friends and German Catholics. The moderate Jewish reform rabbi Ludwig Philippson (1811–1889) epitomized this suspicion, rejecting the dissenting congregations' dismissal of dogma and revelation for a religion of humanity along with their notions that Christianity was a religion that had "evolved" beyond Judaism, as antithetical to the Jewish religion.[62] Nor were Scholl's views on Jewish-Christian ecumenism typical among the dissenting congregations, and he ultimately left the Mannheim German Catholic congregation because of what he saw as its deficiency of rationalism in theology and insufficient radicalism in politics.[63] Nevertheless, only one month after the Frankfurt Parliament had convened, participants at June–August 1848 meetings in Frankfurt that included a German Catholic preacher, a Protestant pastor, a Roman Catholic priest, and several Jewish rabbis, discussed how to cultivate a notion of German unity that was inclusive of the groups represented.[64]

The Free Congregations imagined a unified German nation whose foundation was confessional unity among Catholics and Protestants. Indeed, Ronge recognized the German Question as a by-product of the Reformation and Wars of Religion. The Reformation and the Thirty Years' War had left Germany spiritually and politically disunited.[65] This was a confessional notion of German unity that set aside the question of the political composition of the nation as a Kleindeutschland or Großdeutschland. German liberals preferred a kleindeutsch solution to the German question, but Ronge considered both Austria's close ties to the papacy and the Prussian king's leadership of the Evangelical Church a threat to the survival of the nineteenth-century Reformation. He was wary of the prospect of either Austria or Prussia taking a prominent role in Germany national unification.[66] The dissenting congregations also set aside questions of whether Germany should become a constitutional monarchy or a republic so long as the new government afforded German citizens freedom of religion and conscience. Only if freedom of religion and conscience were recognized could Germany enjoy interconfessional peace. And religious freedom and interconfessional peace were prerequisites for German national freedom and unity. In fact a religious reformation must precede any social and political revolution dedicated to unity (*Einheit*) or freedom (*Freiheit*); interconfessional reconciliation was a prerequisite for the success of any social and political revolutions. If German Catholics and Protestants remained separated opponents of confessional unity, ultramontane Catholics and orthodox Protestants would surely exploit this confessional divide for their own ecclesiastical and political ends.[67] Ronge underlined this point by exclaiming, "Political liberty cannot be realized till the tyranny of Popery is broken to pieces."[68] Indeed, Ronge reminded his supporters that hostilities arising from the confessional divide between German Catholics and Protestants resulted in the Thirty Years' War, which "destroyed the unity and political power of Germany." Thus the Protestant Friends and German-Catholic Movement sought to reclaim German confessional and national unity and popular political power by reuniting the separated confessions.[69]

The German Catholic priest Gustav von Struve succinctly explicated the relationship of religious freedom, confessional unity, and political unification. Struve noted his fears of a rigid ecclesiastical hierarchy sponsored or recognized by the state. He maintained that the one thing more dangerous than the police state was the priest state—it was something against which all friends of the fatherland should unite because there was no more dangerous revolutionary than the theocrat, who desires to control worldly relations by appealing to a higher world order and nurturing superstition and fanaticism in the laity. The theocrat violently defies kings, constitutions, laws, and the civil order and peace in the name of religion. Of course, when Struve and other members of Free Congregations spoke of "theocrats," they were referring to the orthodox Protestants, ultramontane Catholics, and the ecclesiastical hierarchies of those respective churches. Struve warned of impending outbreaks of fanaticism and recommended a union in political relations between "the better liberals and royalists" alongside a union of "the better among us of all religious faiths" in order to defend against threats of religious fanaticism, proscriptions to religious freedom, and the persistence of the confessional divide.[70] Thus Struve, the German Catholics, and the Protestant Friends recognized the absolute need for interconfessional peace and cooperation for a unified German nation.

The German Catholic historian Gervinus acknowledged that a "solid and enduring" German nation could only be grounded in interconfessional cooperation between Catholics and Protestants.[71] Gervinus was well-known throughout Germany as a member of the infamous Göttingen Seven, a group of academics who had been dismissed from the University of Göttingen in 1837 for refusing to profess an oath of loyalty to the new king of Hanover.[72] According to Gervinus, the German confessional divide had "rent in pieces the whole structure of [German] civilization."[73] And so long as ecclesiastical separation persisted in Germany, so too would national division.[74] He argued that the reconciliation of the separated churches "united in the spirit of toleration and love" represented the greatest wish that any German citizen could imagine. Echoing Protestant doubts about Roman intervention into German confessional or civil affairs, Gervinus warned that Catholic ultramontanism would obstruct every attempt for confessional or political union.[75] Ronge called on patriotic German Catholics and Protestants to join together with him out of love for the German people and the fatherland to form a German people's church composed of German Catholics, Protestants, and Jews that would promote German national unity in the current age of confessional discord and religious hatred and bickering.[76] A full three years before the March revolutions of 1848, when politically minded Germans first began to take seriously the possibility of a unified German nation, Ronge had noted that every sign of the times—from new railroads connecting distant cities to the Zollverein customs union—pointed to the imminence of confessional and national unity.[77]

The Free Congregations regarded as insufficient any political model of German national unity that did not address the confessional divide. German humanists, politicians, and socialists shared the common agenda of national unification but lacked unity among themselves and took different routes to achieve their goals. Religion was the most effective means of uniting disparate groups and their agendas because only religion could address the whole being of man rather than merely one aspect of man's existence—such as his intellectual, social, or political existence. Only religion, and the Free Religious movements in particular, could bring harmony to these differences, because they arose from the deepest needs of the era—namely the needs for freedom of conscience and German unity—and because inclusion and unity were at the foundation of their confession. These inclusive notions of German unity and identity were predicated on the need to overcome the confessional divide that resulted from the Reformation. Repairing this divide according to the revolutionary-ecumenical model of the German Catholics and Free Protestants, they believed, was the most effective means of unifying the German nation.[78]

Marriage as a Model for Unity

As a central component of their campaigns for confessional harmony, the Free Congregations demanded the emancipation of women and advocated harmony and equality between the sexes. Appealing to Lutheran notions of marriage and domesticity, the dissenting congregations argued that marriage, and especially mixed marriages, could uniquely contribute to healing the confessional divide by serving as a model domestic relationship, a model that could be applied to society.

The Protestant Friends and German Catholics consciously sought to include women in the communal life and administration of their congregations. German Catholics recommended that female congregants enjoy the same rights and privileges as their male counterparts. Accordingly, German Catholic women served on congregational governing bodies such as councils and synods. They founded charitable associations dedicated to education, social work, and philanthropy.[79] Approximately 40 percent of the members of the dissenting congregations were women, and by 1845 there were thirty women's societies associated with the Free Congregations.[80] The free-religious women's associations were themselves interconfessional and included women associated with the Protestant Friends, German-Catholic women, and other liberal Protestant, Catholic, and Jewish women who were sympathetic to the religious opposition movements but had not broken with their old churches.[81] The women's societies associated with the Free Congregations later became the basis for the women's emancipation movement in Germany.[82]

Ronge had always envisioned "the righteous and independent participation" of women in the German-Catholic Movement. He faulted the revolutions of 1848 for forgetting and failing to respect "the rights of one half of mankind—the rights of the female sex".[83] Indeed, he even faulted the sixteenth-century Reformation for not actively including women.[84] Thus the sixteenth-century Reformation remained incomplete not only because it resulted in a separation of the confessions but also, according to Ronge, because it excluded women from participation in its struggle for spiritual emancipation. The nineteenth-century Reformation would consummate the Reformation of the sixteenth not only by ensuring spiritual freedom and reuniting the confessions, but also by including women in its movement. Indeed, women were integral to the nineteenth-century Reformation and its campaign for interconfessional peace because, according to Ronge, women uniquely possessed "the power of unity, love, and reconciliation."[85]

The German Catholics campaigned for women's emancipation and included women in the administration of the German

Catholic congregations. But German-Catholic conceptions of emancipation and femininity were ambiguous. They demanded greater rights for women within marriage and increased participation for women within their congregations and the social sphere.[86] But these demands were grounded in traditional notions of the feminine as wife, mother, caretaker, and pacifier.[87] On the one hand, Ronge discouraged women from remaining narrowly focused on their families; instead, they must also participate in the life of the community. Women must also turn to that larger community—the nation—and work to arouse and strengthen that national spirit for the well-being and salvation of Germany.[88] But at the same time, Ronge espoused a notion of the feminine that compelled him to believe that women were easily susceptible to manipulation by unscrupulous Catholic priests. He credited his own popular appeal and charisma for the female interest and participation in German Catholic congregations and for "awakening consciousness and religious enthusiasm in the female heart, to act with righteous impulse and free will for the Reformation and for humanity."[89] Women's emancipation, it seemed, turned on a dialectic of empowerment and fragility. It represented an empowerment of women, but within traditional feminine roles.

Women appeared in significant numbers at Ronge's mass religious services and rallies.[90] This specific religious sphere was an accepted realm of the public sphere for women. And they participated in this realm in specifically feminine ways: participating in and making arrangements for religious services and rallies and receiving and presenting visitors with gifts. But they also participated in the religious sphere in ways that had traditionally been the reserve of men: they gave speeches, proposed and gave toasts, collected signatures, and signed petitions.[91] Based on the theories of the education reformer Friedrich Fröbel (1782–1852), German-Catholic women introduced some of the first kindergartens—feminized and deconfessionalized spaces for the education of young children—to Germany.[92] Women associated with the Protestants Friends also participated in the spiritual and social life of their congregations. Sixty Magdeburg women drafted a petition against the impending removal of Leberecht Uhlich from his office for conducting Bible studies that the police had forbidden as "popular assemblies." In this fall 1845 petition, the women expressed their solidarity and agreement with Uhlich and urged the consistory not to remove him.[93]

The dialectic of women's empowerment and fragility at play within the dissenting congregations was resolved in the German Catholics' concept of marriage as a domestic model for the just organization of society. This was a model of unity within unity, a model of national and confessional harmony within the matrimonial union. And it was in this conception of marriage that the relationship among women's powers of unity, love, and reconciliation were manifest.

The German Catholics appealed to Luther's concept of marriage and domesticity to agitate for the acceptance and recognition of confessionally mixed marriages. Whereas the medieval church had lauded celibacy and recognized marriage as an unhappy state that was preferable only to fornication, Luther rejected celibacy while praising marriage and domestic life as virtuous. He supported clerical marriage, condemned the practice of oblation, and advocated the abolition of convents—all practices that separated women from their families. The German Catholics argued that Luther's notions of marriage and domesticity were divinely founded and could serve as bases for a just organization of society and ensuring women's rights.[94] Indeed, through love-based marriages, "The ties of union and brotherly love will be more closely united between community and family; and moreover, the community will prove a moral power, to prevent compulsory marriage, and watch over the equal rights of the female sex."[95] Love-based marriages would serve as the domestic model of the social community. The community would in turn protect this notion of marriage and in so doing ensure the rights of women—who could best exercise these rights within marriage and a supportive community. Mixed marriages between Catholics and Protestants were especially useful domestic models of social community because such unions cut across the confessional divide. Apropos, many of the men and women who joined German Catholic congregations came from confessionally mixed marriages.[96]

The German Catholics considered mixed marriages especially helpful not only for uniting community and family but also for solving so many of Germany's social problems that proceeded from the confessional divide. In 1847 an anonymous pamphlet, *The Controversy over Mixed Marriages and the Sovereign Churches in the Grand Duchy of Baden*, appeared; it supported the dissenting congregations' goal of advocating confessional harmony—and thus improving Germany—through mixed marriage. Among other things, the pamphlet advocated mixed marriage and even implied that the acceptance and recognition of mixed marriages might be a solution to all of nineteenth-century Germany's social, religious, and political problems. Indeed, the author(s) identified the problem of mixed marriages the most pressing ecclesiastical question of the present era and believed it was as important as the national question—a by-product of the confessional divide that was caused by the Reformation.[97]

The author(s) noted that the Reformation put German Catholics and Protestants into separate, antagonistic camps and severed the Christian bonds that Germans had shared before the Reformation. The confessional divide had turned Germans against each other in hostility over and over.[98] But the authors claimed that after centuries of religious strife, German Catholics and Protestants were finally beginning to recognize that only interconfessional coexistence and cooperation could rescue Germany from further violence.[99] They rejected as unworkable the Catholic Church's instructions for mixed marriage, especially those prescribed in Pius VIII's March 5, 1830, breviary to the bishops of the lower Rhine that refused to recognize the marriages of confessionally mixed couples who refused to promise to raise all of their children Catholic.[100] These instructions contributed to the increasing confessional tensions of the Cologne Troubles. Moreover, they would inhibit mixed marriages and spiritual reconciliation between Catholics and Protestants and ultimately German national unity.

The author(s) noted the relationship between spiritual cooperation and German national unity by arguing that the reconciling power of marriage had not only contributed to a strengthening bond of unity between the different confessions in Germany, but had also helped to overcome "the damaging mutual prejudices, antipathies and hesitations, interwoven [in] the physical and spiritual interests of families of different confessions and therefore [mixed marriages] like almost no other thing worked toward the inner unity and strengthening of the life of the state and the life of the Volk."[101] Thus mixed marriages could heal divisions between the confessions but also in German social and political life. Indeed, previous efforts at union failed partly because they did not address the confessional divide in the domestic sphere; that is, they sought to unify the separated confessions from the outside in rather than the inside out—which mixed marriages could uniquely achieve.[102]

The "marriage question" had serious implications for public and private life in nineteenth-century Germany. Every mixed marriage effected a microunion of the separated confessions in the domestic sphere. And by healing the confessional divide in the domestic sphere, one marriage at a time, the confessions became more closely united in the social and national spheres. Thus women's emancipation and the recognition and acceptance of mixed marriages were integral to the success of the nineteenth-century Reformation.

Conclusion

The Protestant Friends' and German Catholics' ecumenical agendas ultimately lost out to the orthodox and ultramontane parties of the Evangelical and Catholic Churches. But at the same time, they attracted tens of thousands of German Catholics and Protestants who had helped to realize confessional, national, and gender harmony in a decade that was dominated by increasing confessional tensions and revolutionary upheaval. Indeed, they were more effective at uniting Germans than the Frankfurt Parliament had been at uniting Germany. And in their campaigns in support of a revolutionary ecumenism, the Protestant Friends and German Catholics invoked memories of Luther to justify ecclesiastical and civil disobedience and to ground the nineteenth-century Reformation—a reformation that aimed to win religious freedom for German dissenters;

emancipation for German women; reunification of the separated confessions; and union of German Catholics, Protestants, and Jews into a single nation. The dissenting congregations' notions of German unity and identity were predicated on the repair of Germany's confessional divide. Their notions of German unity and identity did not turn on the inclusion or exclusion of Prussia and Austria from the German nation nor on the choice between a constitutional monarchy or a republic. These were contested features of the "nation" debated by German liberals and republicans. The dissenting congregations set aside these political questions. Their popular and revolutionary-ecumenical notions of German unity and identity were grounded in, and would only be strengthened by, a reunification of the separated confessions. As a by-product of the Reformation, the dissenting congregations understood the German National Question in confessional terms rather than the liberals' and republicans' political terms.

As such, the dissenting congregations' notions of German unity and identity cannot be neatly categorized with liberal or conservative, confessionally Catholic or Protestant notions of German unity and identity. Jonathan Sperber has recognized confessionally exclusive notions of German unity espoused by German Catholics and Protestants at celebrations of national unity during the 1848 revolutions, noting that "representations of national unity could affirm or reject either of the two Christian confessions."[103] But in the case of the revolutionary ecumenism of the Protestant Friends and German Catholics, representations of national unity could, rather than exclude either of the two confessions, encapsulate them both. Their memories of Luther as a religious revolutionary and the sixteenth-century Reformation as an unfinished process of spiritual emancipation, to be fulfilled by realizing independence from ecclesiastical hierarchies and through a reunification of the separated confessions, grounded the dissenting congregations' ecumenical notions of unity and identity.

3

A HOLY ALLIANCE

Right-Wing Ecumenism and German Nationalism, 1860–1866

AFTER THE FAILURES of the Revolutions of 1848, the German liberal-nationalist movement seemed to be in shambles. Indeed, most standard accounts of German nationalism glide seamlessly from the failures of 1848 onto Bismarck's appointment as Prussian prime minister in 1862 and then onto the Austro-Prussian War of 1866 and the subsequent establishment of the Reich. After all, the conventional narratives of German national unification presume that nationalism had been defeated and that counterrevolution had prevailed. The Prussian king had rebuffed the crown "from the gutter," and his aspirations for a Prussian-dominated German union of north German states had been nipped in the bud by the Austrian Empire at the so-called humiliation of Olmütz. One might assume that in this case the only path to German national unification would be a marginalization of the Austrian Empire. A humiliated Prussia could redeem itself and the rest of the German nation only through war with Austria. At least that is how the conventional accounts of German national unification framed the story. But in fact, German nationalism remained as diffuse in the post-revolutionary period as ever—perhaps even more so. But the marginalization of Austria was not the only proposed solution to the enduring German National Question.

On September 21 and 22, 1860, nine conservative Catholics and four orthodox Lutherans met in Erfurt to discuss the possibility of rapprochement between the separated confessions and to address the German Question in a way that was inclusive of both Catholic Austria and Protestant Prussia. They had been invited to Erfurt by the Westphalian Catholic priest Friedrich Michelis (1815–1886), who convened the conference in reaction to increasing revolutionary activity throughout Europe and the continuing failure to resolve of the German National Question. The conference attendees and its sympathizers, who included Michelis himself, the Catholic theologian Ignaz von Döllinger, the Lutheran historian Heinrich Leo, and the Prussian jurist Ernst Ludwig von Gerlach, among others, envisioned church unity as an association of pious German Catholics and Protestants united to defend Germany against atheism, liberalism, and revolution.[1] They imagined a nation in the confessionally reunited subjects of a German Christian state to be led by a holy alliance of Austria and Prussia whose political authority derived from God.

The group's memories of Luther and the Reformation were essential to how supporters of the Erfurt Conference understood the contemporary confessional divide and the possibility of confessional and German national unity. Attendees and sympathizers of the conference, including its Catholic supporters, recalled Luther as a pious moral reformer of a corrupt medieval church who had forcefully eschewed sectarianism. They absolved Luther of any guilt for the confessional divide—they blamed this on peasant revolutionaries, Anabaptists, other nonconforming clergy and congregations—and invoked Luther's memory to advocate obedience to legitimate political and ecclesiastical authorities and to serve as a bulwark against revolution.

This chapter aims to restore the Erfurt Conference and its supporters to the post-1848 histories of German nationalism. Indeed, of all of the strains of German nationalism proffered between 1848 and 1866, theirs might have been the most irenical. The conventional histories of German nationalism point to the post-1848 period as a mere prelude to the establishment of the German Empire in 1871. But while the contemporary German National Association

(Nationalverein) and German Reform Association (Reformverein) espoused small-German and Greater-German positions, respectively, supporters of the Erfurt Conference proposed a model of unification that acknowledged the political realities of a conservative and multicultural Austria and an increasingly powerful Prussia.[2] Their eschewal of liberal nationalism for a union of Austria and Prussia was consistent with the contemporary political structure of the German Confederation. They explicitly appealed to a balance of power model—harkening back to the Congress of Vienna and the Holy Alliance—that had kept the peace for decades and now suggested how the moribund old regime might address current revolutionary threats. Their großdeutsch nationalism was not animated by anti-Prussian sentiment, as so many models of Greater German nationalism were. And if that were not enough, in 1864—only two years before Prussia would dominate Austria on the field of battle—Bismarck himself would propose a model of German national unity, *sans* ecumenism, that was strikingly similar to that proposed by the Erfurt Conference. But this conference remains practically unknown to historians of German nationalism.

Its obscurity to historians of German nationalism notwithstanding, compared to the better-known National and Reform Unions, the Erfurt program was quite influential. Indeed, the National Union had disbanded in 1867 and the Reform Union had drifted into xenophobia and anti-Semitism as Bismarck's power politics rendered the nationalist movements impotent. But the influence of the Erfurt Conference endured. By pointing to the confessional divide as a national-political problem, as had previous generations of ecumenists, the Erfurt Conference anticipated the consequences of a political unification of a religiously divided nation. This insight—that any unification of the German nation that did not account for the confessional divide must be incomplete—would be picked up by the next generation of ecumenists, but by proponents of the anti-Catholic Kulturkampf as well, and dominated the religious politics of the early German Reich.

The Context and Reception of the Erfurt Conference

The Erfurt Conference occurred within the context of increasing revolutionary activity throughout Europe. Revolutionary outbursts in Italy and the successes of the Risorgimento stoked fears of encroaching atheism, liberalism, and revolution that mid-nineteenth-century European conservatives had decried since 1848. In 1859 Napoleon III, whom archconservatives regarded as a usurper of the legitimate French monarchy, allied with Piedmont-Sardinia against Austria. This alliance eventually contributed to the Italian subjugation of Austrian Lombardy and its annexation into a unified Italian nation. Revolutionary insurrections in Sicily in 1860 precipitated its conquest by Garibaldi and the Redshirts and their subsequent assault on the Kingdom of Naples, a further step in the process of Italian unification. For conservatives like those who would assemble at Erfurt, perhaps the most compelling evidence of the spread of atheism, liberalism, and revolution was the assault on the Papal States by Cavour's armies. Revealing concerns about threats to religious identity beyond the German states, the Erfurt Conference manifesto would describe this "violation" of the Papal States by Italian nationalists as a "shocking, galling injustice."[3] The subsequent unification of Italy under nationalist and revolutionary precepts confirmed European reactionaries' fears of the encroachment of atheism, liberalism, and revolution into European society and politics.

In response to these revolutionary developments, Michelis, a priest and theologian from Münster, convoked the Erfurt Conference. The interconfessional character of the Protestant Awakening and a recent biography of the German publisher Friedrich Perthes (1772–1843) had inspired Michelis to call for an ecumenical meeting of conservative German Catholics and Protestants.[4] Perthes was an irenical German Protestant who had maintained a long correspondence with several pious Catholics. He defended Catholicism from its liberal Protestant critics and argued that disbelief was a greater threat to Christianity than orthodox Catholicism or Protestantism.[5]

Inspired by the examples of the Awakening Movement and the person of Friedrich Perthes, Michelis wrote to several prominent Catholics and Protestants, including the Prussian jurist Ernst Ludwig von Gerlach (1795–1877), the Protestant historian Heinrich Leo (1799–1878), and the conservative politician and Lutheran convert from Judaism, Friedrich Julius Stahl (1802–1861), inviting them to meet, share ideas, and form a common front against revolution and atheism.[6] All three men belonged to a Prussian conservative party centered around the conservative newspaper *Kreuzzeitung* that had emerged from orthodox Lutheran opposition to the 1848 revolutions.[7] Their reactionary bona fides were beyond question.

Unfortunately for Michelis, only one of these pious archconservatives would actually attend the Erfurt Conference. Ludwig von Gerlach, who on his deathbed would profess that what he had wanted most of all was to witness a reunion of the separated confessions,[8] could not attend on account of the marriage of his nephew and instead sent his well wishes. Heinrich Leo accepted the invitation and arrived on the second day. And although he strongly supported the cause of German conservatives such as Gerlach and Leo and usually deemphasized confessional differences between pious Catholics and Protestants, Friedrich Julius Stahl declined the invitation. However strongly Stahl opposed atheism and revolution, he argued that a reunion of the separated confessions was neither a desirable nor a necessary prerequisite for conservative Catholics and Protestants to work toward their shared political interests.[9]

When word of the conference leaked to the religious press, it was met with a mixed reaction. The Catholic press celebrated it as an opportunity, not for authentic reunion, but as one that could bring German Protestants back to Rome.[10] The Protestant press was less enthused. The *Protestant Church Newspaper*, a left-wing Protestant paper, identified the conference as a Catholic plot to convert German Protestants.[11] The conservative Protestant *Kreuzzeitung* acknowledged the German confessional divide as lamentable and recognized that religious separation was the cause of German national disunity.

But, it maintained, the cure for the German confessional and national divide should not be purchased at the price of Protestant freedom. Moreover, claimed the *Kreuzzeitung*, the Roman Catholic Church as it existed in 1860 could offer no asylum to an Evangelical.[12]

Michelis received some affirmative replies to his invitations besides Heinrich Leo's, but when the conference finally convened on September 21, 1860, only two Lutherans and eight Catholics (three priests and five laymen) were in attendance. In addition to Michelis, the prominent attendees included Wilhelm Volk, a Prussian bureaucrat and Catholic convert who produced a history of the Erfurt Conference under the pseudonym Ludwig Clarus, and the Catholic Saxon nobleman Count Cajus zu Stolberg, who was happy to attend any meeting at which friendly Protestants were willing to recognize the assault on the Papal States as an egregious affront to ecclesiastical and political order.[13] On the second day of the conference, Heinrich Leo arrived with Karl Bindewald, a Protestant lawyer in the Prussian ministry of culture who had been won to the cause of the Erfurt Conference by the Berlin High Church Lutheran pastor Friedrich Wilhelm Schulze.[14]

In consultation with the other attendees, Michelis prepared a manifesto for the conference. The manifesto emphasized that the attendees did not seek a reunion of the separated confessions on account of any sense of religious indifferentism, but instead from the conviction that the separation of the churches was a truly lamentable condition. Moreover, the attendees felt compelled by the German people, whom they identified as essentially conservative and Christian, to work toward a rapprochement of German Catholics and Protestants for the cause of a single and undivided fatherland.[15] The attendees acknowledged that a German nation might be politically unified without a reunion of the separated confessions. But, they argued, a German nation so united would remain incomplete, fragile, and susceptible to that unholy trinity of atheism, liberalism, and revolution. Thus confessional reunion was a prerequisite of German national unity.

Heinrich Leo produced an addendum to Michelis's manifesto that further underlined the relationship of confessional reunion to reactionary politics. He identified the paramount threats to the German fatherland as revolution and atheism, embodied in the recent assault on the Papal States by the Risorgimento. That the Papal States, whose sovereignty, Leo argued, was older and more indisputable than that of any European states, could be so violated was proof of the increasing threat of encroaching revolution. Only a unified front of pious German Catholics and Protestants could check the spread of revolution and atheism.[16] A reunion of the separated churches was in the best interests of the German fatherland. Leo envisioned the Erfurt Conference not only as a renewal of the Christian church through a reunion of the separated confessions, but also as a renewal of German conservatism. He maintained that since 1848, German conservatism had attracted too many nefarious characters to its party. Far too many opportunists, Bonapartists, and realpolitiker had joined the conservative cause. A renewed conservatism would proceed from an ecclesiastical basis and expel these profane members from its ranks. And the most effective conservative party was one composed of a union of pious Catholics and Protestants working together to defend Germany from revolution and atheism.[17] The manifesto and Leo's addendum reflected the reactionary-ecumenical tendencies of the Erfurt Conference attendees and its sympathizers. Their paramount goals were to defend Christianity and Germany from atheism and revolution by reuniting the separated confessions. A reunion of Catholics and Protestants along these lines would also strengthen the German fatherland and serve as the basis for their großdeutsch vision of German national unity.

After the conference had disbanded, its attendees and sympathizers continued to discuss the possibility of confessional reunion, their shared opposition to atheism and revolution, and how to properly address the German Question. In their diaries, letters, journals, and monographs, they imagined confessional unity in a reunion of pious Catholics and Protestants united in opposition to atheism and revolution. They considered Catholicism and Protestantism as two complementary constituents of a single, yet separated, catholic Christian church. Piety, opposition to revolution and atheism, and commitment to a unified German fatherland would define this reunion of German Catholics and Protestants. And like the irenical celebrants of the 1817 Reformation anniversaries, and the revolutionary ecumenists of the Vormärz and 1848, the reactionary ecumenists of the Erfurt Conference would appeal to memories of Luther and the Reformation to explicate their notions of confessional and national unity.

The Reactionary-Ecumenical Notion of Church Unity

Since the sixteenth century, Luther and the Reformation had existed as contested sites of memory that functioned as a kind of mnemonic shorthand for the German confessional divide.[18] As such, the participants and sympathizers of the Erfurt Conference could not entertain any ideas of confessional reunion without first addressing memories of Luther and the Reformation. Instead of recognizing Luther and the Reformation as the primary causes of the contemporary confessional divide, the reactionary ecumenists of the Erfurt Conference remembered Luther as a pre-confessional moral reformer who had eschewed sectarianism and had sought to avoid a separation of the church. The Reformation represented an historically necessary correction of the abuses and corruption of the medieval Catholic Church from within the church itself. The schisms that ultimately resulted from the Reformation were never intended to be permanent, nor were they essential to Luther's proposed reforms. As such, the nineteenth-century German Catholic and Evangelical Churches were primed for reunion.

Supporters of the Erfurt Conference argued that the Reformation represented a renewal and purification of the medieval church and a blessing to Catholicism. The Catholic historian and theologian Ignaz von Döllinger (1799–1890), who was one of the earliest advocates of the Erfurt Conference, recalled a Luther who had served as the touchstone for reform of a Roman Catholic Church that refused even to acknowledge, much less reform its abuses.[19] He reaffirmed this sentiment in lectures of 1872 in which he argued that the Reformation represented a "great purification and renewal of the church," but that it could have been accomplished without the schisms that had ultimately resulted.[20] Ludwig von Gerlach, who did not attend but nevertheless defended the Erfurt Conference in the conservative Protestant press, recognized the Reformation as the most magnificent flower of the medieval Catholic Church.[21] He reminded his readers that the Reformation was a necessary correction of abuses—namely, the increasing licentiousness and corruption of the papacy and ecclesiastical hierarchy—within the medieval church. Gerlach noted that the Reformation had also benefited Catholicism because it had compelled the church to reform its abuses and that nonpartisan Catholics recognized its blessings.[22] He countenanced the sixteenth-century Reformation as a shaking up of ecclesiastical authority in its own era and even postulated the need for a contemporary reactionary-ecumenical Counter-Reformation as an answer to secularizing trends of the nineteenth century.[23]

The reactionary ecumenists maintained that the German confessional divide was an accidental, rather than essential, result of the Reformation. Indeed, the Reformation was supposed to be a temporary and provisional state of affairs until the church had been reformed of its abuses. According to Döllinger, the early reformers had never intended permanent separation between the Roman Catholic and Protestant denominations.[24] He regarded the possibility of a reunion of the separated confessions as "a most salutary circumstance" that would repair the confessional divide and whose effects would touch German religion, politics, and society.[25] Heinrich Leo elucidated Döllinger's notion of the accidental nature of the German confessional divide by drawing parallels between Luther and the medieval reforming pontiff Gregory VII.[26] Both Luther's and Gregory's reforms were necessary and ultimately benefited the church, but they were wildly unpopular and fiercely opposed by contemporaries. Any disruptions or schisms within the church that had resulted from Luther's and Gregory's proposed reforms had to be considered incidental to their campaigns. Besides, argued Wilhelm Volk, Luther had no idea that he might be teaching some schismatic heresy—he believed that he was teaching a purified Catholic doctrine. Indeed, Volk noted, contemporary Lutheran doctrine contained vestiges of Catholicism, and in any case, enlightened and free-religious types even identified Lutheranism as a kind of incomplete or partial Catholicism.[27] The theological proximity of Catholicism and Lutheranism suggested a basis for reunion between the two confessions. The reactionary ecumenists located the basis for this theological proximity between Catholics and Lutherans in the Augsburg Confession.

Advocates of the Erfurt Conference program proposed that the Augsburg Confession could serve as the theological foundation for their reactionary-ecumenical church. Gerlach noted that despite the differences between Catholics and Protestants, both confessions had always professed the same fundamental doctrines, as defined by the Apostle's Creed and the first twenty-one articles of the Augsburg Confession.[28] According to Döllinger, the Augsburg Confession constituted "the fundamental creed of the Reformation" and denoted a common symbol and a shared faith between Catholics and Protestants.[29] Wilhelm Volk recalled the goodwill displayed by both Catholics and Protestants at the 1530 Diet of Augsburg as a model for contemporary irenicism.[30] Catholics and Protestants had met in Augsburg at the behest of the emperor Charles V in order to identify their common beliefs and to elucidate the differences that existed between them. And while the Catholic Church issued a confutation of the Augsburg Confession, it affirmed many of the articles defined in the Confession, including those addressing the Trinity, original sin, the episcopal office, baptism, the Real Presence in the Eucharist, and the freedom of the will. So for Volk and other proponents of the Erfurt program, the Augsburg Confession might be read as an irenical, rather than polemical, profession of faith.

The reactionary ecumenists recalled the early Reformation era (1517–1520) as a reformed, yet pre-confessional, catholic Christian community that could serve as the model for their contemporary ecumenical church. Heinrich Leo was a proponent of a pre-confessional

Lutheran Church that he imagined was represented by the Augsburg Confession. According to Leo, this post-Reformation, yet preconfessional, conception of the church embodied by the Augsburg Confession recalled the early Apostolic Church. The Augsburg Confession recognized bishoprics and the sacraments and possessed a liturgy close to that of the old Apostolic Church. Its confessors stood so close to Catholicism that the move toward total reconciliation would be extremely small. Indeed, the Augsburg Confession evoked a Lutheranism that more closely approximated the Apostolic Church and the contemporary Catholic Church than it did later developments of the Reformation.[31]

The Augsburg Confession not only represented the theological basis for a reunion of pious Catholics and Protestants, but also suggested the existence of a single Christian church, albeit split. According to Döllinger, the separation of the confessions was artificial and would only last until the churches had resolved their differences, when they would reunite into a catholic Christian church: "The idea of two rival Churches in Germany arrayed in permanent hostility against each other shocked the [sixteenth-century] mind. All diets and religious conferences of the day were conducted on the assumption that the adherents of the new and the old religion were still members of one universal Church and that a common understanding could and ought to be arrived at, and communion of worship restored."[32] Despite the persistence of the confessional divide, the separated churches remained constituents of a single catholic Christian church. Heinrich Leo further endorsed this idea. According to Leo, the Lutheran Church, despite the separation of the confessions, remained part of the universal (catholic) church, which encompassed the entire Christian world. Both churches were "sick" since their separation from one another, and the only "cure" was mutual cooperation and rapprochement.[33] Indeed, full catholicity could not be found in any of the separated parts of the church, but only in the reactionary-ecumenical church envisioned by the proponents of the Erfurt Conference. Likewise, a German nation could never be fully unified under the auspices of Austria or Prussia alone, but only in a großdeutsch state that encapsulated them both.

The separation of the confessions had hindered Luther's original program of renewal and reform of the sixteenth-century church. The Counter-Reformation and the Council of Trent had later taken up this process of renewal, but the final reformation of the church could only occur in a reunion between Catholics and Protestants. Despite his Protestantism, Heinrich Leo had a favorable perception of the Counter-Reformation and the Council of Trent. The council had addressed a significant number of Luther's and other Protestant reformers' criticisms of the Catholic Church. Indeed, Leo argued that the nineteenth-century Catholic Church had undergone a long process of purification that had begun with Trent, and that if the sixteenth-century church had been what it is today, Luther would have never asserted his opposition to the church so energetically.[34] The memory of Trent represented a basis for reunion for the separated confessions, especially for those Lutherans who remained separated from the Catholic Church because of its historic abuses. Döllinger agreed with Leo's assessment of the Council of Trent and claimed that this irenical sentiment would be the one that reconciled the churches and unified Germany.[35]

To realize this notion of confessional unity, the supporters of the Erfurt Conference program appealed to memories of the early Reformation and invoked a Luther who demanded a reform of the abuses within the church, who eschewed sectarianism, and who never desired a schism. They espoused an ecumenical memory of the Augsburg Confession as an ecumenical profession of faith that recalled the Apostolic Church and underlined the shared beliefs of Catholics and Lutherans. They recalled a Reformation before the separation of the confessions, before its politicization by secular princes, and in short, before confessionalization. These memories of Luther and the Reformation informed their notions of church unity. And their plans for overcoming the confessional divide and reuniting the separated confessions informed how they thought about German national unity.

Confessional Reunion and German National Unity

The reactionary ecumenists explicitly underlined the relationship between confessional reunion and German national unity. It was impossible to unite Germany politically without also addressing the German confessional divide. Friedrich Michelis noted that the separation of the church often manifested itself in the consciousness of the German nation.[36] The German Question was, at its root, an ecclesiastical question and an historical by-product of the Reformation separation of Christianity and the confessionalization of the denominations. Wilhelm Volk claimed that the Erfurt Conference and publication of his history of the conference in 1867 represented the fulfillment of his obligation toward realizing the aspirations for national unification by pursuing a reunion of the separated confessions.[37] Döllinger argued that German unification "requires an ecclesiastical union of all its tribes as the completion, fulfillment, and crowning of the edifice."[38] Heinrich Leo recognized the connection between confessional and German national unity, exclaiming that the history of Germany since the Reformation taught that whoever desired a strong and unified German empire must first reestablish a mighty and unified German church.[39]

Wilhelm Volk noted that the current revolutionary era revealed the need for the establishment of a strong, unified German fatherland. But as the Erfurt Conference suggested, the need for religious reunion was also felt. Volk maintained that the coincidence of the national question and the confessional question was not accidental. These questions had been inextricably linked since the Reformation. And although the current era demanded the establishment of German political unity, it would be disastrous for Germany if its statesmen, motivated by some misguided patriotism, would realize only the unity of the nation without also effecting a reunion of the confessions.[40]

Although the reactionary ecumenists eschewed nationalism as a liberal ideology, they did not remain mute on what defined a nation. The conference participants and their supporters imagined a

German nation in the confessionally reunited subjects of a German Christian state to be led by a holy alliance of Austria and Prussia whose political authority derived from God. Conservatives rejected nationalism as a liberal ideology because it threatened the ostensibly legitimate authority of monarchs and historical states. States were products of the monarchs that ruled over them.[41] Nations—communities with shared languages, ethnicities, and cultures—may exist within states, but they could not represent the foundation of political authority.[42] Heinrich Leo argued that Germany's existence had depended on the church, and since the separation of the confessions during the Reformation, there had been a Catholic and a Protestant Germany. However, Leo maintained, the memory of a confessionally unified Germany persisted. If this memory could be realized in the nineteenth century with a confessionally reunited church, it would provide Germany with the foundation for its political unity.[43]

The reactionary ecumenists recognized the Holy Alliance of 1815 as an ecclesiastical-political model for a confessionally unified German Christian state including Prussia and Austria. Ludwig von Gerlach reminded his readers that nineteenth-century European Catholics and Protestants had shared the same struggles, victories, and defeats before the revolutionary crimes of Napoleon. In reaction to those crimes, the Russian czar, Holy Roman emperor, and Prussian king had formed a holy alliance to provide a common defense of Europe from revolution and atheism.[44] Gerlach sought the revival of such an alliance for the common defense of Christianity and Christian states from atheism and revolution. He recognized an "eternal element" of the Holy Alliance that must be revived.[45] Gerlach lauded its ideal, an alliance of the faithful, without distinction of confession, into an association for the protection of Christian Europe from atheism and revolution. And in particular, he imagined the Holy Alliance as a model for an ecumenical ecclesiastical-political organization.

Gerlach's fond memories of the Holy Alliance informed how he imagined the proper composition of the German state. Gerlach noted that the state precedes the nation. States are not a product of ethnic, confessional, linguistic, cultural, or popular solidarity among a people (that is, the way nineteenth-century nationalists defined a nation), but instead represent the kingdom of God's law within humanity. The medieval Reich had more closely resembled this kingdom because it included many nations within itself and acknowledged its political authority derived from its status as the embodiment of God's law on earth—not from popular solidarity among a people. Accordingly, Gerlach lauded Austria and the Habsburg monarchy, not the least because Austria remained a multiethnic state (*Vielvölkerstaat*) that included many nations. According to this model he similarly saw Prussia not as a nation, but as a stately collection of historical regions, old and new provincial fragments of the old German Reich, for which the provincial corporate relations (*Provinzialständverhältnis*) were alone natural.[46] Accordingly, he resisted nationalist conceptions of German unity for a notion of German unity in which corporate relations were maintained, the confessions were united in a catholic Christian Church, and Austria and Prussia were constituent nations of a single Christian state and aligned in a holy alliance whose authority derived from God.

The German Christian state that Gerlach and other supporters of the Erfurt Conference program envisioned would necessarily exclude Jews, deists, and nonbelievers from its constituency. Instead, political rights in the Christian state would be reserved for members of the confessionally reunited Christian church. Allowing Jews, deists, and nonbelievers to participate in the civil society of a German Christian state whose purpose was to realize Christian values and defend Christian institutions would, in effect, lead to a dechristianization of a state whose very reason for being was predicated on defending the Volk from atheism and revolution.[47] This was, of course, antithetical to those conservatives, like the attendees and sympathizers of the Erfurt Conference, who identified the paramount threats to the German fatherland as the infiltration of atheism, liberalism, and revolution into the German polity and society. Proving that every notion of inclusion and unity comes at the cost of some minority group losing out, later Protestant nationalists and anti-Semites would later employ the notion of the Christian state to marginalize not only

German Jews, but also liberals and German Catholics from the German nation.[48]

The outbreak of the Austro-Prussian War discouraged the reactionary ecumenists' aspirations for a confessionally reunited großdeutsch empire. Indeed, in a July 21, 1866, diary entry, Gerlach claimed to recognize a religious element to the war. He did not want Germany to be overwhelmed by the Prussian-Protestant-Freemasonic (that is, liberal Protestant) faction, nor did he want Germany to become un-Catholic. Accordingly, he opposed kleindeutsch conceptions of German unification. According to Gerlach, that dualism of Protestantism and Catholicism was essential to Germany.[49] Such dualism was lost in a Prussian-dominated German empire that excluded Catholic Austria.

Friedrich Michelis also affirmed the need for a reunion of Catholics and Protestants to bring a peaceful balance between Austria and Prussia. Austria was heir to the imperial idea, inheritor of the legacy of the Holy Roman Empire, and confessionally Catholic, while Prussia was the carrier of the idea of the Reformation and Protestant. According to Michelis, Prussia was a state in which the Protestant church and its continuous Reformation profoundly influenced the national consciousness. Michelis recognized Prussia's most important task as the strengthening of its national-ecclesiastical consciousness and realization of a großdeutsch empire that included Catholic Austria.[50] But he remained ambivalent about the idea of a unification of Germany under a kleindeutsch model of Prussian leadership. Michelis was overjoyed over the emergence of the German Empire, but lamented the ultimate separation of Austria from Germany that the empire entailed.[51] Other reactionary ecumenists were equally ambivalent. Leo imagined a großdeutsch German state composed of Austria and Prussia until Prussia's victory in the Six Weeks War settled the großdeutsch vs. kleindeutsch debate. Ludwig von Gerlach famously opposed German unification and severed his relationship with Bismarck. He would eventually become a member of the Reichstag with the Catholic Center Party, continuing to work for reconciliation between pious Catholics and Protestants.

The confessional divide was an essential component to the solution of the German National Question. But instead of defining a nation and a national identity in a way that excluded Catholics, advocates of the Erfurt Conference imagined that a reunion of separated Catholics and Protestants could serve as the basis for German national unification that included both Austria and Prussia. Their notions of church unity colored how they imagined a unified German nation. And both their ecumenism and their nationalism were informed by their use and abuse of memories of Luther and the Reformation.

The Reactionary-Ecumenical Reclamation of Luther Memory

Supporters of the Erfurt Conference used and abused Luther's memory in their crusades against atheism and revolution and in their campaigns for confessional and political unity. Reactionary ecumenists praised Luther's reform of the abuses within the Catholic Church while absolving him of guilt for the German confessional divide. They invoked fond memories of a pre-confessional Reformation upon which to ground their notions of an Evangelical catholic Church. And they deployed memories of Luther to discourage revolution and to advocate obedience to legitimate political and ecclesiastical sovereigns.

Like other nineteenth-century conservatives, the participants in the Erfurt Conference recalled Luther's fierce opposition to the Peasants' War and emphasized his views on political obedience in order to justify the authority of established powers and to discourage political dissent. By variously appealing to Luther's *To the Christian Nobility of the German Nation* (1520), *On Worldly Authority* (1523), and *Against the Murderous, Robbing Hordes of Peasants* (1525), they affirmed Luther's teaching that secular authority derived from God and that one offended God when one offends his divinely ordained surrogates on Earth.[52]

Despite their frequent invocation of the Lutheran tradition to legitimize ecclesiastical and secular authority, German conservatives faced some difficulty in appropriating Luther's memory in nineteenth-century Germany. One the one hand, it was necessary to confront orthodox Catholic allegations of an identification of Reformation and revolution, and on the other hand it was necessary to distance oneself from the liberal Protestant interpretation of the Reformation as a religious-political emancipation movement.[53] They resolved this by recognizing Luther exclusively as a moral reformer of the church whose shaking up of ecclesiastical hierarchies was justified and by attributing later Reformation-era developments that had challenged the established secular and ecclesiastical authorities as incidental to Luther's reform program.

Ludwig von Gerlach derided conservative Catholics' association of Luther and the Reformation with revolution as erroneous. Even one of the Catholic attendees of the Erfurt Conference, Count Stolberg, had espoused this memory of Luther as fomenter of revolution. But Gerlach argued, by invoking Luther's *To the German Nobility (1520)*, that there were limited cases in which the pious Christian subject—though not the political revolutionary—could legitimately demand a corrupt church answer for its abuses According to Gerlach, this represented the extent of Luther's defiance of secular and ecclesiastical authorities. Besides, the conservative Catholic memory of Luther as revolutionary would inhibit the progress of fellow reactionary ecumenists against atheists and bona fide revolutionaries. In this case Luther's memory became a contested site between conservative reunionists whose shared goal was to impede revolution.[54]

Reactionary ecumenists also deployed Luther's memory to refute memories of Luther and the Reformation espoused by German liberals, nationalists, and revolutionaries. Throughout the Vormärz and 1848, nationalists and radicals had invoked memories of Luther as a revolutionary figure who had emancipated Germany from its oppressive foreign yoke.[55] But Friedrich Michelis recognized Luther's significance not in any struggle for emancipation, but in the reformer's demand for a moral renewal of the church. Thus Michelis expressly disassociated Luther's memory from rebellion against ecclesiastical and secular authority. He claimed that Luther's memory had in fact been usurped by nationalists and revolutionaries, who had misinterpreted Luther's legitimate protest against a corrupt papacy and an immoral church hierarchy as a license for rebellion against divinely ordered institutions of ecclesiastical and secular authority.[56] German liberals, nationalists, and revolutionaries abused this memory of Luther and the Reformation to ground their struggles for emancipation and to justify their enlightened, democratic, and heretical ideas that, reactionary ecumenists argued, would dissolve every divine institution. Although these revolutionary developments may have proceeded from the Reformation, Michelis argued that they should not be attributed to Luther.

Like Michelis, Heinrich Leo maintained a favorable view of Luther and what they both conceived as a "pure" and pre-confessional Reformation. But Leo argued that the epigones of the Reformation—peasant revolutionaries, Anabaptists, other nonconforming clergy and congregations, and even Jean Calvin himself—were the most vile of rabble.[57] Indeed, Leo recognized Calvin's teachings on democratic ecclesiastical organization as the "source and origin of every later disruptive revolutionary event in Europe."[58] Ignaz von Döllinger also expressed distrust for Reformed Christians. Döllinger identified the Reformed religion as foreign to Germany, "artificially fostered by the princes and generally only endured under compulsion."[59] On these grounds, Leo recommended the exclusion of French Reformed from future meetings of the Erfurt Conference. He suggested that the next conference should include Catholics, Lutherans, and German Reformed (Zwinglians) as historical participants at the Diet of Augsburg and historical constituents of the now-defunct Holy Roman Empire. But French Reformed, Anabaptists, and other nonconforming denominations would not be invited, nor would they be permitted to attend future conferences of reactionary ecumenists.[60] Huguenots, Anabaptists, and other religious nonconformists were excluded from the reactionary ecumenists' notions of confessional unity, just as German Jews and nonbelievers were excluded from their ideas of the German Christian state.

Memories of the Reformation as a renewal of the church and of Luther as the legitimate initiator of that reform allowed the supporters of the Erfurt Conference to reclaim Luther's memory from German liberals, nationalists, and revolutionaries who had invoked memories of the Reformation as a period of social and spiritual emancipation and from confessional Catholics who identified Luther with revolution. This repossession of memory was crucial for a reactionary-ecumenical faction that had to reconcile Luther's memory to orthodox Catholics, pious Evangelicals, Austrian proponents of a großdeutsch empire, and Prussian particularists in order to realize their own vision of German confessional and national unity.

Conclusion

In the end, the outbreak of the Austro-Prussian War would deter the reactionary ecumenists' aspirations for a confessionally reunited großdeutsch empire. Nevertheless, the influence of the Erfurt Conference had exceeded its numbers. The ultramontane Catholic press considered this tiny assembly of pious German Catholics and Protestants so compelling that the press believed its example might inspire Protestants to return to their Catholic "Mother Church" en masse. The Evangelical press ascribed a similar importance to the Erfurt Conference, so much so that an alarmed Prince-Regent Wilhelm and Culture Minister Bethmann-Hollweg feared a mass conversion of German Protestants to Catholicism.[61]

After all, the attendees and supporters of the Erfurt Conference were prominent figures: until their falling out, Gerlach had the ears of both Friedrich Wilhelm IV and Bismarck. Proving that Gerlach was not beneath contempt, Bismarck attacked him as a "fanatic in politics and religion."[62] Heinrich Leo was a widely read church historian. Ignaz von Döllinger was a well-known Catholic theologian whose fame only increased when he joined the dissident Old Catholic congregations in protest of the doctrine of papal infallibility. Perhaps the strongest reception of the Erfurt Conference came after the establishment of the German Empire, when the ecumenical epigones of the 1860 conference would become the center of conservative and Catholic opposition to Bismarck and the Kulturkampf.[63] But the real significance of the Erfurt Conference is this: amidst continuing debates over the proper way to unify the German nation, the conference underlined deeply held concerns over the implications of any Germany, be it klein or groß, that was to be unified against the confessional divide.

The confessionalization of the national idea lent itself to confessionally and racially exclusive notions of German national unity. Liberal Protestants and kleindeutsch nationalists espoused a notion of German national unity that elevated Prussia, excluded Austria, and imagined Catholics as internal foreigners and enemies of the German nation.[64] As such, ultramontane and conservative Catholics were forced to negotiate multiple loyalties—a church and a papacy they revered; an Austria they recognized as the standard of Christian-Germanic society; and after 1871, a German nation with which they strongly identified themselves as loyal citizens despite they were persecuted in the Kulturkampf.[65] These exclusive notions of German national unity and identity were predicated on confessional alterity. The German nation imagined by the Erfurt Conference was predicated on confessional unity.

But even the deconfessionalization, or perhaps ecumenization, of the national idea espoused by reactionary ecumenists lent itself to a kind of exclusivity within unity. Indeed, their notions of inclusion excluded others. But this was also the case in 1817, when celebrants of the Reformation anniversaries constructed notions of intra-Protestant unity that excluded orthodox Reformed and Lutherans, and again during the 1840s, when the Free Congregations imagined a reunited German Christian church that excluded the Evangelical hierarchy and ultramontane Catholics. For although the participants and sympathizers of the Erfurt Conference proposed an ecumenical notion of German unity that included Catholics and most Protestants, others remained outside the realm of what it meant to be "German": Reformed Christians, German Jews, and nonbelievers.

Historians of the confessionalization of the national idea have added layers of complexity to the history and historiography of German national unification by exploring how ultramontane and liberal Catholics, orthodox and cultural Protestants, variously imagined

German unity and identity through acts of inclusion and exclusion of confessional, ethnic, and racial Others. But ecumenists, be they radical or reactionary, enlightened or orthodox, also imagined German unity and separation in wildly different ways, including their confessional Others, but excluding their intellectual, ideological, racial, or cultural Others. A similar dynamic of unification through exclusion would come into play after the *Reichsgründung* in 1871. Politically unified, the German nation remained divided by religion. Within a German nation unified under Prussian and Protestant auspices, a new Other was recognized and excluded—German Catholics. Their marginalization underlined the fact that Germany remained divided, which in turn engendered a new generation of ecumenical nationalists to propose a German national idea that was inclusive of both Catholics and Protestants.

4

TRAGEDY AND TRIUMPH

German Unification, the Kulturkampf, and Christian Ecumenism, 1866–1883

FROM 1864 THROUGH 1871, Otto von Bismarck engineered a series of wars that pitted Prussia against the Kingdom of Denmark, the Austrian Empire, and France. These conflicts, collectively known as the German Wars of Unification, ultimately resulted in the establishment of a unified German Empire. The establishment of the empire seemingly ended debate over the German National Question by unifying Germany under Prussian-Protestant hegemony and excluding Catholic Austria from the new Reich. But while Bismarck had made Germany, the task remained to make Germans—there was still no universal agreement about what, exactly, constituted German national identity. How the nation would be unified had been answered—but what it meant to be German remained ambiguous. While the kleindeutsch solution to the German Question effected a political unification of the German lands, it left intact the longstanding confessional divide between German Catholics and Protestants—a divide that nineteenth-century ecumenists had persistently warned must be addressed before the German nation could be properly unified.

An abridged version of this chapter appeared in the journal *Church History* as Stan M. Landry, "That All May be One? Church Unity and the German National Idea, 1866–1883," *Church History* 80, no. 2 (June 2011): 281–301. It is reprinted with permission of Cambridge University Press Journals.

Because confessional identity and difference were pivotal to how contemporary Germans imagined themselves and their nation, the meaning of German national identity remained contested even after unification. But the formation of German national identity during this period was never neutral—nationalists used confessional alterity and antagonism to imagine confessionally exclusive notions of German national identity. Indeed, the establishment of a "small" German Empire under Prussian auspices, the anti-Catholic policies of the Kulturkampf, and the 1883 Luther anniversaries were all stages in a process that conflated Protestantism with German national identity and marginalized German Catholics from the society, culture, and politics of the new Reich. Suggesting that previous generations of ecumenists had been right about the need to heal the confessional divide for the sake of national unity, this process of imposing and enforcing religious and cultural homogeneity was but one solution to the persistence of the confessional divide in a unified German Empire. Many German Catholics responded to their marginalization by withdrawing into confessionally segregated milieus such as social organizations, devotional societies, and the political Catholicism of the Center Party. To be sure, German Catholics had accepted the new Reich from the beginning. Catholics recognized the legitimate authority of the emperor and acknowledged their national and patriotic obligations. They did not rebel against the kleindeutsch organization of the Reich, nor did they question their own identity as constituents of the new empire or the German nation.

But neither Bismarck's unification of the German Empire nor his support for the Kulturkampf legislation and its conflation of Protestantism with German national identity enjoyed universal support from Protestants. Nor did German Catholics withdraw into confessionally and socially isolated spheres en masse. Like those previous instances in German history when the national and confessional questions were tightly interwoven, irenical and ecumenical Germans emerged to propose interconfessional notions of German national identity. And during the early Kaiserreich, an ecumenical group of German Catholics and Protestants called Ut Omnes Unum proposed a means of overcoming Germany's persistent internal divide by reuniting the separated confessions. At the forefront of Catholic and Protestant opposition to the Kulturkampf and the conflation of German identity with Protestantism, Ut Omnes Unum proposed an interconfessional notion of German national identity that was inclusive of both Catholics and Protestants. This chapter recounts the history of the Ut Omnes Unum group and its responses to the confessional consequences of German unification, the exclusion of Catholics from German society and culture through the Kulturkampf, and the Protestant triumphalism of the 1883 anniversaries of Martin Luther's birth. Their efforts on behalf of interconfessional peace belie the idea that the post-unification confessional divide was total and insurmountable or that contemporary Catholic and Protestants were destined to exist in hermetically sealed spheres of existence. Indeed, in its struggle to end the marginalization of German Catholics from the German nation, Ut Omnes Unum worked to counteract the legacy of the Kulturkampf. Its ecumenism represented an assertion of German Catholic identity, interconfessional opposition to the Kulturkampf, and an alternative to its homogenous and confessionally exclusive vision of German national unity and identity—all at a time when confessional antagonism, and by extension the meaning of the German national idea, still remained highly critical.

The Confessionalization of the German National Idea, 1866–1871

Each stage of the process of German unification had underscored the persistent relationship between the confessional divide and the German national idea. In July 1866, Prussia won a decisive victory against Austria at the battle of Königgrätz. This victory effectively ended the Austro-Prussian War and established Prussia's hegemony over German-speaking Europe. German nationalists bragged that Königgrätz represented a confessional victory for Protestantism over Catholicism and redemption for Protestant Germany's terrible losses in the Thirty Years' War.[1] The Prussian victory at Königgrätz also precipitated the dissolution of the German Confederation, an alliance of states that had included Austria and held Germany together since the 1815 Congress of Vienna. In its place, an alliance of overwhelmingly Protestant northern German states was established in 1867. This North German Confederation was dominated by Prussia and excluded Catholic Austria and the southern German states of Baden, Bavaria, Hesse, and Württemberg. And it would become a powerful constituent of the German Empire that was established in 1871.

The old German Confederation had kept the confessional peace during an era of increasing religious integration by issuing and enforcing ecclesiastical policies from the federal level that protected religious minorities. But the North German Confederation stipulated that ecclesiastical policies would be set by individual states rather than by the Confederation itself. Fearing the constituent governments of the overwhelmingly Protestant North German Confederation would restrict the rights of German Catholics in those states where they were minorities, Catholic politicians requested that religious freedom be included in the new constitution of the confederation. But Protestant liberals in the North German parliament vetoed this request and pointed to it as an act of Catholic disloyalty.[2] The establishment of the North German Confederation not only represented a realignment of the confessional demography of Germany—it also pointed to the increasingly Protestant inflection of the nascent German nation.

The Franco-Prussian War (1870–1871) and the subsequent unification of Germany exacerbated confessional tensions between Catholics and Protestants. During the war, German Protestant sermons—whose themes were frequently anti-Catholic—referred to German Protestants as God's chosen people and the French (that is, Catholics) as deserving of defeat and humiliation.[3] Further marrying Protestantism and German national identity, Protestant congregations celebrated the emperor's birthday and the anniversary of the Battle of Sedan (1870), the decisive battle of the Franco-Prussian War, as religious holidays while German Catholics did not.[4] The formation of the German national idea—still in negotiation—continued to turn on confessional difference.

Even after unification in 1871, the German Question still lingered due to the persistence of the confessional divide. While Austria had given the German lands confessional parity, the kleindeutsch unification of the German Empire meant that Protestants outnumbered Catholics by 3 to 2. Politically unified, the German nation still remained split by the confessional divide. And answers to the lingering German Question were increasingly confessionalized in a manner that associated the meaning of being German with Protestantism. The Prussian court pastor Adolf Stoecker (1835–1909) recognized the new German Empire as a distinctively Protestant entity and claimed to see the hand of God at work in 1517 and again in 1871.[5] The *New Evangelical Church Newspaper*—an orthodox Lutheran journal—triumphantly proclaimed that the epoch of German history that had begun with the Reformation in October 1517 had come to a God-ordained fulfillment with the establishment of the German Empire.[6] And the nationalist historian Heinrich von Treitschke (1834–1896) regarded the Franco-Prussian war as a final victory for German Protestantism over German Catholicism. This rhetoric, which imagined German unification as the fulfillment of a process begun during the Reformation, not only underscores the conflation of Protestantism with the German national idea, but also points to a "nationalization of the confessional idea." As the historian Gérald Chaix has pointed out, Martin Luther and the Protestant Reformation functioned as "foundational events, multifaceted usable historical realities and conflict-afflicted sites of memory."[7] The use and abuse of these sites were never confessionally, nor politically, neutral. Instead of standing alone as religious sites of memory, Germany's foundational confessional figures and traditions—namely Martin Luther and the Protestant Reformation—would be nationalized in the service of a Protestant-German idea of the nation.

Even after the war and the successful establishment of the German Empire, German Protestant pastors and German nationalists spoke of the need for a final victory of Germany over France. The total subjection of German Catholics—who represented the "inner

Paris" and the "France within Germany"—was conceived to be a condition for this final victory.[8] By virtue of their confessional difference, German Catholics were imagined as Germany's internal foreigners and increasingly marginalized from German society and politics as enemies of the new Reich.

The lack of German confessional homogeneity provoked different responses from German liberal nationalists and German Catholics. German liberals and cultural Protestants responded to the lack of German internal cohesion by passing the Kulturkampf legislation. The Kulturkampf was precipitated by two main factors: the proclamation of papal infallibility as a dogma of the Catholic Church at the Vatican Council (1869–1870) and the growing influence of the Catholic Center Party in the Reichstag, owing to its electoral successes of 1871. Protestant liberals feared that on account of the newly proclaimed dogma, German Catholics' political loyalty would be directed to Rome rather than the capital of the new nation in Berlin. Bismarck supported the Kulturkampf legislation because of the growing influence of the Catholic Center Party in the Reichstag. He strongly opposed a confessional party whose loyalties to the German nation were ostensibly in question.[9] Invoking the pre-Reformation German collective memory of religion, Bismarck vowed that Germany would never again go to Canossa; that Germany's leaders would never again submit to Roman authority. Cultural Protestants associated Protestantism with science, *Bildung*, progress, and freedom and Catholicism with backwardness and insularity.[10] Thus German liberals envisioned the Kulturkampf as a true "cultural struggle" for German Protestant progress against Catholic backwardness.[11]

Regardless of the motivation behind it, this legislation was intended to compel the integration of Catholics into normative (in other words, Protestant) German society and culture. It included the dissolution of the Catholic Office at the Prussian Culture Ministry, the closure of Catholic seminaries and the assumption of clerical training by the German state, the abolition of religious orders (most famously the Jesuits), the prohibition of Catholic religious education in state schools, the compulsory introduction of civil marriage, the confiscation of church property, and the arrest and exile of thousands of Catholic clergy who opposed these policies. The Kulturkampf represented an internal war waged by the German state against "enemies of the Reich"—as German Catholics were known—to compel the religious homogenization of the German nation and to maintain its tentative unity. But instead of narrowing the confessional divide between German Catholics and Protestants, the Kulturkampf only widened it.

As a result of the Kulturkampf legislation, Catholic distrust of the German state increased and German Catholics withdrew into confessionally segregated milieux—social organizations, devotional societies, the Catholic press, and the political Catholicism of the Center Party.[12] These institutions became the main vehicles of the Catholic milieu and served to reinforce Catholic identity and difference by encouraging a shared Catholic worldview. The German sociologist M. Rainer Lepsius first proposed the idea of the Catholic milieu as a German Catholic social environment or subculture that formed as a response to the increasing power of anticlerical German liberals and the resulting marginalization of Catholics from nineteenth-century German society and politics.[13] But these milieux also had the effect of isolating German Catholics into social and confessional ghettos that restricted their participation in wider German society and politics.[14]

Kaiserreich German Catholics seemed trapped in a double bind between processes that questioned their status as constituents of the German nation and a Catholic milieu that perpetuated their isolation from German society. But there was in fact a third way between the Protestant marginalization of German Catholics and the Catholic withdrawal into a confessionally segregated and socially isolated milieu. This third way—represented by an irenical group of German Catholics and Protestants known as Ut Omnes Unum—suggested the possibility of an ecumenization of the German national idea or an interconfessional notion of the German national idea.

Ut Omnes Unum and the German National Idea

The Ut Omnes Unum group consisted of German Catholic and Protestant clergy and laity dedicated to confessional unity and the realization of a German national idea that was inclusive of both Catholics and Protestants. The group had its origins in devotional societies established by the Lutheran noblewoman Julie von Massow (1824–1901). This initiator and patroness of Ut Omnes Unum was born to the von Behrs, an old Pomeranian noble family. In 1852 she married Wilhelm von Massow (1802–1867), a conservative member of the Prussian upper house and himself from a Lutheran and Pomeranian noble family. The couple's acquaintances included the naturalist Alexander von Humboldt (1769–1859), the legal thinker Carl von Savigny (1779–1861), and Bismarck. In addition to these prominent figures, Julie and her husband maintained close ties with the Prussian jurist Ernst Ludwig von Gerlach (1795–1877); the Protestant historian Heinrich Leo (1799–1878); and the conservative politician and Lutheran convert from Judaism, Friedrich Julius Stahl (1802–1861). Gerlach and Leo, who had participated in the 1860 meeting of conservative Catholics and Protestants in Erfurt, envisioned church unity as an association of pious German Catholics and Protestants united to defend Germany against atheism, liberalism, and revolution.[15] During the early 1860s, the Massows lived in Berlin, where, inspired by the Erfurt Conference, Julie established an informal devotional society in which she, her husband, and a handful of Catholic, Reformed, and Lutheran friends prayed together for an end to the schism between the Christian confessions.

After her husband's death in 1867, Massow moved to Dresden, where she assumed control of the education of her nephew. In Dresden she began to host new meetings of conservative and irenical Catholic and Protestant clergy and laity at her home. This Dresden circle became a celebrated locus of conservative opposition to Bismarck and the Kulturkampf. The leader of the Catholic Center Party, Ludwig Windthorst (1812–1891), quipped that if Massow's new salon had been located in Berlin, it would have been the "center of the Center Party."[16] The ultramontane Catholic press showered accolades on the Dresden circle for its opposition to the Kulturkampf, if not for its irenical tendencies.[17] And the group's efforts in support of church unity won approval from the irenical Bishop of Mainz,

Wilhelm Emmanuel Freiherr von Kettler (1811–1877), who himself had encouraged prayer as a means of healing the German confessional divide.

In addition to attracting ecumenical Catholics who were opposed to the Kulturkampf, Ut Omnes Unum won support from archconservative Protestants opposed to Bismarck's policies of militarism and nationalism. Perhaps the most notable Protestant patron of Massow's salon was Ernst Ludwig von Gerlach. Indeed, Gerlach was typical of the ultra-conservative Protestants attracted to Ut Omnes Unum. A staunch opponent of a kleindeutsch German Empire, Gerlach famously cut ties with his old friend Otto von Bismarck and other moderate conservatives after the outbreak of the Austro-Prussian War.[18] But he later supported Ut Omnes Unum and its interconfessional vision of German national unity. In fact, his dying words—"I wanted nothing more than to witness the unity of the church"—served as the group's motto and were printed on the masthead of the *Ut Omnes Unum* journal Thus in spite of the confessional differences of the attendees, the Lutheran pastor Heinrich Ahrendts (1820–1897) recalled meetings of the Ut Omnes Unum group in Julie von Massow's Dresden home as "an assembly of like-minded and similarly-disposed people, all focused on a single objective: right and justice, truth and freedom for church and society. All in conscious opposition against the ruling party and its destructive tendencies and rapacious policies, which under the name Kulturkampf has been so disastrous for our beloved fatherland."[19] In response to the anti-Catholic legislation of the Kulturkampf and the recognition that an ultimate resolution of the German Question would require bridging the confessional divide, Catholic and Protestant members of Massow's Dresden circle established a journal in 1879 dedicated to promoting "understanding and union" between the separated confessions. The founders proposed the title *Ut Omnes Unum*— "that all may be one." The title—a reference to John 17:21—reflected their ecumenical commitments as well as their hopes for an interconfessional German nation. The journal's founders conceived that the attendees of Julie von Massow's devotional societies and Dresden salon would provide the audience for their ideas.[20] Massow herself continued to preside over meetings of the Dresden circle and frequently contributed to the journal. Other contributors to *Ut Omnes Unum* included ecumenical Catholic and Protestant clergy and laity. The journal also invited and printed letters from orthodox Catholics, Lutherans, and Reformed on the possibilities and limits of church unity.

A recurring theme of *Ut Omnes Unum* was the notion that the German confessional divide had hindered the unification of the German nation for centuries and that it would continue to inhibit real unity even after 1871. In an early article, one anonymous contributor to the journal identified the separation of the confessions as a perpetual sin of Christianity and one that demanded absolution. This sin was especially lamentable for the German nation, because in Germany the confessional divide had become the manifest expression of German identity and difference. Despite the political unification of Germany, the author claimed, the German people remained internally divided. It was thus an obligation of every earnest German Christian, of all German patriots, the Catholic and Protestant clergy, and German princes and statesmen to work toward overcoming the confessional divide for the welfare of the German people and the cause of peace throughout the German Empire.[21]

Adolf Röttscher (1829–1896), the Westphalian Catholic priest and attendee of Massow's Dresden salon, underscored this point and reminded readers that Martin Luther and the Protestant Reformation had only contributed to the centrifugal forces already at work in sixteenth-century Germany.[22] Since that time, Röttscher claimed, foreign and domestic powers had exploited divisions between German Catholics and Protestants in order to render Germany weak and to gain power for themselves.[23] Röttscher invoked memories of Luther and the Reformation similar to the rhetoric employed by Protestant nationalists during the Franco-Prussian War to inflect his own notion of the German national idea. But Röttscher's nationalization of these confessional ideas saw 1871 not as the fulfillment of 1517 but instead as the primary factor in Germany's incomplete unification.

The Silesian Catholic priest Carl Seltmann (1842–1911)—a contributor and editor to the journal in its later stages—also regarded the confessional divide in more than religious terms, calling it a "lamentable misfortune of our fatherland and our people."[24] Seltmann had disdain for Germans whom he believed were guilty of exploiting the confessional divide in order to further their own agendas. Indeed, he accused Bismarck, German liberal nationalists, and those cultural Protestants who supported the exclusion of Catholics from German social and political life as traitors to the German Fatherland and the true cause of German unity.[25]

If church unity was conceived as a prerequisite for German national unity, the question begged was, how should the churches be united? Members of the Ut Omnes Unum group sometimes disagreed on how best to unite the confessions. Church unity meant different things to different figures and sometimes the concept could be amorphous.[26] From its inception, the *Ut Omnes Unum* journal was conceived as a forum that might encourage simple rapprochement between the faiths—mutual understanding, cooperation, and peace. Other members of the group sought to realize church unity by minimizing differences in liturgy and theology between Catholics and Protestants and emphasizing their shared beliefs. Carl Seltmann and the Lutheran church administrator Hermann Opitz (1828–1909) recognized a basis for this notion of church unity in Article VII of the Augsburg Confession of 1530. Article VII defined the church as the congregation of the faithful and stipulated that the only requirements for unity were that the Gospel is preached and the sacraments administered to the faithful. In fact, despite the Augsburg Confession's origins as a Lutheran statement of faith, Seltmann and Opitz read the whole of it as an irenical document.[27]

To illustrate the interconfessional possibilities of the Augsburg Confession, Seltmann appealed to St. Augustine's ecumenical dictum: *in necessariis unitas, in dubiis libertas, in omnibus caritas* (in essential matters unity, in disputed matters liberty, in everything charity).[28] Seltmann argued that with regard to those essential beliefs, Catholics and Protestants were united—the Roman Confutation (1530) had affirmed several articles of the Augsburg Confession, including those articles addressing Catholic beliefs about the Trinity, original sin, the episcopal office, baptism, the Real Presence in the Eucharist, and the freedom of the will. With regard to those disputed beliefs, Seltmann was optimistic that German Catholics and Protestants could peacefully resolve their differences through dialogue.[29] And in all other matters where agreement was not essential or could not be reached, Catholics and Protestants should exercise charity and love toward one another.

Julie von Massow and Adolf Röttscher's plan for realizing church unity consisted in inviting German Protestants to "return" to a Catholic Mother Church that had been splintered by the Reformation.[30] However these figures may have imagined German church unity, they universally agreed that a reunion of the separated confessions was a prerequisite for any authentic form of German national unity. The conception of an interconfessional German nation espoused by Ut Omnes Unum represented an alternative to the Protestant notion of the German national idea that had been expressed by liberal nationalists and cultural Protestants and embodied by Königgrätz, Germany's kleindeutsch unification, and the Kulturkampf. This ecumenization of the national idea suggested a notion of German national identity that was confessionally inclusive rather than exclusive and acknowledged German Catholics as constituents of the German nation. But the Ut Omnes Unum group's vision of an interconfessional German nation would stand in contrast to the strong conflation of Protestantism and the German national idea articulated at the 1883 anniversaries of Martin Luther's birth.

The Luther Anniversaries of 1883

German Protestants and liberal nationalists gave the Prussian victory at Königgratz, the kleindeutsch unification of the German Empire, and the Kulturkampf a Protestant inflection that wrote German Catholics out of the narrative of German unification. Other sites at which the German national idea was articulated and fiercely debated—and the confessional inflection of that idea most apparent—were the 1883 anniversaries of Martin Luther's birth date. These anniversaries, which the historian Thomas A. Brady recognized as a "belated birthday party for the new German Reich,"[31] were sites of memory at which the Protestant celebrants explicitly conflated Protestantism with German national identity. Indeed, the anniversaries were accompanied by highly politicized commemorations of Luther and the Reformation and represented the culmination of the Protestant confessionalization of the German national idea and the symbolic marginalization of German Catholics in Wilhelmine Germany.

Responses to the Protestant-cum-nationalist inflection of the 1883 anniversaries predictably broke along confessional lines. Protestant Germany—including orthodox Lutherans and Cultural Protestants—triumphantly celebrated the memory of Luther as a Protestant-German national hero. German Catholics abstained from the festivities and mourned the anniversary as a day of sorrows that recalled the German confessional divide. The Ut Omnes Unum group expressed solidarity with German Catholics and rejected the instrumentalization of the anniversaries for nationalist purposes. But the group also proposed ways that German Protestants might celebrate the anniversaries without exciting confessional tensions and widening the confessional divide.

Orthodox Lutherans and Cultural Protestants who participated in the 1883 anniversaries celebrated Luther as both a Protestant confessional and a German national hero. Orthodox Lutherans remembered a Luther who was father of the Evangelical Church, herald of a pure Lutheran confession, and the new patron saint of Germany and regarded him as a thirteenth apostle.[32] But Luther was more often remembered as a German national hero than a religious figure at the 1883 anniversaries. German nationalists and Cultural Protestants celebrated him as the quintessential German man, liberator of the German conscience, author of every significant German intellectual and social achievement, and no less than the creator of a new ideal of humanity and as the initiator of modernity. German liberals invoked a Luther who was a hero of freedom, an idol of progress, an intellectual hero, and a fierce opponent of clerical tutelage.[33] Luther was held in the same esteem as German national heroes past and present—from Arminius to Otto von Bismarck—and recognized as the embodiment of Germanness and a foil against foreign (that is, Catholic) influence.[34]

The German Evangelical press strongly affirmed this memory of Luther as a German-Protestant national hero. The conservative *New Prussian Newspaper* recalled Luther as a pious and noble German national hero, the founder of a new German language, an archetype of German domestic life, and a "German man without equal."[35] The liberal *Protestant Church Newspaper for Evangelical Germany* reminded its readers that Luther had standardized and perfected the German language through his translation of the Bible, invented the genre of German literature, and was the benefactor of intellectual Protestantism and its tenets of freedom of conscience and research.[36] Not only was Luther a German national hero in the eyes of these periodicals, he was in fact the author of every significant intellectual and cultural development in German history since the sixteenth century.[37] Both journals—the conservative *New Prussian Newspaper* and the liberal *Protestant Church Newspaper*—conceived modern German society and culture as normatively Lutheran and saw Catholics as excluded from Luther's cultural beneficence to the German nation. The process of fashioning a German national hero might cut across political boundaries, but it remained confessionally exclusive.

The *Protestant Church Newspaper for Evangelical Germany* also suggested that the anniversaries should be celebrated with the purpose of strengthening German Protestant consciousness as a defense against Roman tendencies to interfere in German affairs and against Catholic inclinations to convert German Protestants.[38] Echoing sentiments from the early Kulturkampf era and channeling contemporary anti-ultramontanism, the newspaper claimed that the strength of Rome was historically predicated on Germany's fragmentation and weakness. The paper also lauded Luther for arousing national pride, of which the most recent fruit was the new German Reich. According to the paper, Luther was the greatest representative of German Protestantism and the new German nation because he himself had acted as a bulwark against Roman Catholic interference in German society and politics.[39] But if the establishment of a German Empire was the culmination of a long process of the exclusion of Roman influence, how could German Catholics conceive of themselves as constituents of the new German nation?

Perhaps the most belligerent anti-Catholic expression of a political-national memory of Martin Luther came from the Prussian nationalist historian Heinrich von Treitschke. In his 1883 essay, "Luther and the German Nation," Treitschke maintained that the Luther anniversaries were for German Protestants and that German Catholics had no place there.[40] Treitschke derided Catholics as foreign to German society and claimed to pity them for being unable to comprehend Luther's significance for and contributions to the German nation.[41] Because German Catholics could not share the sense of German-Protestant national consciousness that Luther had originally inspired, Treitschke identified Catholics as decidedly non-German. Like the Jews, who Treitschke would later infamously regard as Germany's "misfortune," German Catholics remained fundamentally alien to Germany.

Treitschke also remembered Luther as the first champion of a German national identity and solidarity. It was Luther who had initially stirred the feelings of German national pride and had liberated Germany from the yoke of an oppressive foreign influence. The kleindeutsch unification of the German nation in 1871 had been the ultimate realization of this achievement. Indeed, Treitschke claimed that Luther's "political" liberation of German Christianity from Roman authority represented a more powerful and enduring act than his Reformation of the church.[42] For Treitschke the origins of German nationalism and the contemporary German nation lay with the Protestant Reformation and with Luther. German history began with Luther, and the establishment of a Protestant-kleindeutsch empire represented the culmination of this history. This confessionally exclusive narrative of German unification—one that began in 1517 and concluded in 1871—explicitly conflated Protestantism with

German national identity, perpetuated the confessional divide, and further marginalized Catholics from German political culture.

The memory of Martin Luther was nationalized at the 1883 anniversaries and Luther and German Protestantism were further conflated with German national identity. But this particular nationalization of a confessional memory was problematic. On its own, the deconfessionalization and nationalization of Luther suggests the possibility of universal access to his memory and tradition. But the construction of Luther as a German National Hero at the 1883 anniversaries was coupled with the conflation of Protestantism and German national identity that had been underway since 1866. The construction of a German national hero in these terms would result in a confessionally exclusive Protestant hero. So the culmination of this process of the identification of Protestantism with German identity—which the 1883 anniversaries represented—rendered Luther still more inaccessible to German Catholics and thus further alienated them from the mnemonic and political culture of the German Empire.

The politicization of Luther's memory at the 1883 anniversaries owes to several factors. By 1883 the Kulturkampf was winding down to an unsatisfactory end for German liberals and cultural Protestants. The anniversaries in general, and the politicization of Luther's memory in particular, represented a way for German Protestants and liberals to revitalize their dying cause—a way of renewing the process of confessional homogenization, social marginalization, and political exclusion of German Catholics that the Kulturkampf was ultimately unsuccessful at realizing.[43] This, along with the recent appearance of fierce Catholic polemics, such as the Catholic historian Johannes Janssen's *History of the German People since the End of the Middle Ages* (1878–1894), precipitated the call from Protestant culture warriors for a final and conclusive defensive war against Catholicism.

Unlike their Protestant counterparts who recalled Luther as a German national hero and cultural benefactor, contemporary German Catholics remembered Luther as a tragic figure who had disrupted the cultural vitality of the late Middle Ages and as a schismatic who had violated German confessional and national unity.[44] The ultramontane faction within the Catholic Church recognized the 1883 Luther anniversaries as a continuation of the policies of the Kulturkampf and as a "call to arms" against German Catholicism.[45] This sentiment was widely shared among German Catholics, who regarded the conflation of Protestantism and German national identity at the 1883 anniversaries as an occasion for sorrow and mourning.[46]

The Ut Omnes Unum group exhibited a dual response to these anniversaries. On the one hand, the group's Catholic members reacted like most confessional Catholics to the polemics—they recognized the political-nationalist commemoration of Luther's memory as a celebration of the confessional divide and as antagonistic to German Catholics as both Christians and as German citizens. But instead of merely attacking the anniversaries as hostile to German Catholicism, Ut Omnes Unum suggested how the anniversaries might be celebrated without alienating Catholics. The group also proposed what it conceived as an interconfessional symbol of German unity and identity—St. Boniface (c. 672–754)—as a substitute for the nationalized memory of Martin Luther commemorated at the 1883 anniversaries.

The Ut Omnes Unum group worried that the conflation of Protestantism with German national identity would inflame passions against German Catholics and further hinder efforts to overcome the confessional and, by extension, national divide. An anonymous Catholic contributor to the journal noted that some of the sermons delivered at the anniversaries had perpetuated old prejudices against the Catholic Church, the pope, indulgences, idolatry, Mary, and the saints. But, the contributor pointed out, friendly Protestants and the Catholic Church itself had refuted these old prejudices. She (or he) also claimed that Catholics were excluded from the festivals, that the festival sermons actively encouraged hatred of Rome and Roman Catholics, and that celebrants commemorated the Reformation while forgetting the confessional strife and painful division that it had engendered.[47] But the repetition of these old prejudices and the uncritical commemoration of Luther and the Reformation only antagonized Catholics and exaggerated confessional divisions between Germans. This would render the memory of Luther—despite efforts to refashion him into a German national hero—still more inaccessible to German Catholics.[48] Thus the contributor wondered how German Catholics could be expected to identify with a German national hero at whose anniversaries they were antagonized and their church attacked.

Another anonymous commentator suggested that the anniversaries had their origins, at least to some extent, in an effort to obscure the failure of the Kulturkampf to nullify Catholic participation in German social and political life. But he (or she) claimed that the move to marginalize German Catholics in 1883 would be as futile as the Kulturkampf. Indeed, the commentator argued that Protestant organizers of the 1883 anniversaries recognized the devotion and fidelity that German Catholics had shown toward their church throughout the Kulturkampf and hoped to reproduce and reawaken such piety in German Protestants, whose faith the author believed had been reduced to political and cultural platitudes.[49] Instead of serving as a foil against authentic German culture, Protestant organizers of the local festivals implied—at least according to this commentator—that German Catholics were in fact a model of German popular devotion.

For their part, Ut Omnes Unum conceded that it was only natural for German Lutherans to want to commemorate the founder of their denomination. It acknowledged that the 1883 Luther anniversaries were celebrations at which German Protestants would commemorate Luther's contributions to the German nation and inspire national pride in German Protestants. And the Ut Omnes Unum group found some of the commemorations of Luther's contributions to German society and culture acceptable. In fact, the journal acknowledged that Luther was one of the most influential men in German history and that he had done great things for the German people.[50] But Ut Omnes Unum implored celebrants of the anniversaries to find a way to express their national pride without showing resentment or hostility toward German Catholics.[51] And it sought to proscribe nationalist memories of Luther that were exclusive to German Protestants and that marginalized German Catholics.

According to Ut Omnes Unum, the German Reformation had ultimately led to the separation of the churches and the confessional division of the German nation. This had left devastating religious wars and suffering in its wake.[52] But in celebrating Luther's contributions to German society and culture, German Protestants had only too gladly forgotten these painful memories of the bitter consequences of the Reformation. A Protestant associate of Julie von Massow hoped that the Luther anniversaries might serve as a forum where German Catholics and Protestants could revisit the histories and traditions of Luther and the Reformation in common. Catholics and Protestants would discuss how each remembered and commemorated Luther and the Reformation and then discuss the persistent positive and negative influences Luther and the Reformation had on the German churches and the German nation—all with an eye toward moving beyond polemics and into more fruitful dialogue about how best to unite the confessions.[53] Ut Omnes Unum maintained that these memories had to be confronted by German Protestants in order for Luther's memorialization as an authentic German national hero—that is, an interconfessional national hero accessible to both Catholics and Protestants—to be complete.[54] But until then, Ut Omnes Unum would appeal to a German national tradition that its members believed might unite Germans across the confessional divide—the memory of St. Boniface.

The commemoration of St. Boniface—Apostle to the Germans—was another contested site of memory between German Protestants and the Ut Omnes Unum group at the 1883 Luther anniversaries. The Protestant celebrants of the 1883 anniversaries envisioned Luther as the culmination of Boniface's ministry. Luther, they claimed, had rightfully inherited the title "Apostle to the Germans" from St. Boniface. For the *New Evangelical Church Newspaper*, the 1883 anniversaries strongly evoked memories of Luther's relationship to St. Boniface. According to this journal, St. Boniface had brought

Christianity to Germany, but Luther had reformed it. Boniface had planted the cross in the German ground, but Luther planted it in the German heart. And while Boniface had been patron saint of the medieval Reich, Luther would be patron saint of the second German Empire—a Protestant empire.[55] By associating Luther with St. Boniface, the journal gave this pre-Reformation and pre-confessional figure of German Christian unity a Protestant inflection. Coupled with the wider conflation of Luther, Protestantism, and German national identity at the anniversaries, the paper's move represented another Protestant nationalization of a confessional idea. German Catholics were again caught in a double bind—Luther was inaccessible as a German national hero but now St. Boniface too was being refashioned as a German Christian prelude to Luther.

But members of the Ut Omnes Unum circle found in St. Boniface the possibility of an interconfessional German national hero. The circle appealed to memories of Boniface as a national-ecumenical symbol of a united German Christianity and confessionally united German nation. Carl Seltmann recalled that anytime he stopped to pray at the tomb of St. Boniface in Fulda—an important pilgrimage site for ecumenical German Christians—he thought immediately of the German confessional divide. So long as the German nation remained divided, he claimed, Boniface could not rest peacefully.[56] Julie von Massow also recognized the tomb of St. Boniface as a site of memory around which both German Catholics and Protestants might work and pray for the reunion of the separated confessions.[57]

A month before the start of the 1883 Luther anniversaries, Massow traveled from Dresden to Fulda to pray at the grave of St. Boniface for an end to the confessional strife that had divided German Christianity and the German nation since the sixteenth century.[58] Massow's diary entry for November 10, 1883, reveals that she looked on what she called the "swindle" of the Dresden Luther anniversaries with great discomfort. Instead of using the anniversaries as an opportunity to foster rapprochement between German Catholics and Protestants, the Protestant-cum-nationalist inflection of the festivals had in fact celebrated the confessional divide and German national disunity. During the anniversaries, Massow remained at Fulda where she fervently prayed for the ideal that she claimed St. Boniface represented: *ut omnes unum sint*—that all may be one.[59] In 1883 Julie von Massow endowed a mass at the tomb of St. Boniface *ad tollendum schism*—to lift the schism between the churches. German Catholics and Protestants in Fulda celebrated these masses together, and so united, Massow argued, would contribute to the dissolution of that "lamentable, sinful, and fearfully unnatural separation" between the confessions that had singularly contributed to the disunity of the German nation.[60] Massow's campaign to unite German Christians would ultimately prove unsuccessful, but it did not go unnoticed. In 1887 Pope Leo XIII (r. 1878–1903) himself lauded Massow and Ut Omnes Unum for their ecumenical efforts and had a commemorative medallion produced in their honor. The medallion was struck with the inscription "Ut Omnes Unum" on one side and an engraving of St. Boniface with the title "One Nation, One Faith" on the other.[61] Massow would eventually bridge the confessional divide in her own person—realizing her notion of church unity as a Protestant return to a Catholic Mother Church—by converting to Catholicism in 1885.

After her conversion, Massow continued to work toward healing the German confessional divide. She was also instrumental in defending the Ut Omnes Unum group from being co-opted by ultramontane Catholics, who had always maintained ambivalence about the group—on the one hand they admired Ut Omnes Unum for its opposition to the Kulturkampf, but on the other they were less than enthused with the group's willingness to accommodate non-Catholics. When Carl Seltmann stepped down as editor of *Ut Omnes Unum* in 1886, the ultramontane Catholic priest Joseph Dell (1831–1893) took over. Under Dell's editorship, the tenor of the articles and editorials became more proselytizing and increasingly hostile toward non-Catholics. Dell, whose own hero was the fiercely ultramontane publicist Joseph Görres (1776–1848), conceived of ecumenism as a means of surreptitiously converting Protestants to Roman Catholicism. Predictably, many of the journal's Lutheran and Reformed contributors severed ties with *Ut Omnes Unum* at this point.[62] In response to the new direction of journal, Julie von Massow founded a competing journal called the *Peace Papers* in 1886 that retained the bona fide ecumenism of the early Ut Omnes Unum group and ran until her death in 1901. Meetings of the Ut Omnes Unum circle ceased after Massow's death, but epigones of the group continued her campaigns for church unity.

Conclusion

The existence of a Catholic-dominated social and religious organization, which together with like-minded German Protestants actively contested the marginalization of German Catholics, points to the group's historical significance. Ut Omnes Unum constituted an ecumenical religious community that neither accepted the idea that their (inter)confessional identities were incompatible with being German nor withdrew into the Catholic milieu. And perhaps most importantly, the group preserved and maintained the ecumenical impulse of German nationalism, arguing that German unity could never fully be realized until the confessional question was properly addressed and until both confessions were recognized as integral parts of the German nation.

The Kulturkampf legislation and other policies directed against German Catholics vindicated the nineteenth-century proponents of church unity as being right all along—a confessionally reunited Germany was a precondition to a politically united Germany. Ecumenists sought this unity via a reunion of the Catholic and Protestant Churches, and Kulturkämpfer through the marginalization of Catholics from German society and politics in the form of discriminatory legislation designed to create and enforce a religious homogeneity that had never existed in the first place. Catholic and Protestant opposition to the Kulturkampf rendered it ineffective at "Germanizing" Catholics or realizing cultural and religious uniformity. The Ut Omnes Unum group strove to complete the religious and cultural unification of Germany—in an irenical rather than exclusive manner—after the failure of the Kulturkampf.[63]

While their ultimate goal of a reunion of the separated confessions was never fully realized, members of the Ut Omnes Unum circle embodied an interconfessional notion of the German national idea. Indeed, members of the Ut Omnes Unum group and contributors to the journal lived this ideal through their participation in a group that recognized German Catholics and Protestants alike as constituents of the German nation. Their ecumenism was not a zero-sum game, and Ut Omnes Unum never maintained that there must be a full reunion of the Catholic and Evangelical confessions or nothing at all. On the way toward their ultimate goal of a final reunion of the churches and an accommodation of German Catholics to the empire, Ut Omnes Unum and other nineteenth-century German ecumenists recognized understanding, mutual respect, and peaceful coexistence between Catholics and Protestants as minor successes and desiderata that were indeed preconditions for the political resolution of the confessional question in Germany. As such they helped to preclude confessional difference as a function of German national identity. Their efforts and accomplishments were acknowledged by no less than Ludwig Windthorst and Pope Leo XIII. Following the lead of Ut Omnes Unum, the following generation of German ecumenists would finalize Germany's incomplete unification at the 1917 Reformation anniversaries—which serve as a coda to this parallel history of German national unification.

5

A TRUCE WITHIN THE WALLS

The Reformation Anniversaries of 1917

IN SPITE OF THE BITTER POLEMICS between German Catholics and Protestants during the early Kaiserreich, the last decade of the nineteenth century and the first decade of the twentieth were marked by increasing confessional peace. The Kulturkampf had failed, the conflation of Protestantism with German national identity had been rejected for the most part, and German Catholics had assimilated into normative German society and culture. The outbreak of war in August 1914 meant that German Catholics would become even more closely united with German Protestants as the pressures of the war compelled confessional Others to unite in common defense of their fatherland.

Indeed, the war compelled adversaries of all kinds within the German Empire to make peace with their opponents. The various political parties of the German Reichstag informally agreed to a truce amongst themselves for the sake of national solidarity.[1] A similar informal truce was consented to amongst the separated confessions. Nowhere was this confessional truce more manifest than at the 1917 Reformation anniversaries, where Catholics and Protestants came together to celebrate Luther as a German national hero who had stoically endured struggles and sacrifice on behalf of the fatherland and the Volk. These anniversaries were the occasion at which the confessional question was parried, once and for all, in the interests of German national solidarity.

Thus, quite unlike the triumphalist Protestant celebration of Luther at the 1883 anniversaries, in 1917 princes, pastors, and professors called on German Catholics and Protestants to recognize one another as fellow German citizens and to unite in common defense of their fatherland. Like previous generations of ecumenists, the celebrants of the 1917 anniversaries sought a rapprochement between Catholics and Protestants for the sake of national concord. To be sure, these celebrations were mostly irenical rather than ecumenical. The confessional "truce" between German Catholics and Protestants did not constitute an agreement to unite the churches. But by then a formal and institutional union of the separated churches would not be necessary to foster a shared sense of German national identity. The unified German state itself could represent that shared national identity. What remained was to agree upon an idea of the German nation and national identity that included both Catholics and Protestants without regard for confessional identity or difference. This was precisely the vision of German identity expressed at the 1917 Reformation anniversaries.

Indeed, the irenical celebration of the 1917 Reformation anniversaries points to the culmination of the efforts of previous generations of the nineteenth-century ecumenical movement. The increasing integration of Catholics into German civil society, World War I, the occasion of the 1917 Reformation anniversaries, and a century of German Christian ecumenism were all integral factors in the final resolution of the confessional problem of German nationalism in favor of an interconfessional notion of German unity and identity. Attempts to define the German national idea in confessionally exclusive terms gained minimal traction after 1917. Thus the irenical sentiments expressed at the 1917 Reformation anniversaries represent the conclusion of this alternative history of German national unification.

Confessional Relations during the Wilhelmine Era

The history of German confessional relations from 1871 through 1917 was a history of Catholic persecution coupled with gradual integration. Alongside the Kulturkampf and other instances of blatant anti-Catholic sentiment, there was evidence of a gradual acceptance of Catholics into German society. Orthodox Protestants, ultramontane Catholics, and Christian ecumenists had after all cooperated to oppose the Kulturkampf. Other German Catholics and Protestants worked together to offer social services at the local level. Catholic missionaries proselytized with Protestants in the German colonies.[2] And for a century, irenical Catholics and Protestants worked together to help realize interconfessional peace for the sake of national unity.

In addition, the increasing participation and prominence of German Catholics and the Catholic Center Party in German civic life seemed to render moot the charge that German Catholics were disloyal citizens and congenital enemies of the empire. Indeed, by the late nineteenth century the Center Party had become one of most powerful parties in Germany and attracted a confessionally diverse constituency. Like the Center Party itself, Catholic youth groups, social organizations, and trade unions had become increasingly interdenominational.[3] Thus by 1914, German Catholics were integrated into a normative German society that was no longer either overwhelmingly liberal or virulently anti-Catholic.[4] The wartime preclusion of the confessional question and the aconfessional nationalization of Luther's memory at the 1917 Reformation anniversaries would accelerate the process of Catholic integration into German society and culture and underscore the idea that the confessional divide as a national-political problem had become a moot point.

One event in particular would presage the wartime preclusion of the confessional question. In an excited speech delivered on August 1, 1914, to Berliners gathered outside Charlottenberg Palace to mark Germany's declaration of war on Russia, Emperor Wilhelm II (r. 1888–1918) exhorted those assembled to unite in defense of the fatherland without distinction of race or religion.[5] The emperor claimed that he recognized no distinct parties, classes, races, or religions—only Germans. On August 2, an interconfessional service was held outside the Reichstag at the foot of the Bismarck monument at which thousands of German Catholics and Protestants attended.[6] German Christians of every confession could now all claim to be proper German citizens. Thus in a single move did the king parry the confessional question, which proponents of church unity had so fiercely aspired to overcome during the previous century. The emperor recognized all Germans, without distinction of race or religion, as constituents of the German nation. Confessional affiliation no longer automatically included or precluded one from membership and participation in the German nation. This was a far cry from the anti-Catholic polemics of the Kulturkampf era and a premonition of how the 1917 Reformation anniversaries would be celebrated.

The 1917 Reformation Anniversaries

The four hundredth anniversary of the Reformation was celebrated quite like the three hundredth—services were held throughout the week, resulting in the festival service. Local and visiting civic and clerical leaders gave speeches. Catholics and Protestants alike observed and attended parades and other festivities. The anniversaries in Wittenberg—the birthplace of the Protestant Reformation and the spiritual center of the 1883 Luther anniversaries—followed the same course. Lutheran confirmands were introduced to their local congregations and communities. Processions from the Luther House to the Castle Church culminated in singing and celebration in front of the Theses Door and around the Luther memorial statue that had been constructed for the 1883 festivities. But even in this holiest site of German Protestantism, the celebrants of these anniversaries recognized German Catholics as their fellow citizens and brothers. Part and parcel of this process was the refashioning of memories of Luther from a Protestant hero to a deconfessionalized German national hero accessible to Catholics and Protestants alike.

Indeed, if there was a single theme—apart from the melancholy of war—that united the sermons and speeches delivered on the occasion of the 1917 Reformation anniversaries, it must be that of the "deconfessionalization of the national idea." German national identity was no longer imagined to be the exclusive reserve of Protestants. Instead, in 1917 Luther was recalled as a German national hero who had endured great struggles and sacrifice on behalf of the German Volk. This aconfessional memory of Luther, with which both German Catholics and Protestants could identify and rally around as a national hero, suggested that the confessional question and the national question, at least among the Christian confessions, had finally been decoupled. From the beginning of the war, German political parties and trade unions had agreed to a *Burgfrieden*, or a temporary "truce within the castle walls" amongst themselves in order to keep the peace, support the government, and serve as a show of solidarity to the German people.[7] Likewise, the 1917 Reformation anniversaries represented a kind of confessional truce between German Catholics and Protestants.[8] But this truce was more than a spontaneous cessation of hostilities between German Catholics and Protestants. Irenical celebrants of the 1917 anniversaries acknowledged the inspiration of previous generations of ecumenists while rejecting confessionally exclusive invocations of Luther's memory. Recognizing a common cause in the defense of their shared German fatherland and culture, members of both confessions invoked Luther as the herald of the German fatherland and a German culture under attack by a world of uncivilized enemies.

Luther was also invoked as a national hero who had demonstrated unconditional fidelity to, and endured great sacrifice for, the German fatherland. His life showed tenacity, toughness, and perseverance. And according to the celebrants of the 1917 Reformation anniversaries, such fidelity, sacrifice, and perseverance were desperately needed in their own dark times.[9] In their anniversary sermons and speeches, Protestant pastors and professors recalled Luther as a man of iron with a stone heart,[10] a stoic who had heroically endured great sacrifices for a better Germany, just as contemporary Germans must remain stoic in the face of their wartime hardships.[11] The Halle theologian D. A. Lang asked his congregation to remember Luther's stand at Worms in particular, where the reformer courageously stood against pope and council, emperor and princes. Lang also exhorted his congregation to remember Luther's resolve during internment in the Wartburg Castle in order to steel themselves against the harsh wartime conditions that they were experiencing.[12] The *Protestant Monthly* echoed this sentiment and added that at Worms, Luther had stood against the Pope and emperor on behalf of the German spirit. The journal lauded contemporary German Catholics and Protestants for standing, like Luther had almost four hundred years prior, against the entire world on behalf of the German spirit and the German fatherland.[13] The *Monthly* also explicitly recalled the 1817 Reformation anniversaries, reminding its readers that Catholics, Reformed, and Lutherans had celebrated together peacefully at those anniversaries. The *Protestant Monthly* proposed that the 1917 anniversary should be celebrated in the same irenical manner for the sake of German national solidarity.[14]

In addition to reminding their congregants of Luther's stoic endurance of hardships, Protestant pastors and professors exhorted their congregations and listeners toward solidarity and unity with their German Catholic brothers. The Lutheran church historian Friedrich Loofs (1858–1928) called for a 1917 Reformation anniversary without polemics, one that did not alienate or antagonize German Catholics, who, Loofs noted, "had remained our comrades throughout this long war."[15] The Berlin theologian Adolf Deißmann (1866–1937) received and published letters in the *Evangelical Weekly Correspondence* from his students and associates on the front who called for interconfessional cooperation between German Catholics and Protestants. One June 1917 letter from an officer on the Western Front noted that there was no confessional animosity or discord among the soldiers and argued that it was imperative that any remaining confessional tensions in Germany be set aside for the success of the German war effort.[16] Another June 1917 letter from a Dresden army chaplain echoed this sentiment. Indeed, the chaplain recognized the coming Reformation anniversaries as an opportunity for rapprochement and understanding between German Catholics and Protestants for the sake of national unity.[17] Deißmann himself regarded these attempts at confessional reconciliation for the sake of national solidarity and unity during the war as the German people's holiest cause.[18]

In his anniversary speech, the Saxon historian Erich Marks acknowledged that the 1883 Luther anniversaries had, in fact, taken a belligerent position against Catholics and that the separation between the confessions remained palpable. Nevertheless, Catholics and Protestants in Germany stood for and with one another during the war. Marks expressed hope that such solidarity would persist well into the century.[19] Thus the 1917 Reformation anniversary would represent the point at which Luther became a national symbol, a site of national memory for the entire German world, not only for the German-Protestant world.[20] Indeed, other sites of memory associated with Luther had already become both deconfessionalized, nationalized, and thus rendered universally accessible. Luther's famous hymn, "Ein' feste Burg," had already been a kind of interconfessional German national anthem. Thus the authors of a popular Hanover anniversary pamphlet cheerfully noted that both Catholic and Protestant German soldiers sang "A Mighty Fortress Is Our God" as they conquered Antwerp, while the stunned Belgian citizens listened in amazement.[21]

In addition to individual pastors and professors, the Evangelical press recognized the need for solidarity with German Catholics. In their issue to mark the 1917 Reformation anniversaries, the *Prussian Church Newspaper* reminded its readers that unity was strength and that this notion of unity necessarily entailed solidarity and unity with German Catholics. The journal underlined the main imperative of the current wartime Reformation anniversary: unity with fellow Germans against the shared enemies of the fatherland.[22] That nominally Protestant England was one of these shared enemies illustrates the marked shift in confessional relations from the previous generation. The Wittenberg writer Max Senf noted that an international Evangelical celebration of the anniversaries would be impossible given the belligerents.[23] Rather than international and Evangelical, the 1917 Reformation anniversaries would remain German and interconfessional. Thus in a single generation the Protestant estimation of German Catholics had gone from internal enemies and congenital foreigners to fellow citizens and the most appropriate co-celebrants of the 1917 Reformation anniversaries. In place of Catholics, English Protestants now constituted the gravest threat to the Fatherland.[24] Likewise, the *German-Evangelical Correspondence* demanded of its readers that any remaining confessional animosities be put to rest before the forthcoming 1917 anniversary. Nothing should be done that could result in the accusation that the anniversary festivals had disturbed the peace, solidarity, and unity between the denominations that the war circumstances had engendered.[25] Even the Evangelical Federation, a national Protestant organization, agreed to keep the confessional peace at the 1917 anniversaries and cautioned its members against any behavior that might upset the truce.[26] For their part, German Catholics resolved to observe a "dignified reticence" toward any polemical tracts that might be produced at the 1917 anniversaries in the interests of internal peace.[27]

Alongside the confessional truce and the irenical celebrations of Luther's memory in German civil society, bona fide Christian ecumenists used the occasion of the 1917 Reformation anniversaries to call for an ecclesiastical union of Lutherans and Catholics. The most prominent of the ecumenical groups active in 1917 was the Lutheran High-Church Movement. An outgrowth of orthodox Lutheranism and the nineteenth-century ecumenical movement, the High-Church Movement stressed fidelity to the 1580 Book of Concord and the salvific power of the sacraments—baptism, the Lord's Supper, and in some nineteenth-century Lutheran circles, confirmation—as the basis of a neo-Lutheran confessional identity that might find concord with Roman Catholicism. The ecumenical tendencies of the High-Church Lutherans were grounded in their emphases on the liturgy and sacraments—emphases they shared with Roman Catholics. These ecumenical proclivities were realized in 1917 when the Lutheran pastor Heinrich Hansen (1861–1940) published his own Ninety-Five Theses advocating liturgical renewal, reminding Lutherans of the significance of the sacraments, and emphasizing church music and church decoration rather than the sermon as important elements of the mass. Hansen argued that these reforms might serve as the basis for a reunion of Lutheran and Roman Catholics in an "evangelical and catholic" church.[28] Indeed, in 1918 a Lutheran High Church Union, which included both ministers and laymen, was formally organized. The Union stressed the importance of the sacraments in place of the preaching of the Word, recommended deemphasizing the sermon, and campaigned to renew the Lutheran liturgy along the lines of Catholic worship. It was also an important precursor to the twentieth-century ecumenical movement.[29]

The Christian ecumenism displayed at the 1917 Reformation anniversaries had little of the nationalist inflection that previous generations of German ecumenists had expressed. This suggests that the confessional divide—while still present in German society and culture—had at least ceased to be a national political problem. And by acknowledging the influence of previous generations of ecumenists and rejecting confessionally exclusive notions of German identity, the irenical celebrants of the 1917 Reformation anniversaries represented the ultimate realization of the ecumenical nationalist impulse—a German national idea that transcended the confessional divide.

Conclusion

The outbreak of World War I compelled German Catholics and Protestants to close ranks in response to a shared external threat. And the 1917 Reformation anniversary festivals functioned as sites of memory at which Catholics and Protestants could mutually invoke Luther as a German hero accessible to all—indeed, a touchstone for an interconfessional German identity. Thus the Reformation anniversaries of 1917 represented the deconfessionalization of the relationship between the national question and the confessional question and the culmination of a century of efforts to fashion an interconfessional notion of German identity. Indeed, the irenical sentiments expressed in 1917 were the culmination of those recurring ecumenical impulses within German nationalism that manifested themselves whenever the German confessional or national questions were at fever pitch. The ecumenists' persistent campaigns on behalf of confessional peace and in favor of an interconfessional German nation kept the issue in the foreground of German society and politics until the time was right to preclude the confessional divide as a national-political problem once and for all. The increasing integration of Catholics into the German Empire, the wartime context, the 1917 Luther anniversaries, and indeed a century of efforts by ecumenical nationalists provided the ideal conditions for the finalization of the process of Germany's incomplete national unification. To be sure, new divides within German society and politics would emerge. The uses of ideology and race as categories to mark identity and difference are the most obvious. But from its inception, the German nationalist movement had acknowledged the confessional divide as a major impediment to German unification. And by fostering mutual understanding and interconfessional peace between Catholics and Protestants for over a century, German ecumenists should be recognized as having been instrumental in overcoming the political implications of that divide and as having contributed to German unification.

While 1917 pointed to a new and interconfessional German national idea, it also pointed to shifting ideas about the relationship between Luther, the Reformation, and German history. The novel invocations of a stoic and deconfessionalized Luther at the 1917 anniversaries pointed to the decline of a tried and true meme of Protestant nationalism: the triumphalist meta-narratives that imagined straight lines leading from Luther to Bismarck and from 1517 to 1871.[30] True believers in the conflation of Protestantism with German national identity—so prevalent during the Kulturkampf and again in 1883—had begun to lose their faith. But the decline of this particular narrative of German religious and political history allows us to see more clearly the successes and failures of those ecumenists who were integral to the histories of German national unification. To be sure, other myths about Luther and the Reformation would take the place of those articulated during the nineteenth century. And Luther's memory would continue to be used, abused, and manipulated throughout the twentieth century. Indeed, memories of Luther and the Reformation were variously invoked during the Weimar period, during the Hitler era by the Nazis, by the two Germanies against one another, and before and after German reunification in 1990.[31] But invocations of Luther to ground confessionally exclusive notions of German national identity faded from German public discourse.

Although the confessional divide still existed, its social, cultural, and political effects were more muted as German Catholics and Protestants grew closer together. And while Luther might still be used and abused in confessionally exclusive ways, his memory had been refashioned from an exclusively confessional symbol to one universally accessible to all Germans. Finally, the confessional divide as a national-political problem had ceased to exist. Short of a formal reunification of the separated churches, these were the goals that nineteenth-century ecumenists had so desperately sought to realize. As such, the 1917 Reformation anniversaries represented the culmination and resolution of the ecumenical impulse within German nationalism. Not because the Catholic and Protestant Churches had been united, but because confessional difference as a primary and determinant category of German national identity had been largely overcome.

CONCLUSION

THE HISTORIAN HAGEN SCHULZE has described the unification of Germany as a process occurring from the top down, bottom up, and from every side.[1] Bismarck's unification of Germany represented a movement from the top down while the kleindeutsch, großdeutsch, and "third" German nationalist movements informed the debate. And alongside recent revisionist accounts of German nationalism that challenge the master narratives, an additional movement deserves to be counted with that diffuse process of German national unification—the nineteenth-century ecumenical movement. If the Bismarckian unification of the German nation represented German nationalism proceeding from the top down, Christian ecumenism represented German nationalism proceeding from either side and from below. And while the German nation might have been formally unified under the auspices of iron and blood, nineteenth-century German ecumenists helped to unite Germans as fellow citizens across an arguably deeper divide than the political disunity of the German lands—the confessional divide between Catholics and Protestants. This should be enough to induce German historians to revisit the standard narratives of German nationalism and national unification and to question our assumptions about the strength of the nineteenth-century German confessional divide. The histories of nineteenth-century German ecumenism and ecumenical nationalism have been overlooked by historians because of their perceived lack of success. But this is in fact a symptom and a result of the old nineteenth-century narratives of national unification that this manuscript aims to correct.

As such, the measure of success of nineteenth-century proponents of church unity should not be limited to the number of churches that they succeeded in formally uniting. Instead, their efforts should be measured according to how well they contributed to interconfessional dialogue, understanding, and peaceful coexistence among their fellow Germans. After all, the confessional divide had been a national-political problem for as long as German nationalism had existed. The ecumenical impulse within German nationalism, often with a significant popular reception, recurred whenever the national question was most fiercely debated. This suggests that German ecumenism was far from a marginal political movement. Instead, it was intrinsic to the German National Question.

For Christian ecumenists past and present, a union of the separated churches had been the ultimate ideal of their campaigns. But along the way, ancillary goals such as the encouragement of rapprochement, mutual respect, and peaceful cooperation were worked toward. In the case of nineteenth-century German ecumenism, these secondary goals facilitated German religious and national harmony, even if a general Christian church was never realized. Short of a formal and institutional union of the Catholic and Protestant churches in Germany, ecumenists at least blunted the sharpest edges of the confessional divide for the sake of national concord. And by using that metric, the nineteenth-century German ecumenists were more successful than historians have given them credit. This suggests why persistent efforts to heal the confessional divide were so popular. Because these ecumenists recognized that Germany need not be unified through iron, blood, and the exclusion of minorities but could also be united by appealing to shared histories and traditions to overcome long-standing internal divides.

Indeed, the reception of the ecumenical impulse at the 1817 Reformation anniversaries was generally positive. A union of the Reformed and Lutheran churches was effected in Prussia and other German states with popular, clerical, and state support. Catholics, Protestants, and in limited instances Jews celebrated an ecumenical memory of Luther and the Reformation in an early expression of German nationalism. If confessional and political tensions again flared in the 1830s and 1840s, they were diffused during the Vormärz and revolutionary periods when German Catholics and Protestants united by the tens of thousands to express common frustration with their respective church hierarchies and to support Leberecht Uhlich's and Johannes Ronge's visions of German confessional, national, and gender unity. Except for the ultramontane and orthodox wings of the Catholic and Protestant churches respectively, the reception of these dissenting congregations was overwhelmingly popular. While the Free Congregations had united themselves in an ecumenical bond, they were unsuccessful in formally uniting the established Catholic and Protestant churches in Germany. But Leberecht Uhlich, Johannes Ronge, and their sympathizers played an enormous role in making religious dissenters, persecuted congregations, men and women in interconfessional relationships, and the children of confessionally mixed marriages feel like they were part of an inclusive German nation not split by confession. The same may be said for the 1860 Erfurt Conference. The participants in the Conference never did realize a Christian state of pious German Catholics and Protestants whose authority derived from God. But amidst debates over a kleindeutsch versus großdeutsch notion of German unity, the conference did successfully articulate their deeply held concern that any notion of German unity that did not take the confessional divide into account was necessarily incomplete. The Kulturkampf would finally acknowledge the truth of the problem that ecumenists had long recognized, if not its solution. The Erfurt Conference also initiated irenical dialogues between influential German Catholics and Protestants that inspired the next generation of ecumenists. And while Ut Omnes Unum never convinced German Protestants to return to their Catholic Mother Church en masse, it did create a space for both the affirmation of German Catholic identity and for interconfessional dialogue and cooperation during a period in which German Catholics were increasingly persecuted. Their efforts toward church unity and toward realizing a notion of German national identity and unity that was inclusive of Catholics as well as Protestants were lauded by no less than the Catholic politician Ludwig Windthorst and Pope Leo XIII. And the celebrants of the postconfessional 1917 Reformation anniversaries, rejecting religious antagonism and uniting for the sake of German national solidarity, explicitly recognized previous generations of ecumenists as benefactors of the current religious truce.

These ecumenical figures did not realize a formal union of the separated confessions nor was their ecumenical model of the German nation adopted. However, they point to an interconfessional history of German nationalism that has so far been an afterthought of nineteenth-century German history. Indeed, their efforts represent one of the unacknowledged ways that nineteenth-century German nationalism played out, in Schulze's terminology, from the side and on the ground. Not through the marginalization and exclusion of difference, the method that so many nationalist movements had adopted, but by imagining a means of uniting Germans across longstanding internal divides.

Nineteenth-century ecumenical-nationalist groups were most effective in helping Catholics and Protestants overcome the German religious divide by fostering mutual respect, understanding, and peaceful coexistence between the confessions. They helped to "prime" the nation for an interconfessional notion of what it meant to be German. But it was this ecumenical impulse itself—this desire to unite the separated confessions as a precondition of German national unification—that led to the completion of Germany's unfinished unification. Ecumenical nationalists persistently responded to this impulse until the national-cum-confessional question was resolved. The Reformation anniversaries of 1917 represented not only a culmination of the previous century of ecumenism. In addition, they represented a final resolution of the confessional question as a national-political problem in favor of an interconfessional notion of German unity and identity.

As such, these histories of ecumenism reveal what has been obscured in the master narratives of German national unification and work to complement revisionist accounts of German nationalism and its relationship to the confessional divide. Like other revisionist accounts of German nationalism that consider how local, regional, dynastic, and socioeconomic factors informed the construction of the German national idea, the history of ecumenism suggests that German nationalism was a diffuse process throughout the nineteenth century and that it cannot be reduced to a simple dualism between a Großdeutschland or Kleindeutschland. And while religious affiliation was essential to how Germans imagined their national identities, the history of ecumenical nationalism demonstrates that there was in fact another side to the confessionalization of the national idea.

As a result of the efforts of these ecumenical nationalists, Catholics as well as Protestants could be conceived as fellow Germans. Not because the institutional churches had been formally united, but because by using Luther as a touchstone, the confessional divide as a determinant of national identity had been overcome. That is not to say that old animosities did not persist. But thanks to generations of ecumenists, German Christians of both faiths were less often excluded from the German national idea on the basis of religious difference alone. To be sure, nineteenth-century German proponents of church unity had failed to reunite the separated churches. But by rendering the confessional divide superfluous to German national identity, they succeeded in helping to reunite a nation.

NOTES

BIBLIOGRAPHY

INDEX

NOTES

Introduction

1. On the myths and master narratives of the Protestant Reformation, see C. Scott Dixon, *The German Reformation: The Essential Readings* (Oxford: Blackwell, 1999), and R. W. Scribner and C. Scott Dixon, *The German Reformation*, 2nd ed. (Basingstoke, UK: Palgrave Macmillan, 2003).

2. Robert Southard, *Droysen and the Prussian School of History* (Lexington: University Press of Kentucky, 1995), and Stefan Berger, *The Search for Normality: National Identity and Historical Consciousness in Germany since 1800* (New York: Berghahm Books, 1997).

3. Margaret Lavinia Anderson, "Living Apart and Together in Germany," in *Protestants, Catholics, and Jews in Germany, 1800–1914*, ed. Helmut Walser Smith (Oxford: Berg, 2001), 320.

4. Olaf Blaschke, "Das 19. Jahrhundert: Ein Zweites Konfessionelles Zeitalter?," *Geschichte und Gesellschaft* 26 (2000): 38–75. See also Olaf Blaschke, ed., *Konfessionen im Konflikt: Deutschland zwischen 1800 und 1970; Ein zweites konfessionelles Zeitalter* (Göttingen, Germany: Vandenhoeck and Ruprecht, 2002).

5. For a sample of recent scholarship on German nationalism that challenges the master narratives of German national unification from regional, gendered, and sociocultural perspectives, see Abigail Green, *Fatherlands: State-Building and Nationhood in Nineteenth-Century Germany* (Cambridge: Cambridge University Press, 2001); Karen Hagemann, *"Männlicher Muth und Teutsche Ehre": Nation, Militär und Geschlecht zur Zeit der Antinapoleonischen Kriege Preussens* (Paderborn, Germany: Schöningh, 2002); Michael Rowe, *From Reich to State: The Rhineland in the Revolutionary Age, 1780–1830* (New York: Cambridge University Press, 2003); and Katherine B. Aaslestad, *Place and Politics: Local Identity, Civic Culture and German Nationalism in North Germany during the Revolutionary Era* (Leiden: Brill, 2005).

6. For the confessionalization of the German national idea during the nineteenth century, see Wolfgang Altgeld, *Katholizismus, Protestantismus, Judentum:*

Über religiös begründete Gegensätze und nationalreligiöse Ideen in der Geschichte des deutschen Nationalismus (Mainz, Germany: Matthias-Grünewald, 1992); Joel F. Harrington and Helmut Walser Smith, "Confessionalization, Community, and State Building in Germany, 1555–1870," *Journal of Modern History* 69, no. 1 (March 1997): 77–101; Helmut Walser Smith, *German Nationalism and Religious Conflict: Culture, Ideology, Politics, 1870–1914* (Princeton, NJ: Princeton University Press, 1995); Heinz-Gerhard Haupt and Dieter Langewiesche, eds., *Nation und Religion in der deutschen Geschichte* (Frankfurt a.M.: Campus Verlag, 2001); and Keith H. Pickus "Native Born Strangers: Jews, Catholics and the German Nation," in *Religion und Nation, Nation und Religion: Beiträge zu einer unbewältigten Geschichte*, ed. Micheal Geyer and Hartmut Lehmann (Göttingen, Germany: Wallstein, 2004).

7. William Adolf Visser 't Hooft, "The Word 'Ecumenical'—Its History and Use," in *A History of the Ecumenical Movement, 1517–1948*, 2nd ed., ed. Ruth Rouse and Stephan Charles Niell (Philadelphia: Westminster Press, 1967), 735–37.

8. In addition to the predominantly used terms *Ecumenism* (*Ökumene*) and *Irenicism* (*Irenik*), nineteenth-century German proponents of church unity variously used the terms *Convergence* (Annäherung), *Unity Efforts* (*Einheitsbestrebung*), *Concord* (*Eintracht*), *Union Attempts* (*Unionsversuche*), *Union* (*Vereinigung*), *Understanding* (*Verständigung*), and *Reunion* (*Wiedervereinigung*) to refer to their causes.

9. For the one and only general history of German ecumenism from the Reformation through the twentieth century, see Manfred P. Fleischer, *Katholische und lutherische Ireniker: Unter besonderer Berücksichtigung des 19. Jahrhunderts* (Göttingen, Germany: Musterschmidt, 1968).

10. See Smith, ed., *Protestants, Catholics, and Jews.*

11. See Helmut Walser Smith, *The Continuities of German History: Nation, Religion, and Race across the Long Nineteenth Century* (Cambridge: Cambridge University Press, 2008), and Konrad H. Jarausch and Michaël Geyer *Shattered Past: Reconstructing German Histories* (Princeton, NJ: Princeton University Press, 2003).

12. George S. Williamson, "A Religious Sonderweg? Reflections on the Sacred and the Secular in the Historiography of Modern Germany," *Church History* 75, no. 1 (March 2006): 142. While starting with the confessional divide, Williamson himself had already moved beyond that point. His *The Longing for Myth in Germany: Religion and Aesthetic Culture from Herder to Nietzsche* (Chicago: University of Chicago Press, 2004) recounted how German mythology provided a shared sense of intellectual and cultural community to Germans across the confessional divide.

13. Thomas Nipperdey, *Germany from Napoleon to Bismarck, 1800–1866*, trans. Daniel Nolan (Princeton, NJ: Princeton University Press, 1996), 1. See also Tim Blanning, "Napoleon and German Identity," *History Today* 48, no. 4 (April 1998): 37–43, and John Breuilly, "The Response to Napoleon and German Nationalism," in *The Bee and the Eagle: Napoleonic France and the End of the Holy Roman Empire*, ed. Alan Forrest and Peter H. Wilson (Basingstoke, UK: Palgrave Macmillan, 2009), 256–83. For a revisionist account that challenges Napoleon's importance to the formation of early German nationalism, see Ute Planert, *Der Mythos vom Befreiungskrieg: Frankreichs Kriege und der deutsche Süden; Alltag, Wahrnehmung, Deutung, 1792–1841* (Paderborn, Germany: Ferdinand Schöningh Verlag, 2007).

14. For two original and definitive expositions of the confessionalization thesis, see Wolfgang Reinhard, "Gegenreformation als Modernisierung? Prolegomena zu einer Theorie des konfessionellen Zeitalters," *Archiv für Reformationsgeschichte* 68 (1977): 226–52, and Heinz Schilling, *Konfessionskonflikt und Staatsbildung: Eine Fallstudie iiber das Verhdltnis von religiosem und sozialem Wandel in der Frühneuzeit am Beispiel der Grafschaft Lippe* (Güttersloh, Germany: Mohn, 1981). For a comprehensive historiography of the confessionalization thesis up to 1989, see R. Po-Chia Hsia, *Social Discipline in the Reformation: Central Europe, 1550–1750* (London: Routledge, 1989). On the relationship of the confessionalization thesis to modern German history, see the April 2005 H-German Forum "Confessionalization," available at http://www.h-net.org/~german/discuss/Confessionalization/Confess_index.htm.

15. Maurice Halbwachs, *On Collective Memory*, trans. Lewis A. Coser (Chicago: University of Chicago Press, 1992), 50.

16. Ibid., 54.

17. Ibid., 78.

18. Jan Assmann, *Religion and Cultural Memory: Ten Studies*, trans. Rodney Livingstone (Stanford, CA: Stanford University Press, 2006), 11.

19. Ibid., 94, and Jan Assmann and John Czaplicka, "Collective Memory and Cultural Identity," *New German Critique* 65 (Spring–Summer 1995): 127.

20. Assmann and Czaplicka, "Collective Memory and Cultural Identity," 130.

21. Pierre Nora, ed., *Realms of Memory: Rethinking the French Past*, trans. Arthur Goldhammer (New York: Columbia University Press, 1996), xvii.

22. Ibid., x, 6.

23. Ibid., 7, 15–16.

24. Gérald Chaix, "Die Reformation," trans. Reinhard Tiffert, in *Deutsche Erinnerungsorte*, ed. Etienne François and Hagen Schluze, vol. 2 (Munich: C. H. Beck, 2001), 9, 27.

1. For the Sake of the German Fatherland: Church Unity and the German National Idea at the 1817 Reformation Anniversaries

1. For revisionist accounts of the response to the Napoleonic Wars inside and outside of Prussia, which complicate the Prussian origins of German nationalism, see Karen Hagemann, *"Männlicher Muth und Teutsche Ehre": Nation, Militär und Geschlecht zur Zeit der Antinapoleonischen Kriege Preussens* (Paderborn, Germany: Schöningh, 2002); Michael Rowe, *From Reich to State: The Rhineland in the Revolutionary Age, 1780–1830* (New York: Cambridge University Press, 2003); Katherine B. Aaslestad, *Place and Politics: Local Identity, Civic Culture and German Nationalism in North Germany during the Revolutionary Era* (Leiden: Brill, 2005); Ute Planert, *Der Mythos vom Befreiungskrieg. Frankreichs Kriege und der deutsche Süden: Alltag, Wahrnehmung, Deutung, 1792–1841.* (Paderborn, Germany: Ferdinand Schöningh Verlag, 2007); and John Breuilly, "The Response to Napoleon and German Nationalism," in *The Bee and the Eagle: Napoleonic France and the End of the Holy Roman Empire*, ed. Alan Forrest and Peter H. Wilson (Basingstoke, UK: Palgrave Macmillan, 2009) 256–83.

2. Eric Dorn Brose, *German History, 1789–1871: From the Holy Roman Empire to the Bismarckian Reich* (Providence, RI: Berghahn, 1997), 63.

3. For the Prussian response to Jena and Auerstedt, see Peter Paret, *The Cognitive Challenge of War: Prussia 1806* (Princeton, NJ: Princeton University Press, 2009).

4. For the "political Protestantism" of the Wartburgfest, see D. G. Kieser, *Das Wartburgfest am 18. October 1817: In seiner Entstehung, Ausführung und Folgen* (Jena: Frommann, 1818), and Lutz Winckler, *Martin Luther als Bürger und Patriot: Das Reformationsjubiläum von 1817 und der politische Protestantismus des Wartburgfestes* (Lübeck, Germany: Mathiesen, 1969).

5. See Dieter Düding, Peter Friedemann, and Paul Münch, eds., *Öffentliche Festkultur: Politische Feste in Deutschland von der Aufklärung bis zum Ersten Weltkrieg* (Hamburg: Rowohl, 1988); Emil Brix and Hannes Stekl, eds., *Der Kampf um das Gedächtnis: Öffentliche Gedenktage in Mitteleuropa* (Vienna: Böhlau, 1997); and Jan Assman, "Collective Memory and Cultural Identity," trans. John Czaplicka, *New German Critique*, no. 65 (Spring–Summer 1995).

6. E. W. Zeeden, *The Legacy of Luther: Martin Luther and the Reformation in the Estimation of the German Lutherans from Luther's Death to the Beginning of the Age of Goethe*, trans. Ruth Mary Bethell (London: Hollis and Carter, 1954), 36.

7. Friedrich Loofs, "Die Jahrhundertfeier der Reformation an den Universitäten Wittenberg und Halle, 1617, 1717, und 1817," *Zeitschrift des Vereins für Kirchengeschichte in der Provinz Sachsen*, 14 (1917): 66–67.

8. Ibid., 55–56.

9. Nigel Aston, *Christianity and Revolutionary Europe c. 1750–1830* (Cambridge: Cambridge University Press, 2002), 11–12, 18–20, and Rudolf Vierhaus, *Germany in the Age of Absolutism*, trans. Jonathan B. Knudsen (Cambridge: Cambridge University Press, 1988), 63–64.

10. Aston, *Christianity and Revolutionary Europe*, 12, 19.

11. Ibid., 198, 207.

12. Susan Crane, "Holy Alliances: Creating Religious Communities after the Napoleonic Wars," in *Die Gegenwart Gottes in der modernen Gesellschaft: Transzendenz und Religiöse Vergemeinschaftung in Deutschland*, ed. Michael Geyer and Lucian Hölscher (Göttingen, Germany: Wallstein, 2006), 37–59.

13. Jacob Gottlieb Planck, *Über die Trennung und Wiedervereinigung der getrennten christlichen Haupt-Partheyen* (Tübingen: Cotta, 1803).

14. Friedrich Samuel Gottfried Sack, *Ueber die Vereinigung der beiden protestantischen Kirchenparteien in der Preußischen Monarchie* (Berlin: Friedrich Maurer, 1812).

15. These increasing confessional tensions are often pointed to as evidence that the nineteenth century represented a "second confessional age." See Olaf Blaschke, "Das 19. Jahrhundert: Ein Zweites Konfessionelles Zeitalter?," *Geschichte und Gesellschaft* 26, no. 1 (2000): 38–75, and Olaf Blaschke, ed., *Konfessionen im Konflikt: Deutschland zwischen 1800 und 1970; Ein zweites konfessionelles Zeitalter* (Göttingen, Germany: Vandenhoeck and Ruprecht, 2002). For a critique of Blaschke's thesis, see Anthony J. Steinhoff, "Ein zweites konfessionelles Zeitalter? Nachdenken über die Religion im langen 19. Jahrhundert," *Geschichte und Gesellschaft* 30, no. 4 (October–December 2004), 549–70.

16. Lucian Hölscher, "The Religious Divide: Piety in Nineteenth-Century Germany," in *Protestants, Catholics, and Jews in Germany, 1800–1914*, ed. Helmut W. Smith (Oxford: Berg, 2001), 42.

17. Lucian Hölscher, *Geschichte der protestantischen Frömmigkeit in Deutschland* (Munich: C. H. Beck, 2005), 211.

18. Walter H. Conser Jr., *Church and Confession: Conservative Theologians in Germany, England, and America, 1815–1866* (Macon, GA: Mercer University Press, 1984), 16–17.

19. Carl Immanuel Nitzsch, "Kabinettsordre Friedrich Wilhelm III: Vom 27 September 1817," in *Urkundenbuch der Evangelischen Union mit Erläuterungen*, by Carl Immanuel Nitzsch (Bonn: Adolph Marcus, 1853), 125.

20. "Official Declaration of the Synod of Berlin Concerning the Celebration of Holy Communion Which It Will Hold on 30 October 1817," in *Friedrich Schleiermacher on Creeds, Confessions, and Church Union: That They May be One*, ed. Iain G. Nicol (Lewiston, NY: Edwin Mellen Press, 2004), 20.

21. Ibid., 23.

22. Klaus Wappler, "Reformationsjubiläum und Kirchenunion (1817)," in *Die Geschichte der Evangelischen Kirche der Union*, ed. J. F. Gerhard Goeters and Rudolf Mau, vol. 1 (Leipzig: Evangelische Verlagsanstalt, 1992), 112–13.

23. Nitzsch, "Kabinettsordre Friedrich Wilhelm III: Vom 27 September 1817," 125.

24. For the confessional politics of Johann Sigismund's conversion and the significance of the decision of his wife, Anna of Saxony, to remain Lutheran, see Bodo Nischan, *Prince, People, and Confession: The Second Reformation in Brandenburg* (Philadelphia: University of Pennsylvania Press, 1994).

25. Walter Grossmann, "Religious Toleration in Germany, 1648–1750," *Studies on Voltaire and the Eighteenth Century* 201 (1982): 124–25.

26. Andrew Landale Drumond, "Church and State in Protestant Germany before 1918: With Special Reference to Prussia," *Church History* 13, no. 3 (September 1944): 213–14.

27. Grossmann, "Religious Toleration," 126.

28. K. R. Hagenbach, *History of the Church in the Eighteenth and Nineteenth Centuries*, trans. John F. Hurst (New York: Charles Scribner and Sons, 1869), 350.

29. Nitzsch, "Kabinettsordre Friedrich Wilhelm III. vom 27 September 1817," 126.

30. Ibid., 125–26.

31. Christopher Clark, "Confessional Policy and the Limits of State Action: Frederick William III and the Prussian Church Union 1817–1840," *Historical Journal* 39, no. 4 (December 1996): 989.

32. Robert M. Bigler, *The Politics of German Protestantism: The Rise of the Protestant Church Elite in Prussia, 1815–1848* (Berkeley: University of California Press, 1972), 37.

33. Carl Immanuel Nitzsch, "Vereinigungsurkunde für die Gemeinde Unterbarmen vom J. 1822," in *Urkundenbuch der Evangelischen Union mit Erläuterungen*, by Carl Immanuel Nitzsch (Bonn: Adolph Marcus, 1853), 137

34. Christian Schreiber, Valentin Karl Veillodter, and William Hennings, eds., *Allgemeine Chronik der dritten Jubel-Feier der deutschen evangelischen Kirche: Im Jahre 1817* (Erfurt and Gotha: Hennings, 1819), vol. 1, 35.

35. Clark, "Confessional Policy," 986.

36. Gerhard Friederich, ed., *Chronik der dritten Jubelfeier der Reformation in Frankfurt am Main* (Frankfurt am Main: Sauerländer, 1817), 5.

37. "Die Lokalunion in Bergzabern, 2 Dezember 1817," in *Kirchenunionen im 19. Jahrhundert*, ed. Gerhard Ruhbach (Guterslöh, Germany: Gerd Mohn, 1967), 45.

38. Friedrich Schleiermacher, "Address Celebrating the Third Centennial of the Reformation of the Church by Luther at the University of Berlin Held on 3 November 1817," in *Friedrich Schleiermacher*, ed. Iain G. Nicol, 45.

39. Friedrich Schleiermacher, quoted in James J. Sheehan, *German History, 1770–1866* (Oxford: Oxford University Press, 1993), 379.

40. For nineteenth-century German associational life, see Thomas Nipperdey, "Verein als soziale Struktur in Deutschland im späten 18. und frühen 19. Jahrhundert. Eine Fallstudie zur Modernisierung," in *Gesellschaft, Kultur, Theorie: Gesammelte Aufsätze zur neueren Geschichte*, ed. Thomas Nipperdey (Göttingen, Germany: Vandenhoeck and Ruprecht, 1976), 176–205, and Otto Dann, "Vereinswesen und bürgerliche Gesellschaft in Deutschland," *Historische Zeitschrift* 9 (1984).

41. Valentin Karl Veillodter, *Zwei Predigten am dritten Säkularfeste der Reformation im Jahre 1817* (Nuremberg: Riegel and Wießner, 1817), 8.

42. Ibid., 24.

43. Ibid., 7–8.

44. E. A. Clarus, *Erinnerung an die dritte Säcularfeier des Reformationsfestes in der evangelischen Stadtkirche zu Bamberg* (Bamberg: E. F. Kunz, 1817), 11.

45. Ibid., 15.

46. Ibid., 27.

47. Ibid., 27–28.

48. Ibid., 26–27.

49. Gottlieb Philipp Christian Kaiser, "Zwei Preidgten am Reformations-Jubelfeste 1817 in der Stadtkirche der evangelisch, lutherischen Neustadt zu Erlangen," in *Allgemeine Chronik*, ed. Christian Schreiber et al., vol. 2, 108, 112.

50. Ibid., 109.

51. Clarus, *Erinnerung*, 5–6.

52. Ibid., 6.

53. Ibid., 36.

54. Ibid., 51, 60–66.

55. Ibid., 66.

56. Ibid., 84.

57. Alon Confino, *The Nation as a Local Metaphor: Württemberg, Imperial Germany, and National Memory, 1871–1918* (Chapel Hill, NC: University of North Carolina Press, 1997). See also Celia Applegate, *A Nation of Provincials: The German Idea of Heimat* (Berkeley: University of California Press, 1990), and Abigail Green, *Fatherlands: State-Building and Nationhood in Nineteenth-Century Germany* (Cambridge: Cambridge University Press, 2001).

58. Maximilian Prechtl, *Seitenstück zur Weisheit Dr. Martin Luthers zum Jubeljahre der Lutherischen Reformation* (Sulzbach: J. C. Seidel, 1817), iii. See also Maximilian Prechtl, *Friedens-Benehmen zwischen Boussuet, Leibniz und Molanus* (1815), and his *Friedensworte an die katholische und protestantische Kirche für ihre Wiedervereinigung* (1820).

59. Prechtl, *Seitenstück vii*–viii.

60. Georg Arndt, *Das Reformationsjubelfest in vergangenen Jahrhunderten* (Berlin: Evangelical Federation, 1917), 28–29.

61. Prechtl, *Seitenstück*, x.

62. Ibid., xvi.

63. Arndt, *Das Reformationsjubelfest*, 29.

64. On the Hep-Hep Riots and post-Napoleonic German anti-Semitism in general, see Stefan Rohrbacher "The 'Hep-Hep' Riots of 1819: Anti-Jewish Agitation, and Violence," in *Exclusionary Violence: Anti-Semitic Riots in Modern Germany History*, ed. Christhard Hoffman, Werner Bergmann, and Helmut Walser Smith (Ann Arbor: University of Michigan Press, 2002), 23–42. See also Eleonore O. Sterling, "Anti-Jewish Riots in Germany in 1819: A Displacement of Social Protest," *Historia Judaica* 12 (October 1950): 105–42, and Jakob Katz, *Die Hep-Hep-Verfolgungen des Jahres 1819* (Berlin: Metropol, 1994).

65. Christian Wiese, "Überwinder des Mittelalters? Ahnherr des Nationasozialismus? Zur Vielstimmigkeit und Tragik der jüdischen Lutherrezeption im wilhelmischen Deutschland und in der Weimarer Republik," in *Lutherinszenierung und Reformationserinnerung*, ed. Stefan Laube and Karl-Heinz Fix (Leipzig: Evangelische Verlagsanstalt, 2002), 169–71.

66. Johannes Wallmann, "The Reception of Luther's Writings on the Jews from the Reformation to the End of the 19th Century," *Lutheran Quarterly* 1 (Spring 1987): 86–87.

67. An anonymous Catholic, *D. Martin Luthers Verdienste um die katholische Kirche in Teutschland* (Erlangen, 1818), 6–7.

68. Ibid., 11.

69. L. F. Schmidt, *Zwey Predigten am Säkularfeste der Kirchenreformation* (Munich: J. G. J. Seybold, 1817), III.

70. Ibid., IV–V.

71. G. H. Kayser, *Wie feyern wir Luthern und die Reformation am Stiftungstage der letzern am Würdigsten?* (Augsburg: August Bäumer, 1817), 28–29.

2. The Ecumenical Vanguard: Ecumenism, Nationalism, and Luther-Worship in the German Revolutions of 1848

1. For a corrective to this view, see David Blackbourn and Geoff Eley, *The Peculiarities of German History: Bourgeois Society and Politics in Nineteenth-Century Germany* (Oxford: Oxford University Press, 1984).

2. See Jonathan Sperber, *Popular Catholicism in Nineteenth-Century Germany* (Princeton, NJ: Princeton University Press, 1984), and Helmut Walser Smith, *German Nationalism and Religious Conflict: Culture, Ideology, Politics, 1870–1914* (Princeton, NJ: Princeton University Press, 1995).

3. For the German-language literature on the German Catholics, see Wolfgang Leesch, *Die Geschicte des Deutschkatholizismus in Schlesien (1844–1852), unter besonderer Berücksichtigung seiner politischen Haltung* (Breslau, Germany: Priebatsch, 1938); Günter Kolbe, "Demokratische opposition in Religiösem Gewande und Antikirchliche bewegeng im Königreich Sachsen" (PhD diss., University of Leipzig, 1964); Jörn Brederlow, *"Lichtfreunde" und "Freie Gemeinden": Religiöser Protest und Freiheitsbewegung im Vormärz und in der Revolution von 1848/1849* (Munich: Oldenbourg, 1976); Friedrich Wilhelm Graf, *Die Politisierung des religiösen Bewußtseins: Die bürgerlichen Religionsparteien im deutschen Vormärz; Das Beispiel des Deutschkatholizismus* (Stuttgart: Friedrich Frommann, 1978); Peter Bahn "Deutschkatholiken und Freireligiöse: Geschichte und Kultur einer religiös-weltanschaulichen Dissidentgruppe, dargestellt am Beispiel der Pfalz" (PhD diss., University of Mainz, 1991); and Andreas Holzem, *Kirchenreform und Sektenstiftung: Deutschkatholiken, Reformkatholiken und Ultramontane am Oberrhein 1844–1866* (Paderborn, Germany: Schöningh, 1994).

4. On Young Germany and the Hambach Festival, see Helmut Koopmann, *Das Junge Deutschland: Eine Einführung* (Darmstadt, Germany: Wiss. Buchgesellschaft, 1993), and Cornelia Foerster, "Das Hambacher Fest 1832: Volksfest und Nationalfest einer oppositionellen Massenbewegung," in *Öffentliche Festkultur: Politische Feste in Deutschland von der Aufklärung bis zum Ersten Weltkrieg*, ed. Dieter Düding, Peter Friedemann, and Paul Münch (Hamburg: Rowohl, 1988), 113–31.

5. Nicholas Hope, *German and Scandinavian Protestantism 1700 to 1918* (Oxford: Oxford University Press, 1995), 446–47.

6. Thomas Nipperdey, *Germany from Napoleon to Bismarck, 1800–1866*, trans. Daniel Nolan (Princeton, NJ: Princeton University Press, 1996), 337–38.

7. Hope, *German and Scandinavian Protestantism*, 449.

8. Nipperdey, *Germany from Napoleon to Bismarck*, 362–63.

9. Eric Dorn Brose, *German History, 1789–1871: From the Holy Roman Empire to the Bismarckian Reich* (Providence, RI: Berghahn, 1997), 129.

10. For the pre-history of nineteenth-century Catholic opposition to ultramontanism, see Michael Printy, *Enlightenment and the Creation of German Catholicism* (Cambridge: Cambridge University Press, 2011).

11. Robert M. Bigler, *The Politics of German Protestantism: The Rise of the Protestant Church Elite in Prussia, 1815–1848* (Berkeley: University of California Press, 1972), 193, and Hajo Halborn, *A History of Modern Germany, 1648–1840* (Princeton, NJ: Princeton University Press, 1964), 508.

12. Bigler, *Politics of German Protestantism*, 194–95.

13. The definitive social history of the Trier pilgrimages is still Wolfgang Schieder's "Kirche und Revolution: Sozialgeschichtliche Aspekte der Trier Wallfahrt von 1844," *Archiv fur Sozialgeschichte* 14 (1974): 419–54.

14. Jonathan Sperber, *Rhineland Radicals: The Democratic Movement and the Revolution of 1848–1849* (Princeton, NJ: Princeton University Press, 1991), 126.

15. *John Ronge, the Holy Coat of Treves, and the New German-Catholic Church* (New York: Harper, 1845), 18.

16. Johannes Ronge, "Urteil eines katholischen Priesters uber den Heiligen Rock zu Trier" (October 1, 1844), in *Freireligiöse Quellenbuch 1844–1926: Eine Sammlung grundlegender Texte über Inhalt und Ziele Freier Religion*, ed. Lothar Geis (Mainz, Germany: Freireligiöse Gemeinde, 2007), 17–22.

17. Manfred P. Fleischer, *Katholische und lutherische Ireniker: Unter besonderer Berücksichtigung des 19. Jahrhunderts* (Göttingen, Germany: Musterschmidt, 1968), 119.

18. Samuel Laing, *Notes on the Rise, Progress, and Prospects of the Schism from the Church of Rome, called the German-Catholic Church* (London: Longman, 1846), 76.

19. Ibid., 76–96.

20. Lucian Hölscher, *Geschichte der protestantischen Frömmigkeit* (Munich: Beck, 2005), 358–59.

21. Johannes Ronge, *The Reformation of the Nineteenth Century*, vol. 1 (London: E. Deutsch, 1852), 8.

22. Ibid., ix.

23. Leberecht Uhlich, *The Protestant Friends: A Circular Addressed to Christians throughout Germany*, trans. G. C. Hebbe (New York: Charles Müller, 1846).

24. Gustav Tschirn, *Zur 60jährigen Geschichte der freireligiösen Bewegung* (Gottesberg, Germany: Hensels, 1904), 25.

25. *Sonntags-Blätt*, no. 62, December 8, 1850

26. Leberecht Uhlich, *Hier stehe ich, ich kann nicht anders* (Magdeburg: Creutz, 1845), 16.

27. Ronge, *Reformation of the Nineteenth Century*, vol. 1, 48.

28. Gustav [von] Struve, *Politisches Taschenbuch für das deutsche Volk* (Frankfurt a.M.: Rütten, 1846), 204.

29. Ronge, *Reformation of the Nineteenth Century*, vol. 1, 6.

30. Ibid.

31. Ibid., vol. 1, 38.

32. Johannes Ronge, *Rede, gehalten am 23. September 1845 in der Münsterkirche zu Ulm* (Ulm: Ernst Nübling, 1845), 8.

33. Uhlich, *Protestant Friends.*

34. Ibid.

35. "Offener Brief an die protestantische Geistlichkeit Deutschlands," *Zeitung für freie Gemeinden. Materialien zur Geschichte und Fortbildung der freien Gemeinden*, 2, no. 2 (March 28, 1851): 32–34.

36. Bigler, *Politics of German Protestantism*, 222, and Ronge, *Reformation of the Nineteenth Century*, vol. 1, 38–39.

37. Uhlich, *Protestant Friends.*

38. Tschirn, *Zur 60jährigen Geschichte der freireligiösen Bewegung*, 53–54.

39. Hölscher, *Geschichte der protestantischen Frömmigkeit*, 360.

40. G. G. Gervinus, *The Mission of the German Catholics* (London: Chapman, 1846), 33.

41. Johannes Ronge, *An meine Glaubensgenossen und Mitbürger* (Altenburg, 1845), 4.

42. See Brian E. Vick, *Defining Germany: The 1848 Frankfurt Parliamentarians and National Identity* (Cambridge, MA: Harvard University Press, 2002).

43. Bigler, *Politics of German Protestantism*, 197, 205.

44. Arnold Ruge, *Hallische Jahrbücher*, 1838, cited in Bigler, *Politics of German Protestantism*, 211. For the Left Hegelians, see John Edward Toews, *Hegelianism: The Path toward Dialectical Humanism, 1805–1841* (Cambridge: Cambridge University Press, 1985).

45. Nipperdey, *Germany from Napoleon to Bismarck*, 364.

46. Tschirn, *Zur 60jährigen Geschichte der freireligiösen Bewegung*, 21–25.

47. Ronge, *Rede zu Ulm*, 4.

48. Ibid., 7.

49. Johannes, *Die Neue Reformation oder die deutsch-katholische Bewegung* (Leipzig: Naumburg, 1845), 6.

50. Ferdinand Kampe, *Geschichte der religiösen Bewegung der neuern Zeit: Vierter Band; Geschichte des Deutschkatholicismus und freien Protestantismus in Deutschland und Nordamerika von 1848–1858* (Leipzig: Franz Wagner, 1860), 44, 53.

51. A. Andresen, *Luther Revived: or, a Short Account of Johannes Ronge, the Bold Reformer of the Catholic Church in Germany* (London: Chapman, 1845), 33.

52. Ronge, *Reformation of the Nineteenth Century*, vol. 1, viii.

53. Tschirn, *Zur 60jährigen Geschichte der freireligiösen Bewegung*, 30.

54. Catherine Magill Holden Prelinger, "A Decade of Dissent in Germany: An Historical Study of The Society of Protestant Friends and The German-catholic Church, 1840–1848" (PhD diss., Yale University, 1954), 75.

55. For an account of Christian-Jewish relations during the "long" nineteenth century that navigates between integration and persecution, see Amos Elon, *The Pity of It All: A Portrait of the German-Jewish Epoch, 1743–1933* (New York: Picador, 2003). For debates over the emancipation of Jews at the Frankfurt Parliament, see Werner E. Mosse, ed., *Revolution and Evolution: 1848 in German-Jewish History* (Tübingen, Germany: Mohr Siebeck, 1981); Michael Brenner, "From Subject to Citizen," in *German-Jewish History in Modern Times: Emancipation*

and Acculturation, 1780–1871, ed. Michael A. Meyer et al. (New York: Columbia University Press, 1998), 251–76; and Brian E. Vick, "The German Nation and the German Jews," in *Defining Germany: The 1848 Frankfurt Parliamentarians and National Identity*, by Brian E. Vick (Cambridge, MA: Harvard University Press, 2002), 83–109.

56. Carl Scholl, *Drei Vorträge gehalten vor der deutschkatholischen Gemeinde Mannheim, zugleich also Rechtfertigung meines Anschlusses* (Darmstadt: Pabst, 1846), 27.

57. Hermann Greive, "Religious Dissent and Tolerance in the 1840s," in *Revolution and Evolution: 1848 in German-Jewish History*, ed. Werner E. Mosse (Tübingen, Germany: Mohr Siebeck, 1981), 345–46.

58. Michael A. Meyer, "Alienated Intellectuals in the Camp of Religious Reform: The Frankfurt Reformfreunde, 1842–1845," *Association for Jewish Studies Review* 6 (1981): 83–86.

59. Ibid., 85.

60. Ibid., 84.

61. On the "Problematics of Philosemitism," see Dagmar Herzog, *Intimacy and Exclusion: Religious Politics in Pre-Revolutionary Baden* (Princeton, NJ: Princeton University Press, 1996), 111–39

62. Michael A. Meyer et al., *German-Jewish History in Modern Times: Emancipation and Acculturation, 1780–1871* (New York: Columbia University Press, 1998), 197.

63. Herzog, *Intimacy and Exclusion*, 123.

64. Kampe, *Geschichte der religiösen Bewegung der neuern Zeit*, vol. 4, 8.

65. Johannes Ronge, *Religion und Politik* (Frankfurt a.M., 1850), repr. in Graf, *Die Politisierung des religiösen Bewußtseins*, 354.

66. Ronge, *Reformation of the Nineteenth Century*, vol. 1, 38.

67. Ronge, *An meine Glaubensgenossen und Mitbürger*, 11.

68. Ronge, *Reformation of the Nineteenth Century*, vol. 1, 58.

69. Ibid., 6.

70. Struve, *Politisches Taschenbuch*, 75–76.

71. Gervinus, *Mission of the German Catholics*, 24.

72. On the Göttingen Seven, see Miriam Saage-Maaß, *Die Göttinger Sieben- demokratische Vorkämpfer oder nationale Helden?: Zum Verhältnis von Geschichtsschreibung und Erinnerungskultur in der Rezeption des Hannoverschen Verfassungskonfliktes* (Göttingen, Germany: Vandenhoeck and Ruprecht, 2007).

73. Ibid., 35.

74. Ibid., 37–38.

75. Ibid., 37.

76. Johannes Ronge, *Ein Wort der Verständigung über die deutsche Volkskirche als die höhere nationale Einheit von Protestantismus und Katholizismus* (Stuttgart: Sonnewald, 1845), 4.

77. Ronge, *Rede zu Ulm*, 4.

78. *Zeiting für freie Gemeinden*, no. 1 (January 4, 1850).

79. Ronge, *Reformation of the Nineteenth Century*, vol. 1, 90.

80. Sylvia Paletschek, "Religiöse Emanzipation und Frauenemanzipation: Was bedeutet Religionskritik Mitte des 19. Jahrhunderts für Frauen?" *Sozialwissenschaftliche Information* 18, no. 4 (1989): 3.

81. Sylvia Paletschek, *Frauen und Dissens: Frauen im Deutschkatholizismus und in den freien Gemeinden 1841–1852* (Göttingen, Germany: Vandenhoeck and Ruprecht, 1990), 194.

82. See Catherine M. Prelinger, *Charity, Challenge, and Change: Religious Dimensions of the Mid-Nineteenth-Century Women's Movement in Germany* (Westport, CT: Greenwood, 1987).

83. Ronge, *Reformation of the Nineteenth Century*, vol. 1, 90.

84. Ibid., 89.

85. Ronge, *The Reformation of the Nineteenth Century*, vol. 2, 92.

86. Heinrich Thiel, *Der Inhalt des Deutsch-Katholizismus: Den denkenden Deutsch-Katholiken gewidmet* (Dessau: Neubürger, 1846), 68–69.

87. Herzog, *Intimacy and Exclusion*, 86.

88. Ronge, *Rede zu Ulm*, 12.

89. Ronge, *Reformation of the Nineteenth Century*, vol. 1, 90.

90. Ibid., 48.

91. Ibid., 52.

92. Prelinger, *Charity, Challenge, and Change*, ix.

93. Paletscheck, *Frauen und Dissens*, 36.

94. Ronge, *Reformation of the Nineteenth Century*, vol. 2, 88.

95. Ibid., 68.

96. Alexandra Lotz, "*Die Erlösung des weiblichen Geschlechts*: Frauen in deutschkatholischen Gemeinden," in *Schimpfende Weiber und patriotische Jungfrau: Frauen im Vormärz und in der Revolution 1848/1849*, ed. Carola Lipp (Moos, Germany: Elster, 1986), 232.

97. *Der Streit über Gemischte Ehen und das Kirchenhoheitsrecht im Großherzogthum Baden* (Karlsruhe, Germany: G. Braun, 1847), xvi.

98. Ibid., xv.

99. Ibid., ix.

100. Ibid., xxvii

101. Ibid., xvii. Also cited in Herzog, *Intimacy and Exclusion*, 47.

102. Ibid., xi.

103. Jonathan Sperber, "Festivals of National Unity in the German Revolution of 1848–1849," *Past and Present*, no. 136 (August 1992): 137.

3. A Holy Alliance: Right-Wing Ecumenism and German Nationalism, 1860–1866

1. On Michelis, see Willi Belz, *Friedrich Michelis und seine Bestreitung der Neuscholastik in der Polemik gegen Joseph Kleutgen* (Leiden: E. J. Brill: 1978). On Döllinger, see Peter Neuener, *Döllinger als Theologe der Ökumene: Beiträge zur ökumenischen Theologie* (Padernborn, Germany: Schöningh, 1979), and Peter Neuener, "Ignaz von Döllinger: Katholizität und Anti-ultramontanismus," in *Theologen des 19. Jahrhunderts: Eine Einführung*, ed. Peter Neuner and Gunther Wenz (Darmstadt, Germany: Wissenschaftliche Buchgesellschaft, 2002), 75–93. On Leo, see Carolyn Rebecca Henderson, "Heinrich Leo: A Study in German Conservatism" (PhD diss., University of Wisconsin-Madison, 1977), and Christoph Freiherr von Maltzahn, *Heinrich Leo (1799–1878): Ein politisches Gelehrtenleben zwischen romantischem Konservatismus und Realpolitik* (Göttingen, Germany: Vandenhoeck and Ruprecht, 1979). On Gerlach, see Hans-Christof Kraus, *Ernst Ludwig von Gerlach: Politisches Denken und Handeln eines preussischen Altkonservativen*, vol. 1 (Göttingen, Germany: Vandenhoeck and Ruprecht, 1994).

2. For the full range of approaches to national unity between 1848 and 1871, especially with respect to the *Nationalverein* and *Reformverein*, see Willy Real, *Der Deutsche Reformverein: Grossdeutsche Stimmen und Kräfte zwischen Villafranca und Königgrätz* (Lübeck, Germany: Matthiesen, 1966), and Shlomo Na'aman, *Der Deutsche Nationalverein: Die politische Konstituierung des deutschen Bürgertums 1859–1867* (Düsseldorf: Droste Verlag, 1987).

3. Ludwig Clarus [Wilhem Volk], *Die Zusammenkunft gläubiger Protestanten und Katholiken zu Erfurt im Herbste 1860 und deren Verlauf: Eine auf eigene Theilnahme und sämmtliche bekannt gewordene Quellen gegründete Darstellung und Mahnung zur Fortsetzung des Werkes* (Paderborn: Junsermann, 1867), 10–12.

4. Willi Belz, *Friedrich Michelis und seine Bestreitung der Neuscholastik in der Polemik gegen Joseph Kleutgen* (Leiden: E. J. Brill, 1978), 25.

5. Clemens Theodor Perthes, *Life and Times of Friedrich Perthes: Patriot and Man of Business* (London: William P. Nimmo, 1858), 396–97.

6. Clarus, *Die Zusammenkunft*, 6.

7. Marjorie Lamberti, "Lutheran Orthodoxy and the Beginning of Conservative Party Organization in Prussia," *Church History* 37, no. 4 (December 1968): 452–53.

8. *Ut Omnes Unum*, no. 3 (December 1, 1879).

9. Clarus, *Die Zusammenkunft*, 63. On Stahl, see Robert A. Kann, "Friedrich Julius Stahl: A Re-examination of his Conservatism," *Leo Baeck Institute*

Yearbook 12, no. 1 (1967): 55–74; Hans Peter Pyclik, *Friedrich Julius Stahl: A Study of the Development of German Conservative Thought, 1802–1861* (Minneapolis: University of Minnesota, 1972), and Christian Wiegand, *Über Friedrich Julius Stahl (1801–1862): Recht, Staat, Kirche* (Paderborn, Germany: Schöningh, 1981).

10. Manfred P. Fleischer, *Katholische und lutherische Ireniker: Unter besonder Berücksichtigung des 19. Jahrhunderts* (Göttingen, Germany: Musterschmidt, 1968), 135–36.

11. Ibid., 146.

12. Clarus, *Die Zusammenkunft*, 32.

13. Ibid., 17.

14. Fleischer, *Katholische und lutherische Ireniker*, 141.

15. Clarus, *Die Zusammenkunft*, 10–12.

16. Ibid., 14–15.

17. Heinrich Leo to Philipp von Nathusius, Erfurt, September 24, 1860, in Hans-Joachim Schoeps, *Das Andere Preussen: Konservative Gestalten und Probleme im Zeitalter Friedrich Wilhelms IV*, 3rd ed. (Berlin: Haude and Spenersche, 1964), 322–23.

18. Gérald Chaix, "Die Reformation," trans. Reinhard Tiffert, in *Deutsche Erinnerungsorte*, ed. Etienne François and Hagen Schluze, vol. 2 (Munich: C. H. Beck, 2001).

19. A. G. Dickens and John M. Tonkin, with Kenneth Powell, *The Reformation in Historical Thought* (Cambridge, MA: Harvard University Press, 1985), 183.

20. Ignaz von Döllinger, *Lectures on the Reunion of the Churches*, trans. Henry Nutcombe Oxenham (New York: Dodd and Mead, 1872), 14.

21. Ludwig von Gerlach, "Die Evangelische-katholische Zusammenkunft in Erfurt," *Volksblatt für Stadt und Land* 18, no. 16 (February 1861), repr. in Schoeps, *Das Andere Preussen*, 346.

22. Ibid., 346–47.

23. Hans-Christof Kraus, *Ernst Ludwig von Gerlach: Politisches Denken und Handeln eines preussischen Altkonservativen*, vol. 1 (Göttingen, Germany: Vandenhoeck and Ruprecht, 1994), 230.

24. Döllinger, *Lectures*, 74–75.

25. Ignaz von Döllinger, *The Church and the Churches; or the Papacy and the Temporal Power: An Historical and Political Review*, trans. William Bernard MacCabe (London: Hurst and Blackett, 1862), 12.

26. Heinrich Leo to Ernst Ludwig von Gerlach, July 1, 1852, repr. in *Ernst Ludwig von Gerlach: Aufzeichnungen aus seinem Leben und Wirken, 1795–1877*, ed. Jakob von Gerlach, vol. 2 (Schwerin, Germany: Bahn, 1903), 151–52.

27. Clarus, *Die Zusammenkunft*, 132–33.

28. Gerlach, "Die Evangelische-katholische Zusammenkunft in Erfurt," repr. in Schoeps, *Das Andere Preussen*, 348.

29. Döllinger, *Church and the Churches*, 14, and Döllinger, *Lectures*, 75–76.

30. Clarus, *Die Zusammenkunft*, 132.

31. Heinrich Leo, *Lehrbuch der Universalgeschichte*, vol. 3 (Halle: Eduard Anton, 1853), 300.

32. Döllinger, *Lectures*, 74.

33. Heinrich Leo, cited in Schoeps, *Das Andere Pruessen*, 201.

34. Heinrich Leo, [untitled], *Neue Preußische Zeitung* (September 27, 1861), cited in Döllinger, *Church and the Churches*, 16.

35. Döllinger, *Church and the Churches*, 16.

36. Friedrich Michelis, *Augsburger Postzeitung* 1861, No. 92-111, repr. in Schoeps, *Das Andere Pruessen*, 336.

37. Clarus, *Die Zusammenkunft*, 4.

38. Döllinger, *Lectures*, 161.

39. Henderson, "Heinrich Leo," 242.

40. Clarus, *Die Zusammenkunft*, 85–86.

41. Thomas Nipperdey, *Germany from Napoleon to Bismarck, 1800–1866*, trans. Daniel Nolan (Princeton, NJ: Princeton University Press, 1996), 279.

42. Manfred P. Fleischer, "*Deus Praesens in Jure*: The Politics of Ludwig von Gerlach," *Zeitschrift für Religions- und Geistesgeschichte* 39 (1987): 15.

43. Henderson, "Heinrich Leo," 180–81.

44. Gerlach, "Die Evangelische-katholische Zusammenkunft in Erfurt," repr. in Schoeps, *Das Andere Preussen*, 347.

45. Jakob von Gerlach, *Aufzeichnungen*, 151.

46. Schoeps, *Das Andere Preussen*, 64.

47. Christopher Clark, "The 'Christian' State and the 'Jewish Citizen' in Nineteenth-Century Prussia," in *Protestants, Catholics, and Jews in Germany, 1800–1914*, ed. Helmut Walser Smith (Oxford: Berg, 2001), 79–81.

48. Uriel Tal, *Christians and Jews in Germany: Religion, Politics, and Ideology in the Second Reich, 1870–1914*, trans. Noah Jonathan Jacobs (Ithaca, NY: Cornell University Press, 1975), 137.

49. Ludwig von Gerlach, "Tagebuch 21 Juli 1866," repr. in *Von der Revolution zum Norddeutschen Bund: Politik und Ideengut der preußischen Hochkonservativen; Aus dem Nachlaß von Ernst Ludwig von Gerlach*, ed. Hellmut Diwald, vol. 1 (Göttingen, Germany: Vandenhoeck and Ruprecht, 1970), 482.

50. Friedrich Michelis, *Preußens Beruf für Deutschland und die Weltgeschichte* (Paderborn, 1863), 13, 20, cited in Belz, *Friedrich Michelis*, 37.

51. Belz, *Friedrich Michelis*, 38.

52. Doron Avraham, "The Social and Religious Meaning of Nationalism: The Case of Prussian Conservatism, 1815–1871," *European History Quarterly*, no. 38 (2008): 537; Hartmut Lehmann, "Martin Luther as a National Hero in the Nineteenth Century" in *Romantic Nationalism in Europe*, ed. J. C. Eade (Canberra: Australian National University, 1983), 183; Uriel Tal, *Christians and Jews in Germany*, 121–22.

53. Kraus, *Ernst Ludwig von Gerlach*, vol. 1, 230.

54. Ludwig von Gerlach to Adolf von Thadden, Berlin, January 14, 1851, repr. in *Von der Revolution*, ed. Hellmut Diwald, vol. 2, 733.

55. See Chaix, "Die Reformation," 17–18; Lehmann, "Martin Luther as National Hero," 182; and the preceding chapter of this volume.

56. Michelis, *Augsburger Postzeitung* 1861, No. 92-111, repr. in Schoeps, *Das Andere Preussen*, 335–36.

57. Heinrich Leo to Ludwig [von] Gerlach, January 3, 1853, repr. in Diwald, *Von der Revolution*, vol. 2, 832.

58. Leo, *Lehrbuch*, vol. 3, 308.

59. Döllinger, *Lectures*, 63.

60. Leo to Nathusius, Erfurt, September 24, 1860, repr. in Schoeps, *Das Andere Preussen*, 323.

61. Fleischer, "Lutheran and Catholic Reunionists," 46–47.

62. Otto von Bismarck, *Bismarck: The Man and the Statesman*, trans. A. J. Butler, vol. 2 (New York: Harper, 1899), 305.

63. See Hans-Joachim Schoeps, "CDU vor 75 Jahren: Die sozialpolitischen Bestrebungen des Reichsfreiherrn Friedrich Carl von Fechenbach (1836 bis 1907)," *Zeitschrift für Religions- und Geistesgeschichte* 9 (1957): 267.

64. Keith H. Pickus, "Native Born Strangers: Jews, Catholics and the German Nation," in *Religion und Nation, Nation und Religion: Beiträge zu einer unbewältigten Geschichte*, ed. Micheal Geyer and Hartmut Lehmann (Göttingen, Germany: Wallstein, 2004), 146.

65. Helmut Walser Smith, *German Nationalism and Religions Conflict: Culture, Ideology, Politics, 1870–1914* (Princeton, NJ: Princeton University Press, 1995), 237–38, and George G. Windell, *The Catholics and German Unity, 1866–1871* (Minneapolis: University of Minnesota Press, 1954), 7–8.

4. Tragedy and Triumph: German Unification, the Kulturkampf, and Christian Ecumenism, 1866–1883

1. Anthony J. Steinhoff, "Christianity and the Creation of Germany," in *The Cambridge History of Christianity: World Christianities, c. 1815–1914*, ed. Sheridan Gilley and Brian Stanley (Cambridge: Cambridge University Press, 2006), 293,

and Thomas Nipperdey, *Religion im Umbruch: Deutschland 1870–1918* (Munich: C. H. Beck, 1998), 92.

2. Steinhoff, "Christianity and the Creation of Germany," 293.

3. Hartmut Lehmann, "The Germans as Chosen People: Old Testament Themes in German Nationalism," *German Studies Review* 14, no. 2 (May 1991): 261, 265.

4. Steinhoff, "Christianity and the Creation of Germany," 298.

5. Kurt Nowak, *Geschichte des Christentums in Deutschland: Religion, Politik und Gesellschaft vom Ende der Aufklärung bis zur Mitte des 20. Jahrhunderts* (Munich: C. H. Beck, 1995), 158.

6. *Neue Evangelische Kirchenzeitung*, January 7, 1871, 1 cited in Günter Brakelmann, "Der Krieg 1870/1871 und die Reichsgründung im Urteil des Protestantismus," in *Kirche zwischen Krieg und Frieden: Studien zur Geschichte des deutschen Protestantismus*, ed. Wolfgang Huber and Johannes Schwerdtfeger (Stuttgart: Ernst Klett, 1976), 303.

7. Gérald Chaix "Die Reformation," trans. Reinhard Tiffert, in *Deutsche Erinnerungsorte*, ed. Etienne François and Hagen Schluze, vol. 2 (Munich: C. H. Beck, 2001), 9, 27.

8. Brakelmann, "Der Krieg 1870/1871," 310–11.

9. Gordon A. Craig, *Germany, 1866–1945* (Oxford: Oxford University Press, 1978), 71.

10. Michael B. Gross, "Kulturkampf and Unification: German Liberalism and the War against the Jesuits," *Central European History* 30, no. 4 (1997): 546. See also Michael B. Gross, *The War against Catholicism: Liberalism and the Anti-Catholic Imagination in Nineteenth-Century Germany* (Ann Arbor, MI: University of Michigan Press, 2004).

11. David Blackbourn, *The Long Nineteenth Century: A History of Germany, 1780–1918* (Oxford: Oxford University Press, 1997), 261–62.

12. For the concept of the *Catholic milieu*, see M. Rainer Lepsius, "Parteiensystem und Sozialstrukture: Zum Problem der Demokritasierung der deutschen Gesellschaft," in *Wirtschaft, Geschichte und Wirtschaftsgeschichte; Festschrift zum 65. Geburtstag von Friedrich Lutge*, ed. Wilhelm Abel et al. (Stuttgart: G. Fischer, 1966), 371–93. For the social, religious, and political reactions of German Catholics to the establishment of the German Empire, see George G. Windell, *The Catholics and German Unity, 1866–1871* (Minneapolis: University of Minnesota Press, 1954); Margaret Lavinia Anderson, *Windthorst: A Political Biography* (Oxford: Oxford University Press, 1981); Jonathan Sperber, *Popular Catholicism in Nineteenth-Century Germany* (Princeton, NJ: Princeton University Press, 1984); David Blackbourn, *Marpingen: Apparitions of the Virgin Mary in Nineteenth-Century Germany* (Oxford: Clarendon Press, 1993); Thomas Mergel, *Zwischen*

Klasse und Konfession: Katholisches Bürgertum im Rheinland 1794–1914 (Gottingen, Germany: Vandenhoeck and Ruprecht, 1994); and Thomas Mergel, "Ultramontanism, Liberalism, Moderation: Political Mentalities and Political Behavior of the German Catholic Bürgertum, 1848–1914," *Central European History* 29 (1996): 151–74.

13. Lepsius, "Parteiensystem und Sozialstrukture." For a theoretical reassessment of the Catholic milieu, see Johannes Horstmann and Antonius Liedhegener, eds. *Konfession, Milieu, Moderne: Konzeptionelle Positionen und Kontroversen zur Geschichte von Katholizismus und Kirche im 19. und 20. Jahrhundert* (Schwerte, Germany: Katholische Akademie Schwerte, 2001).

14. For a corrective to the social and methodological "ghettoization" of Wilhelmine German Catholics, see Oded Heilbronner, "From Ghetto to Ghetto: The Place of German Catholic Society in Recent Historiography," *Journal of Modern History* 72 (June 2000): 453–95, and Helmut Walser Smith, ed. *Protestants, Catholics, and Jews in Germany, 1800–1914* (Oxford: Berg, 2001).

15. For the manifesto of the 1860 Erfurt Conference, see Hans Joachim Schoeps, "Die Erfurter Konferenz von 1860 (Zur Geschichte des katholisch-protestantischen Gesprächs)," *Zeitschrift für Religions- und Geistesgeschichte* 4 (1953): 135–59.

16. Manfred P. Fleischer, *Katholische und lutherische Ireniker: Unter besonderer Berucksichtigung des 19. Jahrhunderts* (Göttingen, Germany: Musterschmidt, 1968), 198.

17. "Die irenische Monatsschrift 'Ut omnes unum' und die Anderen," *Historich-Politische Blätter für das katholische Deutschland* 91 (1883): 494.

18. For the confessional politics of Ernst Ludwig von Gerlach, see Hans Joachim Schoeps, *Das Andere Preussen: Konservative Gestalten und Probleme im Zeitalter Friedrich Wilhelms IV*, 3rd ed. (Berlin: Haude and Spener, 1964).

19. Heinrich Ahrendts, quoted in Maria Bernardina, *Julie von Massow, geborene von Behr: Ein konvertitenbild aus dem 19. Jahrhundert* (Freiburg im Breisgau, Germany: Herder, 1902), 191.

20. Manfred P. Fleischer, *Katholische und lutherische Ireniker: Unter besonderer Berucksichtigung des 19. Jahrhunderts* (Göttingen, Germany: Musterschmidt, 1968), 192–94.

21. "Wiedervereinigung der getrennten Confessionen," *Ut Omnes Unum* 1 (December 1879): 34–36.

22. Adolf Röttscher, *Unionsversuche zwischen Katholiken und Protestanten Deutschlands* (Frankfurt a.M.: Foesser, 1885), 1.

23. Ibid., 1.

24. Carl Seltmann, *Zur Wiedervereinigung der getrennten Christen, zunächst in deutschen Landen* (Breslau, Germany: Aderholz, 1903), 391.

25. Ibid., 391.

26. For the historical use of the term *ecumenism*, see William Adolf Visser 't Hooft, "The Word 'Ecumenical'—Its History and Use," in *A History of the Ecumenical Movement, 1517–1948*, ed. Ruth Rouse and Stephan Charles Niell, 2nd ed., ed. Ruth Rouse and Stephan Charles Niell (Philadelphia: Westminster Press, 1967), 735–37.

27. Seltmann, *Zur Wiedervereinigung*, iv–v, 389–90; *Ut omnes unum: auf daß Alle Eins seien* (December 1, 1900), 3320–21. For the Roman Catholic reception and ecumenical potential of the Augsburg Confession, see Avery Dulles, "The Catholicity of the Augsburg Confession," *Journal of Religion* 63, no. 4 (October 1983): 337–54; Robert Kress, "The Roman Catholic Reception of the Augsburg Confession" *The Sixteenth Century Journal* 11, no. 3 (June 1980): 115–28; and Lewis Spitz, "The Augsburg Confession: 450 Years of History," *The Sixteenth Century Journal* 11, no. 3 (June 1980): 3–9.

28. Seltmann, *Zur Wiedervereinigung*, 96–97.

29. Ibid., 389.

30. Röttscher, *Unionsversuche*, 2, and Bernardina, *Julie von Massow*, 274.

31. Thomas A. Brady Jr., *The Protestant Reformation in German History*, Occasional Paper no. 22 of the German Historical Institute (Washington DC: German Historical Institute, September 1998), 15.

32. Hans-Volker Herntrich, "Ein deutsch-nationaler Freiheitsheld: Wie Martin Luther vor hundert Jahren gefeiert wurde," *Lutherische Monatshefte*, no. 21 (1982): 275.

33. Ibid., 275.

34. In addition to Martin Luther, nineteenth-century Protestant nationalists had also recognized the Swedish solider-king and martyr of the Battle of Lützen, Gustavus Adolphus (1594–1632), as a German-Protestant national hero. See Kevin Cramer, "The Cult of Gustavus Adolphus: Protestant Identity and German Nationalism," in *Protestants, Catholics, and Jews in Germany, 1800–1914*, ed. Helmut Walser Smith (Oxford: Berg, 2001), 97–120, and Kevin Cramer, *The Thirty Years War and German Memory* (Lincoln: University of Nebraska Press, 2007). For other nineteenth-century German national symbols, see George L. Mosse, *The Nationalization of the Masses: Political Symbolism and Mass Movements in Germany from the Napoleonic Wars through he Third Reich* (New York: Howard Fertig, 1975).

35. *Neue preußische Zeitung* (aka *Kreuzzeitung*), no. 256 (November 2, 1883).

36. *Protestantische Kirchenzeitung für das evangelische Deutschland*, no. 29 (July 18, 1883): 642.

37. *Neue preußische Zeitung*, no. 263 (November 10, 1883).

38. *Protestantische Kirchenzeitung für das evangelische Deutschland*, no. 21 (May 23, 1883), 471; ibid., no. 26 (June 27, 1883), 582–83.

39. Ibid., no. 47 (November 21, 1883), 1060.

40. Heinrich von Treitschke, "Luther und die deutsche Nation," *Preußische Jahrbücher* 52 (1883): 470.

41. Ibid., 470.

42. Ibid., 475.

43. Gottfried Maron, "1883—1917—1933—1983: Jubiläen eines Jahrhundert," in *Die ganze Christenheit auf Erden: Martin Luther und seine ökumenische Bedeutung*, ed. Gerhard Müller and Gottfried Seebaß (Göttingen, Germany: Vandenhoeck and Ruprecht, 1993), 190.

44. Hartmut Lehmann, "Das Lutherjubiläum 1883," in *Luthers bleibende Bedeutung*, ed. Jürgen Becker (Husum, Germany: Husum Druck- und Verlagsgruppe, 1983), 110.

45. *Historisch-Politische Blätter*, 119 (1883): 488.

46. *Allgemeine evangelisch-lutherische Kirchenzeitung* (1883): 1090, cited in Hans Düfel, "Das Lutherjubiläum 1883: Ein Beitrag zum Luther- und Reformationsverständnis des 19. Jahrhunderts, seiner geistesgeschichtlichen, theologischen und politischen Voraussetzungen, unter besonder Berücksichtigung des Nationalismus," *Zeitschrift für Kirchengeschichte* 95, no. 1 (1984): 77–78.

47. *Ut omnes unum: auf daß Alle Eins seien*, no. 53 (February 1, 1884), 645.

48. Ibid., 646.

49. Ibid., 645.

50. Ibid., no. 45 (June 1, 1883), 547.

51. Ibid., 547.

52. Ibid.

53. Julie von Massow, *Dorotheen-Körblein: Beiträge zur Reunionsfrage a. d. Zeitschrift "Ut omnes Unum" mit Erlaubnis der Verfasserin*, ed. Josef Beer (Augsburg, Germany: Huttler, 1896), 156–57. On ecumenism as a process of confronting divisive histories, memories, and traditions, see G. R. Evans, "Ecumenical Historical Method," *Journal of Ecumenical Studies* 31, no. 1–2 (Winter–Spring 1994): 93–110.

54. *Ut omnes unum*, no. 53 (February 1, 1884), 646.

55. *Neue Evangelische Kirchenzeitung*, no. 39 (September 29, 1883), 621.

56. Seltmann, *Zur Wiedervereingigung*, 391.

57. Massow, *Dorotheen-Körblein*, 160–62.

58. Bernardina, *Julie von Massow*, 203.

59. Ibid., 203–4.

60. Ibid., 204.

61. Manfred Fleischer, "Lutheran and Catholic Reunionists in the Age of Bismarck," *Church History* 38, no. 1 (March 1969): 55. In a 1919 encyclical to the archbishops of Germany titled *In Hac Tanta*, Pope Benedict XV would also invoke

the memory of St. Boniface as "the perfect herald and the model" of German religious unity and peace. For other instances of the German Catholic veneration of St. Boniface in mid-nineteenth-century Germany, see Sigfried Weichlein, "Die Bonifatiustradition und die Rekonfessionalisierung des deutschen Katholizismus zur Mitte des 19. Jahrunderts," in *Religionskrieg in der Moderne? Renaissance und Rückgang des Konfessionalismus von 1800 bis heute*, ed. Olaf Blaschke (Göttingen, Germany: Vandenhoeck and Ruprecht, 2001).

62. Hans Jörg Urban and Harald Wagner, eds. *Handbuch der Ökumenik* (Paderborn, Germany: Verlag Bonifatius Druckerei, 1985), 319.

63. On the failure of the Kulturkampf, see Ronald J. Ross, *The Failure of Bismarck's Kulturkampf: Catholicism and State Power in Imperial Germany, 1871–1887* (Washington, DC: The Catholic University of America Press, 1998).

5. A Truce within the Walls: The Reformation Anniversaries of 1917

1. On German *Burgfriedenspolitik*, see Susanne Miller, *Burgfrieden und Klassenkampf: Die deutsche Sozialdemokratie im Ersten Weltkrieg* (Düsseldorf: Droste, 1974), and Wolfgang Kruse, *Krieg und nationale Integration: Eine Neuinterpretation des sozialdemokratischen Burgfriedensschlusses 1914/15* (Essen, Germany: Klartext, 1993).

2. Thomas Nipperdey, *Deutsche Geschichte 1866–1918, Erster Band: Arbeitswelt und Bürgergeist* (Munich: C. H. Beck, 1990), 456–57.

3. Margaret Lavinia Anderson, "Interdenominationalism, Clericalism, Pluralism: The *Zentrumsstreit* and the Dilemma of Catholicism in Wilhelmine Germany," *Central European History* 21, no. 4 (December 1998): 350–78.

4. Thomas Nipperdey, *Religion im Umbruch: Deutschland 1870–1918* (Munich: C. H. Beck, 1998), 50.

5. *Verhandlungen des Reichstags* 1 (August 4, 1914): 1–2, cited in Anthony J. Steinhoff, "Christianity and the Creation of Germany," in *The Cambridge History of Christianity: World Christianities, c. 1815–1914*, ed. Sheridan Gilley and Brian Stanley (Cambridge: Cambridge University Press, 2006), 300.

6. Modris Eksteins, *Rites of Spring: The Great War and the Birth of the Modern Age* (New York: Houghton-Mifflin, 1989), 61–62.

7. Gottfried Maron, "Luther 1917: Beobachtungen zur Literatur des 400. Reformationsjubiläums," *Zeitschrift für Kirchengeschichte* 93 (1982): 191–92.

8. Martin Greschat regarded the 1917 Reformation anniversaries as examples of a "questionable symbiosis of politics and theology." As if the Reformation anniversaries of 1817 and 1883 were not sites of memory at which religion, theology, and political culture intersected! Martin Greschat, "Reformationsjubiläum 1917, Exempel einer fragwürdigen Symbiose von Politik und Theologie," *Wissenschaft und Praxis in Kirche und Gesellschaft* 61 (1972): 419–29.

9. Maron, "Luther 1917," 192.

10. Max L. Baeumer, "Lutherfeiern und ihre politische Manipulation," in *Deutsche Feiern*, ed. Reinhold Grimm and Jost Hermand (Wiesbaden: Athenaion, 1977), 56.

11. Karl Schwarzlose, *Zum 400jährigen Gedächtnis der Reformation: Drei Predigten* (Frankfurt a.M.: Knauer, 1917), 20–21.

12. D. A. Lang, *Die Reformation: Festschrift zum 31. Oktober 1917* (Detmold, Germany: Meyer, 1917), 18.

13. *Protestantische Monatschrift* 21 (1917): 71–72.

14. Ibid., 74–75.

15. Friedrich Loofs, "Die Jahrhundertfeier der Reformation an den Universitäten Wittenberg und Halle, 1617, 1717, und 1817," *Zeitschrift des Vereins für Kirchengeschichte in der Provinz Sachsen* 14 (1917): 68.

16. Adolf Deißmann, [untitled], *Evangelische Wochenbriefe*, no. 25/26 (1917), cited in *Der deutsche Protestantismus im Epochenjahr 1917*, ed. Günter Brakelmann (Wittenberg, Germany: Luther-Verlag, 1974), 247.

17. Ibid., 246.

18. Ibid., 249.

19. Erich Marks, *Luther und Deutschland: Eine Reformationsrede im Kriegsjahr 1917* (Leipzig: Meyer, 1917), 36.

20. Ibid., 1–2.

21. Martin Peters and Karl Henninger, *Hannoversches Reformationsbüchlein: Festgabe zum vierhundertjährigen Gedenktage der Reformation: 31 Oktober 1917* (Hanover, Germany: Spoonholtz, 1917), 7.

22. Albert Klein, "Zum Reformationsfest 1917," *Preußische Kirchenzeitung* 13, nos. 41–42 (October 14, 1917): 323.

23. Max Senf, *Die Reformationsfeier zu Wittenberg 1917* (Wittenberg, Germany, 1917), 7.

24. Matthew Stibbe, *German Anglophobia and the Great War, 1914–1918* (Cambridge: Cambridge University Press, 2001).

25. *Deutsch-Evangelische Korrespondenzblatt*, 13 (March 30, 1916).

26. Georg Arndt, *Gegenreformation einst und heute: Heft 11; Deutsche Reformation, Deutsche Protesantismus, Deutsche Kultur in katholischer Beleuchtung* (Berlin: Säemann, 1933), 19–20.

27. Hartmann Grisar, "Die Literatur des Lutherjubiläums 1917, ein Bild des heutigen Protestantismus," *Zeitschrift für katholische Theologie* 42 (1918): 810.

28. Leonard J. Swidler, *The Ecumenical Vanguard: The History of the Una Sancta Movement* (Pittsburgh: Duquesne University Press, 1966), 74–75.

29. Bernard E. Meland, "The Modern Liturgical Movement in Germany," *Journal of Religion* 11, no. 4 (October 1931): 522–23.

30. Brady, *The Protestant Reformation in German History*, 16.

31. For the use and abuse of Luther's memory during the Weimar period and the *Hilterzeit* and in the German Democratic Republic and the Federal Republic of Germany, see, inter alia, Gérald Chaix "Die Reformation," trans. Reinhard Tiffert, in *Deutsche Erinnerungsorte*, ed. Etienne François and Hagen Schluze, vol. 2 (Munich: C. H. Beck, 2001); Heiko Obermann, "The Nationalist Conscription of Martin Luther," in *The Impact of the Reformation: Essays*, by Heiko Obermann (Grand Rapids, MI: W. B. Eerdman's Co., 1994), 69–78; Horst Zilleßen, ed., *Volk, Nation, Vaterland: Der deutsche Protestantismus und der Nationalismus* (Gütersloh, Germany: G. Mohn, 1970); and Max L. Baeumer, "Lutherfeiern und ihre politische Manipulation," in *Deutsche Feiern*, ed. Reinhold Grimm and Jost Hermand (Wiesbaden: Athenaion, 1977).

Conclusion

1. Hagen Schulze, *The Course of German Nationalism: From Frederick the Great to Bismarck, 1763–1867*, trans. Sarah Hanbury-Tenison (Cambridge: Cambridge University Press, 1991), 2.

BIBLIOGRAPHY

Periodicals

AP	*Augsburger Postzeitung*, 1861
DEK	*Deutsch-Evangelische Korrespondenzblatt*, 1916
EW	*Evangelishe Wochenbriefe*, 1917
HPB	*Historisch-Politische Blätter*, 1883
NEK	*Neue Evangelische Kirchenzeitung*, 1871
NPZ	*Neue preußische Zeitung*, 1861, 1883
PJ	*Preußische Jahrbücher*, 1883
PK	*Protestantische Kirchenzeitung für das evangelische Deutschland*, 1883
PM	*Protestantische Monatschrift*, 1917
PreK	*Preußische Kirchenzeitung*, 1917
SB	*Sonntags-Blätt*, 1850
UOU	*Ut omnes unum: auf daß Alle Eins seien*, 1879, 1883–1884, 1900
ZKT	*Zeitschrift für katholische Theologie*, 1918
ZFG	*Zeitung für freie Gemeinden: Materialien zur Geschichte und Fortbildung der freien Gemeinden*, 1851

Primary Sources

Andreson, A. *Luther Revived: or, a Short Account of Johannes Ronge, the Bold Reformer of the Catholic Church in Germany*. London: Chapman, 1845.

Anonymous. *Der Streit über Gemischte Ehen und das Kirchenhoheitsrecht im Großherzogthum Baden*. Karlsruhe: G. Braun, 1847.

An anonymous Catholic. *D. Martin Luthers Verdienste um die katholische Kirche in Teutschland*. Erlangen, Germany, 1818.

John Ronge, the Holy Coat of Treves, and the New German-Catholic Church. New York: Harper, 1845.

Arndt, Georg. *Das Reformationsjubelfest in vergangenen Jahrhunderten*. Berlin: Evangelical Federation, 1917.

Bernardina, Maria. *Julie von Massow, geborene von Behr ein Konvertitenbild aus dem 19. Jahrhundert nach authentischen Quellen dargest.* Freiburg, Germany: Herder, 1902.

Bismarck, Otto von. *Bismarck: The Man and the Statesman*. Translated by A. J. Butler. New York: Harper, 1899.

Blum, Robert, and Franz Wigard, eds. *Die erste allgemeine Kirchenversammlung der deutsch-katholischen Kirche*. Leipzig: Robert Friese, 1845.

Bretschneider, Karl Gottlieb. *Aphorismen über die Union der beiden evanglischen Kirchen in Deutschland, ihre gemeinschaftliche Abendmahlsfeier, und den Unterschied ihrer Lehre*. Gotha: Justus Perthes, 1819.

Carrington, James W. *The German Reformation of the Nineteenth Century: A Sketch of the Rise, Progress, and Present Position of Those Who Have Recently Separated Themselves from the Church of Rome*. London: John Snow, 1846.

Clarus, E. A. *Erinnerung an die dritte Säcularfeier des Reformationsfestes in der evangelischen Stadtkirche zu Bamberg*. Bamberg: E. F. Kunz, 1817.

Clarus, Ludwig [Wilhelm Volk]. *Die Zusammenkunft gläubiger Protestanten und Katholiken zu Erfurt im Herbste 1860 und deren Verlauf*. Paderborn: Junfermann, 1867.

[Dittmar, Wilhelm?]. *Pax vobiscum! Die kirchliche Wiedervereinigung der Katholiken und Protestanten, historisch-pragmatisch beleuchtet von einem Protestanten*. Bamberg: 1863.

Döllinger, Johann Joseph Ignaz von. *The Church and the Churches; or the Papacy and the Temporal Power: An Historical and Political Review*. Translated by William Bernard MacCabe. London: Hurst and Blackett, 1862.

———. *Lectures on the Reunion of the Churches*. Translated by Henry Nutcombe Oxenham. New York: Putt and Young, 1872.

Friederich, Gerhard, ed. *Chronik der dritten Jubelfeier der Reformation in Frankfurt am Main*. Frankfurt am Main: Sauerländer, 1817.

Gerlach, Jakob von, ed. *Ernst Ludwig von Gerlach: Aufzeichnungen aus seinem Leben und Wirken, 1795–1877*. Schwerin, Germany: Bahn, 1903.

Gervinus, Georg Gottfried. *The Mission of the German Catholics*. Translated by anonymous. London: Chapman Brothers, 1846.

Grisar, Hartmann. "Die Literatur des Lutherjubiläums 1917, ein Bild des heutigen Protestantismus." *Zeitschrift für katholische Theologie* 42 (1918): 591–628, 785–814.

Hasse, Hermann. *Grundlinien christlicher Irenik: Aufruf und Beitrag zum Frieden unter den christlichen Confessionen und Nationen*. Leipzig: J. Lehmann, 1882.

Hecker, Friedrich. *Die staatsrechtlichen Verhältnisse der Deutschkatholiken mit besonderem Hinblick auf Baden*. Heidelberg: Julius Groos, 1845.

Hering, Carl Wilhelm. *Geschichte der kirchlichen Unions-Versuche seit der Reformation bis auf unsere Zeit*. Leipzig: Fleischer, 1836–1838.

Johannes. *Die Neue Reformation oder die deutsch-katholische Bewegung*. Leipzig: Naumburg, 1845.

Kampe, Ferdinand. *Geschichte der religiösen Bewegung der neuern Zeit. Vierter Band: Geschichte des Deutschkatholicismus und freien Protestantismus in Deutschland und Nordamerika von 1848–1858*. Leipzig: Franz Wagner, 1860.

Kampe, Friedrich Ferdinand. *Das Wesen des Deutschkatholicismus, mit besonder Rücksicht auf sein Verhältnis zur Politik*. Tübingen: Fues, 1850.

Kayser, G. H. *Wie feyern wir Luthern und die Reformation am Stiftungstage der letzern am Würdigsten?*. Augsburg: August Bäumer, 1817.

Keyser, Friedrich, ed. *Reformations-Almanach für Luthers Verehrer auf das evangelische Jubeljahr 1817*. Erfurt: Keyser, 1817.

Kieser, D. G. *Das Wartburgfest am 18. October 1817: In seiner Entstehung, Ausführung und Folgen*. Jena: Frommann, 1818.

Krafft, Karl Georg. *Kirchliche Wiedervereinigung: Versuch einer zeitgemass popularen Darstellung des zwischen Katholiken und Protestanten obwaltenden Glaubensunterschiedes*. Mainz: Kupferberg, 1871.

———. *Zwölf Thesen behufs einer möglichen Kirchlichen Wiedervereinigung in Deutschland von Karl Georg Krafft*. Neuberg: Prechter, 1874.

———. *Zwölf weitere Thesen zur Herbeiführung einer wirklichen kirchlichen Wiedervereinigung von Karl Georg Krafft*. Neuberg: Prechter, 1874.

Laing, Samuel. *Notes on the Rise, Progress, and Prospects of the Schism from the Church of Rome, Called the German-Catholic Church*. London: Longman, 1846.

Lang, D. A. *Die Reformation: Festschrift zum 31. Oktober 1917.* Detmold, Germany: Meyer, 1917.

Leo, Heinrich. *Lehrbuch der Universalgeschichte.* Vol. 3. Halle: Eduard Anton, 1853.

Loofs, Friedrich. "Die Jahrhundertfeier der Reformation an den Universitäten Wittenberg und Halle, 1617, 1717, und 1817." *Zeitschrift des Vereins für Kirchengeschichte in der Provinz Sachsen* 14 (1917): 1–68.

Marks, Erich. *Luther und Deutschland: Eine Reformationsrede im Kriegsjahr 1917.* Leipzig: Meyer, 1917.

Massow, Julie von. *Dorotheen-Körblein: Beiträge zur Reunionsfrage a. d. Zeitschrift; Ut omnes Unum mit Erlaubnis der Verfasserin herausgegeben von Josef Beer.* Augsburg, Germany, 1896.

Nitzsch, Carl Immanuel. *Urkundenbuch der Evangelischen Union mit Erläuterungen.* Bonn: Adolph Marcus, 1853.

Opitz, Hermann. *Ein Wort zum Frieden in dem confessionellen Kampf der Gegenwart.* Frankfurt, 1894,.

Perthes, Clemens Theodor. *Life and Times of Friedrich Perthes: Patriot and Man of Business.* London: William P. Nimmo, 1858.

Peters, Martin, and Karl Henninger. *Hannoversches Reformationsbüchlein: Festgabe zum vierhundertjährigen Gedenktage der Reformation; 31 Oktober 1917.* Hanover: Spoonholtz, 1917.

Planck, Jacob Gottlieb. *Über die Trennung und Wiedervereinigung der getrennten christlichen Haupt-Partheyen.* Tübingen: Cotta, 1803.

Prechtl, Maximilian. *Seitenstück zur Weisheit Dr. Martin Luthers zum Jubeljahre der Lutherischen Reformation.* Sulzbach: J. C. Seidel, 1817.

Ronge, Johannes. *An meine Glaubensgenossen und Mitbürger.* Altenburg: 1845.

———. *Ein Wort der Verständigung über die deutsche Volkskirche als die höhere nationale Einheit von Protestantismus und Katholizismus.* Stuttgart: Sonnewald, 1845.

———. *John Ronge, the Holy Coat of Treves, and the New German-Catholic Church.* New York: Harper, 1845.

———. *Rede, gehalten am 23. September 1845 in der Münsterkirche zu Ulm.* Ulm: Ernst Nübling, 1845.

———. *The Reformation of the Nineteenth Century.* London: E. Deutsch and Company, 1852.

———. *Religion und Politik.* Frankfurt: Rütten, 1850.

———. *Vindication of John Ronge: The Luther of the 19th Century*. Translated by Robert Taylor. London: William E. Painter, 1845.

Röttscher, Adolph. *Unionsversuche zwischen Katholiken und Protestanten Deutschlands*. Frankfurt: Foesser, 1886.

Sack, Friedrich Samuel Gottfried. *Ueber die Vereinigung der beiden protestantischen Kirchenparteien in der Preußischen Monarchie*. Berlin: Friedrich Maurer, 1812.

Schmidt, L. F. *Zwey Predigten am Säkularfeste der Kirchenreformation*. Munich: J. G. J. Seybold, 1817.

Scholl, Carl. *Die freien religiösen Gemeinden und die Social-Demokratie: E. Wort zum Frieden*. Heidelberg, 1877.

———. *Drei Vorträge gehalten vor der deutschkatholischen Gemeinde Mannheim, zugleich also Rechtfertigung meines Anschlusses*. Darmstadt: Pabst, 1846.

Schreiber, Christian, Valentin Karl Veillodter, and William Hennings, eds. *Allgemeine Chronik der dritten Jubel-Feier der deutschen evangelischen Kirche: Im Jahre 1817*. Erfurt: Hennings, 1819.

Schubert, E. *Die deutsch- evangelischen Einheitsbestrebungen vom Beginn des. 19. Jahrhunderts bis zur Gegenwart*. Berlin: Evangelischen Bundes, 1919.

Schulze, Friedrich Wilhelm. *Über romanisierende Tendenzen, ein Wort zum Frieden*. Berlin, 1870.

Schwarzlose, Karl. *Zum 400jährigen Gedächtnis der Reformation: Drei Predigten*. Frankfurt a.M.: Knauer, 1917.

Seltmann, Carl. *Kritiken und Neues zur Wiedervereinigung*. Breslau, Germany: Aderholz, 1906.

———. *Zur Wiedervereinigung der getrennten Christen: Zunächst in deutschen Landen*. Breslau, Germany: Aderholz, 1903.

Senf, Max. *Die Reformationsfeier zu Wittenberg 1917*. Wittenberg, Germany, 1918.

Stahl, Friedrich Julius. *What Is the Revolution? With The Reformation and the Revolution*. Translated by Timothy David Taylor. State College, PA: Blenheim, 1977.

Struve, Gustav von. *Politisches Taschenbuch für das deutsche Volk*. Frankfurt a.M.: Rütten, 1846.

Thiel, Heinrich. *Der Inhalt des Deutsch-Katholizismus: Den denkenden Deutsch-Katholiken gewidmet*. Dessau: Neubürger, 1846.

Treitschke, Heinrich von. "Luther und die deutsche Nation." *Preußische Jahrbücher* 52 (1883): 469–86.

Uhlich, Leberecht. *Hier stehe ich, ich kann nicht anders.* Magdeburg: Creutz, 1845.

———. *Leberecht Uhlich in Magdeburg: Sein Leben von ihm selbst beschrieben.* 2nd ed. Gera, Germany: Paul Strebel, 1872.

———. *The Protestant Friends: A Circular Addressed to Christians throughout Germany.* Translated by Gustav Clemens Hebbe. New York: Charles Muller, 1846.

Veillodter, Valentin Karl. *Zwei Predigten am dritten Säkularfeste der Reformation im Jahre 1817.* Nuremberg: Riegel and Wießner, 1817.

Secondary Sources

Aaslestad, Katherine B. *Place and Politics: Local Identity, Civic Culture, and German Nationalism in North Germany during the Revolutionary Era.* Leiden: Brill, 2005.

Altgeld, Wolfgang. *Katholizismus, Protestantismus, Judentum: Über religiös begründete Gegensätze und nationalreligiöse Ideen in der Geschichte des deutschen Nationalismus.* Mainz, Germany: Matthias-Grünewald, 1992.

Anderson, Benedict. *Imagined Communities: Reflections on the Origin and Spread of Nationalism.* Rev. ed. London: Verso, 1991.

Anderson, Margaret Lavinia. "Interdenominationalism, Clericalism, Pluralism: The *Zentrumsstreit* and the Dilemma of Catholicism in Wilhelmine Germany." *Central European History* 21, no. 4 (1990): 350–78.

———. "The Kulturkampf and the Course of German History." *Central European History* 19, no. 1 (1986): 82–115.

———. "The Limits of Secularization: On the Problem of the Catholic Revival in Nineteenth-Century Germany." *Historical Journal* 38, no. 3 (1995): 647–70.

———. "Piety and Politics: Recent Work in German Catholicism." *Journal of Modern History* 63, no. 4 (December 1991): 681–716.

———. *Windthorst: A Political Biography.* Oxford: Oxford University Press, 1981.

Applegate, Celia. *A Nation of Provincials: The German Idea of Heimat.* Berkeley: University of California Press, 1990.

Assmann, Aleida. *Erinnerungsräume: Formen und Wandlungen des kulterellen Gedächtnis*. Munich: C. H. Beck, 1999.

———. *Religion and Cultural Memory: Ten Studies*. Translated by Rodney Livingstone. Stanford, CA: Stanford University Press, 2006.

———. "Texts, Traces, Trash: The Changing Media of Cultural Identity." *Representations* 56 (Autumn 1996): 123–34.

———, and John Czaplicka. "Collective Memory and Cultural Identity." *New German Critique* 65 (Spring–Summer 1995): 125–33.

Aston, Nigel. *Christianity and Revolutionary Europe c. 1750–1830*. Cambridge: Cambridge University Press, 2002.

Avraham, Doron. "The Social and Religious Meaning of Nationalism: The Case of Prussian Conservatism, 1815–1871." *European History Quarterly*, no. 38 (2008): 525–50.

Bahn, Peter. "Deutschkatholiken und Freireligiöse: Geschichte und Kultur einer religiös-weltanschaulichen Dissidentgruppe, dargestellt am Beispiel der Pfalz." PhD diss., University of Mainz, 1991.

Becker, Jürgen, ed. *Luthers bleibende Bedeutung*. Husum, Germany: Husum Druck- und Verlagsgesellschaft, 1983.

Belz, Willi. *Friedrich Michelis und seine Bestreitung der Neutscholastik in der Polemik gegen Joseph Kleutigen*. Leiden: Brill, 1978.

Berger, Stefan. *Inventing the Nation: Germany*. London: Arnold, 2004.

———. *The Search for Normality: National Identity and Historical Consciousness in Germany since 1800*. New York: Berghahm Books, 1997.

Bigler, Robert M. *The Politics of German Protestantism: The Rise of the Protestant Church Elite in Prussia, 1815–1848*. Berkeley: University of California Press, 1972.

Blackbourn, David. *The Long Nineteenth Century: A History of Germany 1789–1918*. Oxford: Oxford University Press, 1997.

———, and Geoff Eley. *The Peculiarities of German History: Bourgeois Society and Politics in Nineteenth-Century Germany*. Oxford: Oxford University Press, 1984.

Blanning, Tim. "Napoleon and German Identity." *History Today* 48, no. 4 (April 1998): 37–43.

Blaschke, Olaf. "Das 19. Jahrhundert: Ein Zweites Konfessionelles Zeitalter?" *Geschichte und Gesellschaft* 26 (2000): 38–75.

———, ed. *Konfessionen im Konflikt: Deutschland zwischen 1800 und 1970; ein zweites konfessionelles Zeitalter.* Göttingen, Germany: Vandenhoeck and Ruprecht, 2002.

———, ed. *Religionskrieg in der Moderne? Renaissance und Rückgang des Konfessionalismus von 1800 bis heute.* Göttingen, Germany: Vandenhoeck and Ruprecht, 2001.

———, and Frank-Michael Kuhlemann, eds. *Religion im Kaiserreich: Milieus, Mentalitäten, Krisen.* Gütersloh, Germany: Kaiser, 1996.

Boettcher, Susan R. "Luther Year 2003? Thoughts on an Off-Season Comeback." *Sixteenth Century Journal* 35 (2004): 795–809.

Bornkamm, Heinrich. *Luther im Spiegel der deutschen Geistesgeschichte.* 2nd ed. Göttingen, Germany: Vandenhoeck and Ruprecht, 1970.

Brady, Thomas A. *German Histories in the Age of Reformations, 1400–1650.* Cambridge: Cambridge University Press, 2009.

———. *The Protestant Reformation in German History.* Occasional Paper No. 22 of the German Historical Institute. Washington DC: German Historical Institute, September 1998.

Brakelmann, Günter, ed. *Der deutsche Protestantismus im Epochenjahr 1917.* Wittenberg, Germany: Luther-Verlag, 1974.

Brederlow, Jörn. *"Lichtfreunde" und "Freie Gemeinden": Religiöser Protest und Freiheitsbewegung im Vormärz und in der Revolution von 1848/1849.* Munich: Oldenbourg, 1976.

Breuilly, John. "Nation and Nationalism in Modern German History." *The Historical Journal* 33, no. 3 (1990): 659–75.

Brinks, Jan Herman. "Luther and the German State." *The Heythrop Journal* 39, no. 1 (1998): 1–17.

Brix, Emil, and Hannes Stekl, eds. *Der Kampf um das Gedächtnis: Öffentliche Gedenktage in Mitteleuropa.* Vienna: Böhlau, 1997.

Brose, Eric Dorn. *German History, 1789–1871: From the Holy Roman Empire to the Bismarckian Reich.* Providence, RI: Berghahn Books, 1997.

Butler, Thomas, ed. *Memory: History, Culture, and the Mind.* Oxford: Blackwell, 1989.

Chickering, Roger, ed. *Imperial Germany: A Historiographical Companion.* Westport, CT: Greenwood Press, 1996.

Clark, Christopher. "Confessional Policy and the Limits of State Action: Frederick William III and the Prussian Church Union 1817–1840." *The Historical Journal* 39, no. 4 (December 1996): 985–1004.

———. "The Wars of Liberation in Prussian Memory: Reflections on the Memorialization of War in Early Nineteenth-Century Germany." *Journal of Modern History* 68, no. 3 (September 1996): 550–76

Confino, Alon. "Collective Memory and Cultural History: Problems of Method." *American Historical Review* 102 (December 1997): 1386–1403.

———. *Germany as a Culture of Remembrance: Promises and Limits of Writing History.* Chapel Hill, NC: University of North Carolina Press, 2006.

———. *The Nation as Local Metaphor: Württemberg, Imperial Germany, and National Memory, 1871–1918.* Chapel Hill, NC: University of North Carolina Press, 1997.

———, and Peter Fritzsche, eds. *The Work of Memory: New Directions in the Study of German Society and Culture.* Urbana: University of Illinois Press, 2002.

Connerton, Paul. *How Societies Remember.* Cambridge: Cambridge University Press, 1989.

Conser, Walter H., Jr. *Church and Confession: Conservative Theologians in Germany, England, and America, 1815–1866.* Macon, GA: Mercer University Press, 1984.

Craig, Gordon A. *Germany, 1866–1945.* Oxford: Oxford University Press, 1978.

Cramer, Kevin. *The Thirty Years War and German Memory.* Lincoln, NE: University of Nebraska Press, 2007.

Dann, Otto. "Vereinswesen und bürgerliche Gesellschaft in Deutschland." *Historische Zeitschrift* 9 (1984).

Dickens, A. G., and John M. Tonkin. *The Reformation in Historical Thought.* Cambridge, MA: Harvard University Press, 1985.

Diwald, Hellmut, ed. *Von der Revolution zum Norddeutschen Bund: Politik und Ideengut der preußischen Hochkonservativen; Aus dem Nachlaß von Ernst Ludwig von Gerlach.* Göttingen, Germany: Vandenhoeck and Ruprecht, 1970.

Dixon, C. Scott. *The German Reformation: The Essential Readings.* Oxford: Blackwell, 1999.

Drumond, Andrew Landale. "Church and State in Protestant Germany before 1918: With Special Reference to Prussia." *Church History* 13, no. 3 (September 1944): 210–29.

———. *German Protestantism since Luther.* London: Epworth Press, 1951.

Düding, Dieter, Peter Friedemann, and Paul Münch, eds. *Öffentliche Festkultur: Politische Feste in Deutschland von der Aufklärung bis zum Ersten Weltkrieg.* Hamburg: Rowohl, 1988.

Düfel, Hans. "Das Lutherjubiläum 1883: Ein Beitrag zum Luther- und Reformationsverständnis des 19. Jahrhunderts, seiner geistesgeschichtlichen, theologischen und politischen Voraussetzungen, unter besonder Berücksichtigung des Nationalismus." *Zeitschrift für Kirchengeschichte* 95, no. 1 (1984): 1–94.

Dulles, Avery. "The Catholicity of the Augsburg Confession." *Journal of Religion* 63, no. 4 (October 1983): 337–54.

Eade, J. C., ed. *Romantic Nationalism in Europe.* Canberra: Australian National University, 1983.

Eibach, Joachim, and Marcus Sandl, eds. *Protestantische Identität und Erinnerung: Von der Reformation bis zur Bürgerrechtsbewegung in der DDR.* Göttingen, Germany: Vandenhoeck and Ruprecht, 2003.

Eksteins, Modris. *Rites of Spring: The Great War and the Birth of the Modern Age.* New York: Houghton-Mifflin, 1989.

Elon, Amos. *The Pity of It All: A Portrait of the German-Jewish Epoch, 1743–1933.* New York: Picador, 2003.

Evans, G. R. "Ecumenical Historical Method." *Journal of Ecumenical Studies* 31, nos. 1–2 (Winter–Spring 1994): 93–110.

Fleischer, Manfred. "Lutheran and Catholic Reunionists in the Age of Bismarck." *Church History* 38, no. 1 (March 1969): 43–66.

Fleischer, Manfred P. "*Deus Praesens in Jure*: The Politics of Ludwig von Gerlach." *Zeitschrift für Religions- und Geistesgeschichte* 39 (1987): 1–23.

———. *Katholische und lutherische Ireniker: Unter besonder Berücksichtigung des 19. Jahrhunderts.* Göttingen, Germany: Musterschmidt, 1968.

Fleetham, Deborah Lee. "In the Shadow of Luther: The Reshaping of Protestantism in Berlin, 1817–1848." PhD diss., University of Rochester, 2001.

Forrest, Alan, and Peter H. Wilson, eds. *The Bee and the Eagle: Napoleonic France and the End of the Holy Roman Empire.* Basingstoke, UK: Palgrave Macmillan, 2009.

François, Etienne, and Hagen Schulze, eds. *Deutsche Erinnerungsorte.* Munich: C. H. Beck, 2001.

Führman, Rainer. "Das Reformationsjubiläum 1817: Martin Luther und die Reformation im Urteil der protestantischen Festpredigt des Jahres 1817.".PhD diss., Eberhard Karls University of Tübingen, 1973.

Geis, Lothar, ed. *Freireligiöses Quellenbuch: 1844–1926; Eine Sammlung grundlegender Texte über Inhalt und Ziele Freier Religion.* 2nd ed. Mainz, Germany: Freireligiöse Gemeinde Mainz, 2007.

Geyer, Michael, and Hartmut Lehmann, eds. *Religion und Nation, Nation und Religion: Beiträge zu einer unbewältigten Geschichte.* Göttingen, Germany: Wallstein, 2004.

———, and Lucian Hölscher, eds. *Die Gegenwart Gottes in der modernen Gesellschaft: Transzendenz und Religiöse Vergemeinschaftung in Deutschland.* Göttingen, Germany: Wallstein, 2006.

Gillis, John R. *Commemorations: The Politics of National Identity.* Princeton, NJ: Princeton University Press, 1994.

Goeters, J. F. Gerhard, and Rudolf Mau, eds. *Die Geschichte der Evangelischen Kirche der Union.* Leipzig: Evangelische Verlagsanstalt, 1992.

Graf, Friedrich Wilhelm. *Die Politisierung des religiösen Bewußtseins: Die bürgerlichen Religionsparteien im deutschen Vormärz; Das Beispiel des Deutschkatholizismus.* Stuttgart: Friedrich Frommann, 1978.

———, ed. *Profile des neuzeithlichen Protestantismus: Kaiserreich.* Gütersloh, Germany: Gerd Mohn, 1992.

Green, Abigail. *Fatherlands: State-Building and Nationhood in Nineteenth-Century Germany.* Cambridge: Cambridge University Press, 2001.

Greschat, Martin. "Reformationsjubiläum 1917: Exempel einer fragwürdigen Symbiose von Politik und Theologie." *Wissenschaft und Praxis in Kirche und Gesellschaft* 61 (1972): 419–29.

Grimm, Reinhold, and Jost Hermand, eds. *Deutsche Feiern.* Wiesbaden: Athenaion, 1977.

Gross, Michael B. "Kulturkampf and Unification: German Liberalism and the War against the Jesuits." *Central European History* 30, no. 4 (1997): 545–66.

———. *The War against Catholicism: Liberalism and the Anti-Catholic Imagination in Nineteenth-Century Germany.* Ann Arbor, MI: University of Michigan Press, 2004.

Grossmann, Walter. "Religious Toleration in Germany, 1648–1750." *Studies on Voltaire and the Eighteenth Century*, no. 201 (1982): 115–41.

Hagemann, Karen. *"Männlicher Muth und Teutsche Ehre": Nation, Militär und Geschlecht zur Zeit der Antinapoleonischen Kriege Preussens*. Paderborn, Germany: Schöningh, 2002.

Hagenbach, K. R. *History of the Church in the Eighteenth and Nineteenth Centuries*. Translated by John F. Hurst. New York: Charles Scribner and Co., 1869.

Halborn, Hajo. *A History of Modern Germany, 1648–1840*. Princeton, NJ: Princeton University Press, 1964.

Halbwachs, Maurice. *On Collective Memory*. Translated by Lewis A. Coser. Chicago: University of Chicago Press, 1992. Repr., Paris: Presses Universitaires de France, 1941.

Hammer, Karl. *Deutsche Kriegstheologie (1870–1918)*. Munich: Kösel-Verlag, 1971.

Hannay, Eberhard. "Der Gedanke der Wiedervereinigung der Konfessionen in den Anfängen der konservative Bewegung." PhD diss., Friedrich-Wilhelm University Berlin, 1936.

Harrington, Joel F., and Helmut Walser Smith. "Confessionalization, Community, and State Building in Germany, 1555–1870." *Journal of Modern History* 69, no. 1 (March 1997): 77–101.

Haupt, Heinz-Gerhard, and Dieter Langewiesche, eds. *Nation und Religion in der deutschen Geschichte*. Frankfurt: Campus Verlag, 2001.

Heilbronner, Oded. "From Ghetto to Ghetto: The Place of German Catholic Society in Recent Historiography." *Journal of Modern History* 72, no. 2 (June 2000) 453–95.

Henderson, Carolyn Rebecca. "Heinrich Leo: A Study in German Conservatism." PhD diss., University of Wisconsin-Madison, 1977.

Herntrich, Hans-Volker. "Ein deutsch-nationaler Freiheitsheld: Wie Martin Luther vor hundert Jahren gefeiert wurde." *Lutherische Monatshefte*, no. 21 (1982): 274–76.

Hervieu-Leger, Daniele. *Religion as a Chain of Memory*. Translated by Simon Lee. New Brunswick, NJ: Rutgers University Press, 2000.

Herzog, Dagmar. *Intimacy and Exclusion: Religious Politics in Pre-Revolutionary Baden*. Princeton, NJ: Princeton University Press, 1996.

Hoffman, Chrishard, Werner Bergmann, and Helmut Walser Smith, eds. *Exclusionary Violence: Anti-Semitic Riots in Modern German History*. Ann Arbor: University of Michigan Press, 2002.

Hölscher, Lucian. *Geschichte der protestantischen Frömmigkeit in Deutschland.* Munich: Beck, 2005.

Holzem, Andreas. *Kirchenreform und Sektenstiftung: Deutschkatholiken, Reformkatholiken und Ultramontane am Oberrhein 1844–1866.* Paderborn, Germany: Schöningh, 1994.

Hope, Nicholas. *German and Scandinavian Protestantism, 1700–1918.* Oxford: Oxford University Press, 1999.

Horstmann, Johannes, and Antonius Liedhegener, eds. *Konfession, Milieu, Moderne: Konzeptionelle Positionen und Kontroversen zur Geschichte von Katholizismus und Kirche im 19. und 20. Jahrhundert.* Schwerte, Germany: Katholische Akademie Schwerte, 2001.

Howard, Thomas Albert. "Commentary—A 'Religious Turn' in Modern European Historiography?" *Church History* 75, no. 1 (2006): 157–62.

Huber, Wolfgang, and Johannes Schwerdtfeger, eds. *Kirche zwischen Krieg und Frieden: Studien zur Geschichte des deutschen Protestantismus.* Stuttgart: Ernst Klett, 1976.

Hyde, Simon. "Roman Catholicism and the Prussian State in the Early 1850s." *Central European History* 24, no. 2 (1991): 95–121.

Jarausch, Konrad H., and Michael Geyer. *Shattered Past: Reconstructing German Histories.* Princeton, NJ: Princeton University Press, 2003.

Kann, Robert A. "Friedrich Julius Stahl: A Re-examination of his Conservatism" in *Leo Baeck Institute Yearbook* 12, no. 1 (1967): 55–74

Kantzenbach, Friedrich Wilhelm. *Einheitsbestrebungen im Wandel der Kirchengeschichte.* Gütersloh, Germany: Mohn, 1980.

Katz, Jakob. *Die Hep-Hep-Verfolgungen des Jarhes 1819.* Berlin: Metropol, 1994.

Klueting, Harm, ed. *Irenik und Antikonfessionalismus im 17. und 18. Jahrhundert.* Hildesheim, Germany: Georg Olms, 2003.

Kolbe, Günter. "Demokratische opposition in Religiösem Gewande und Antikirchliche bewegeng im Königreich Sachsen." PhD diss., University of Leipzig, 1964.

Koop, Helmut. *Das Junge Deutschland: Ein Einführung.* Darmstadt, Germany: Wiss. Buchgesellschaft, 1993.

Kraus, Hans-Christof. *Ernst Ludwig von Gerlach: Politisches Denken und Handeln eines pruessischen Altkonservativen.* Göttingen, Germany: Vandenhoeck and Ruprecht, 1994.

Kress, Robert. "The Roman Catholic Reception of the Augsburg Confession." *The Sixteenth Century Journal* 11, no. 3 (June 1980): 115–28.

Krumeich, Gerd, and Hartmut Lehmann, eds. *"Gott mit uns": Nation, Religion, und Gewalt im 19. und frühen 20. Jahrhundert.* Göttingen, Germany: Vandenhoeck and Ruprecht, 2000.

Kruse, Wolfgang. *Krieg und nationale Integration: Eine Neuinterpretation des sozialdemokratischen Burgfriedensschlusses 1914/15.* Essen, Germany: Klartext, 1993.

Kuhlmann, Thomas Stamm. *König in Preußens großer Zeit: Friedrich Wilhelm III. der Melancholiker aud dem Thron.* Berlin: Siedler, 1992.

Landry, Stan M. "That All May be One? Church Unity and the German National Idea, 1866–1883." *Church History* 80, no. 2 (June 2011): 281–301.

Lamberti, Marjorie. "Lutheran Orthodoxy and the Beginning of Conservative Party Organization in Prussia." *Church History* 37, no. 4 (December 1968): 439–53.

Laube, Stefan. *Das Lutherhaus Wittenberg: Eine Museumgeschichte von Stefan Laube.* Leipzig: Evangelische Verlagsanstalt, 2003.

———. *Fest, Religion, und Erinnerung: konfessionalles Gedächtnis in Bayern von 1804 bis 1917.* Leipzig: Evangelische Verlagsanstalt, 1999.

———, and Karl-Heinz Fix, eds. *Lutherinzenierung und Reformationserinnerung.* Leipzig: Evangelische Verlagsanstalt, 2002.

Leesch, Wolfgang. *Die Geschicte des Deutschkatholizismus in Schlesien (1844–1852), unter besonderer Berücksichtigung seiner politischen Haltung.* Breslau, Germany: Priebatsch, 1938.

LeGoff, Jacques. *History and Memory.* Translated by Steven Rendall and Elizabeth Claman. New York: Columbia University Press, 1992.

Lehmann, Hartmut. "The Germans as Chosen People: Old Testament Themes in German Nationalism." *German Studies Review* 14, no. 2 (May 1991): 261–73.

———. "Martin Luther als deutscher Nationalheld im 19. Jahrhundert." *Luther: Zeitschrift der Luther-Gesellschaft* 55, no. 2 (1984): 53–65.

———. *Martin Luther in the American Imagination.* Munich: W. Fink 1988.

———. "Pietism and Nationalism: The Relationship between Protestant Revivalism and National Renewal in Nineteenth-Century Germany." *Church History* 51, no. 1 (March 1982): 39–53.

Lepsius, Rainer M. "Parteiensystem und Sozialstrukture: Zum Problem der Demokritasierung der deutschen Gesellschaft," in *Wirtschaft, Geschichte und Wirtschaftsgeschichte: Festschrift zum 65. Geburtstag von Friedrich Lutge*, ed. Wilhelm Abel et al., 371–93. Stuttgart: G. Fischer, 1966.

Levinger, Matthew. *Enlightened Nationalism: The Transformation of Prussian Political Culture, 1806–1848*. Oxford: Oxford University Press, 2000.

Liedtke, Rainer, and Stephan Wendehorst, eds. *The Emancipation of Catholics, Jews, and Protestants: Minorities and the Nation-State in Nineteenth-Century Europe*. Manchester, UK: Manchester University Press, 1999.

Lipp, Carola, ed. *Schimpfende Weiber und patriotische Jungfrau: Frauen im Vormärz und in der Revolution 1848/1849*. Moos, Germany: Elster, 1986.

Maltzahn, Christoph Freiherr. *Heinrich Leo (1799–1878): Ein politisches Gelehrtenleben zwischen romantischem Konservatismus und Realpolitik*. Göttingen, Germany: Vandenhoeck and Ruprecht, 1979.

Maron, Gottfried. *Die ganze Christenheit auf Erden: Martin Luther und seine ökumenische Bedeutung*. Edited by Gerhard Müller and Gottfried Seebaß. Göttingen, Germany: Vandenhoeck and Ruprecht, 1993.

———. "Luther 1917: Beobachtungen zur Literature des 400. Reformationsjubiläums." *Zeitschrift fuur Kirchengeschichte* 93 (1982): 177–221.

Martin, Alfred von, ed. *Luther in ökumenischer Sicht*. Stuttgart: Frommanns, 1929.

May, Georg. *Interkonfessionalismus in Bayern in der ersten Hälfte des 19. Jahrhunderts*. Paderborn, Germany: Schöningh, 1969.

McKim, Donald M., ed. *The Cambridge Companion to Martin Luther*. Cambridge: Cambridge University Press, 2003.

McLeod, Hugh, ed. *European Religion in the Age of Great Cities, 1830–1930*. London: Routledge, 1995.

Meding, Wichmann von. "Jubel ohne Glauben? Das Reformationsjubiläum 1817 in Württemburg." *Zeitschrift für Kirchengeschichte* 93, no. 1 (1982): 119–60.

Meding, Wichmann von. *Kirchenverbesserung: Die deutschen Reformationspredigten des Jahre 1817*. Bielefeld, Germany: Luther-Verlag, 1986.

Menge, Gisbert. *Versuche zur Wiedervereinigung Deutschlands im Glauben*. Steyl, Germany: Missionsdruckerei, 1920.

Mergel, Thomas. "Ultramontanism, Liberalism, Moderation: Political Mentalities and Political Behavior of the German Catholic *Bürgertum*, 1848–1914." *Central European History* 29 (1996): 151–74.

———. *Zwischen Klasse und Konfession: Katholisches Bürgertum im Rheinland 1794–1914*. Gottingen, Germany: Vandenhoeck and Ruprecht, 1994.

Meyer, Carl S., ed. *Luther for an Ecumenical Age: Essays in Commemoration of the 450th Anniversary of the Reformation*. St. Louis: Concordia Publishing House, 1967.

Meyer, Michael A. "Alienated Intellectuals in the Camp of Religious Reform: The Frankfurt Reformfreunde, 1842–1845." *Association for Jewish Studies Review* 6 (1981): 61–86.

———, et al. *German-Jewish History in Modern Times: Emancipation and Acculturation, 1780–1871*. New York: Columbia University Press, 1998.

Miller, Susanne. *Burgfrieden und Klassenkampf: Die deutsche Sozialdemokratie im Ersten Weltkrieg*. Düsseldorf: Droste, 1974.

Misztal, Barbara A. *Theories of Social Remembering*. London: Open University Press, 2003.

Mosse, George L. *The Nationalization of the Masses: Political Symbolism and Mass Movements in Germany from the Napoleonic Wars through the Third Reich*. New York: Howard Fertig, 1975.

Mosse, Werner E., ed. *Revolution and Evolution: 1848 in German-Jewish History*. Tübingen, Germany: Mohr Siebeck, 1981.

Na'aman, Shlomo. *Der Deutsche Nationalverein: Die politische Konstituierung des deutschen Bürgertums 1859–1867*. Düsseldorf: Droste Verlag, 1987.

Neuener, Peter. *Döllinger als Theologe der Ökumene: Beiträge zur ökumenischen Theologie*. Padernborn, Germany: Schöningh, 1979.

———, and Gunther Wenz, eds. *Theologen des 19. Jahrhunderts: Eine Einführung*. Darmstadt, Germany: Wissenschaftliche Buchgesellschaft, 2002.

Nicol, Iain G., ed. *Friedrich Schleiermacher on Creeds, Confessions, and Church Union: That They May be One*. Lewiston, NY: Edwin Mellen Press, 2004.

———, ed. *Reformed But Ever Reforming: Sermons in Relation to the Celebration of the Handing Over of the Augsburg Confession (1830).* Lewiston, NY: Edwin Mellen Press, 1997.

Nipperdey, Thomas. "Der Kölner Dom als Nationaldenkmal." *Historische Zeitschrift* 231 (1981): 595–613.

———. *Deutsche Geschichte 1866–1918, Erster Band: Arbeitswelt und Bürgergeist.* Munich: C. H. Beck, 1990.

———. *Deutsche Geschichte 1866–1918, Zweiter Band: Machstaat vor der Demokratie.* Munich: C. H. Beck, 1992.

———. *Germany from Napoleon to Bismarck, 1800–1866.* Translated by Daniel Nolan. Princeton, NJ: Princeton University Press, 1996.

———. *Religion im Umbruch: Deutschland 1870–1918.* Munich: C. H. Beck, 1998.

———, ed. *Gesellschaft, Kultur, Theorie: Gesammelte Aufsätze zur neuren Geschicthe.* Göttingen, Germany: Vandenhoeck and Ruprecht, 1976.

Nischan, Bodo. *Prince, People, and Confession: The Second Reformation in Brandenburg.* Philadelphia: University of Pennsylvania Press, 1994.

Nora, Pierre, ed. *Realms of Memory: Rethinking the French Past.* Translated by Arthur Goldhammer. New York: Columbia University Press, 1996.

Nowak, Kurt. *Geschichte des Christentums in Deutschland: Religion, Politik und Gesellschaft vom Ende der Aufklärung bis zur Mitte des 20. Jahrhunderts.* Munich: C. H. Beck, 1995.

Oberman, Heiko A. *The Impact of the Reformation: Essays.* Grand Rapids, MI: W. B. Eerdman's Co., 1994.

Paletschek, Sylvia. *Frauen und Dissens: Frauen im Deutschkatholizismus und in den freien Gemeinden 1841–1852.* Göttingen, Germany: Vandenhoeck and Ruprecht, 1990.

———. "Religiöse Emanzipation und Frauenemanzipation: Was bedeutet Religionskritik Mitte des 19. Jahrhunderts für Frauen?" *Sozialwissenschaftliche Information* 18, no. 4 (1989): 228–36.

Paret, Peter. *The Cognitive Challenge of War: Prussia 1806.* Princeton, NJ: Princeton University Press, 2009.

Pinson, Koppel S. *Pietism as a Factor in the Rise of German Nationalism.* New York: Columbia University Press, 1934.

Planert, Ute. *Der Mythos vom Befreiungskrieg: Frankreichs Kriege und der deutsche Süden; Alltag, Wahrnehmung, Deutung, 1792–1841.* Paderborn, Germany: Schöningh, 2007.

Po-Chia Hsia, R. *Social Discipline in the Reformation: Central Europe, 1550–1750*. London: Routledge, 1989.

Prelinger, Catherine M. *Charity, Challenge, and Change: Religious Dimensions of the Mid-Nineteenth-Century Women's Movement in Germany*. Westport, CT: Greenwood, 1987.

Prelinger, Catherine Magill Holden. "A Decade of Dissent in Germany: An Historical Study of The Society of Protestant Friends and The German-catholic Church, 1840–1848." PhD diss., Yale University, 1954.

Printy, Michael. *Enlightenment and the Creation of German Catholicism*. Cambridge: Cambridge University Press, 2011.

Pyclik, Hans Peter. *Friedrich Julius Stahl: A Study of the Development of German Conservative Thought, 1802–1861*. Minneapolis: University of Minnesota, 1972.

Raab, Heribert. "'Ad reuniendos dissidents': Zur Geschichte der kirchlichen Reunionsbestrebungen im ausgehenden 18. und im beginnenden 19. Jahrhundert." *Jahrbuch für das Bistum Mainz* 8 (1960): 128–47.

Real, Willy. *Der Deutsche Reformverein: Grossdeutsche Stimmen und Kräfte zwischen Villafranca und Königgrätz*. Lübeck, Germany: Matthiesen, 1966.

Reardon, Bernard M. G. *Religion in the Age of Romanticism: Studies in Early Nineteenth Century Thought*. Cambridge: Cambridge University Press, 1985.

Reinhard, Wolfgang. "Gegenreformation als Modernisierung? Prolegomena zu einer Theorie des konfessionellen Zeitalters." *Archiv für Reformationsgeschichte* 68 (1977): 226–52.

Roensch, Manfred, and Werner Klän, eds. *Quellen zur Entstehung und Entwicklung selbständiger evangelisch-lutherischer Kirchen in Deutschland*. Frankfurt am Main: Peter Lang, 1987.

Ross, Ronald J. *The Failure of Bismarck's Kulturkampf: Catholicism and State Power in Imperial Germany, 1871–1887*. Washington, DC: The Catholic University of America Press, 1998.

Rouse, Ruth, and Stephen Charles Neill, eds. *A History of the Ecumenical Movement, 1517–1948*. 2nd ed. Philadelphia: Westminster Press, 1967.

Rowe, Michael. *From Reich to State: The Rhineland in the Revolutionary Age, 1780–1830*. Cambridge: Cambridge University Press, 2003.

Ruhbach, Gerhard, ed. *Kirchenunionen im 19. Jahrhundert*. Guterslöh, Germany: Gerd Mohn, 1967.

Saage-Maaß, Miriam. *Die Göttinger Sieben-demokratische Vorkämpfer oder nationale Helden? Zum Verhältnis von Geschictsschreibung und Erinnerungskultur in der Rezeption des Hannoverischen Verfassungskonfliktes.* Göttingen, Germany: Vandenhoeck and Ruprecht, 2007.

Schieder, Wolfgang. "Kirche und Revolution: Sozialgeschichtliche Aspekte der Trier Wallfahrt von 1844." *Archiv fur Sozialgeschichte* 14 (1974): 419–54.

Schilling, Heinz. "Alternatives to the Lutheran Reformation and the Rise of Lutheran Identity." In *Germania Illustria: Essays on Early Modern Germany Presented to Gerald Strauss*, eds. Andrew C. Fix and Susan C. Karant-Nunn, 99–120. Kirksville, MO: Sixteenth-Century Journal Publishers, 1992.

———. *Konfessionalkonflikt und Staatsbildung: Eine Fallstudie über das Verhältnis von religiosem und sozialem Wandel in der Frühenzeit am Beispiel der Grafschaft Lippe.* Gütersloh, Germany: Mohn, 1981.

Schmid, Harald, and Justyna Krzymianowska, eds. *Politische Erinnerung: Geschichte und kollektive Identität.* Würzburg, Germany: Königshausen and Neumann, 2007.

Schnabel, Franz. *Deutsche Geschichte im neunzehnten Jahrhundert: Bd. 4; Die religiösen Kräfte.* 3rd ed. Freiburg, Germany: Herder, 1955.

———. *Deutschlands geschichtliche Quellen und Darstellungen in der Neuzeit: Das Zeitalter der Reformation 1500–1550.* Leipzig: Teubner, 1931.

Schneider, Georg. *50 Jahre freireligiösen Gemeindelebens: Festschrift zur Feier des fünfzigjährigen Bestehens der freireligiösen Gemeinde in Mannheim.* Mannheim, Germany: Mannheimer Aktiendruckerei, 1895.

Schoeps, Hans-Joachim. "CDU vor 75 Jahren: Die sozialpolitischen Bestrebungen des Reichsfreiherrn Friedrich Carl von Fechenbach (1836 bis 1907)." *Zeitschrift für Religious- und Geistesgeschichte* 9 (1957): 266–77.

———. *Das andere Preussen: Konservative Gestalten und Probleme im Zeitalter Friedrich Wilhelms IV.* 3rd ed. Berlin: Haude and Spenersche, 1964.

———. "Die Erfurter Konferenz von 1860 (Zur Geschichte des katholisch-protestantischen Gesprächs)." *Zeitschrift für Religions- und Geistesgeschicthe* 4 (1953): 135–59.

———. "Die lutherische Hochorthodoxie Preussens und der Katholizismus." *Zeitschrift für Religions- und Geistesgeschichte* 4 (1952): 311–37.

Schulin, Ernst. "Luther's Position in German History and Historical Writing." *Australian Journal of Politics and History* 30, no.1 (1984): 85–98.

Schulze, Hagen. *The Course of German Nationalism: From Frederick the Great to Bismarck, 1763–1867*. Translated by Sarah Hanbury-Tenison. Cambridge: Cambridge University Press, 1991.

Schwaiger, Georg, ed. *Zwischen Polemik und Irenik: Untersuchungen zum Verhältnis der Konfessionen im späten 18. Jahrhundert und frühen 19. Jahrhundert*. Göttingen, Germany: Vandenhoeck and Ruprecht, 1977.

Scribner, R. W. "Incombustible Luther: The Image of the Reformer in Early Modern Germany." *Past and Present* 110 (February 1986): 38–68.

———. *Religion and Culture in Germany (1400–1800)*. Edited by Lyndal Roper. Leiden: Brill, 2001.

———, and C. Scott Dixon. *The German Reformation*. 2nd ed. Basingstoke, UK: Palgrave Macmillan, 2003.

Sheehan, James J. *German History, 1770–1866*. Oxford: Oxford University Press, 1989.

Smith, Helmut Walser. *The Continuities of German History: Nation, Religion, and Race across the Long Nineteenth Century*. Cambridge: Cambridge University Press, 2008.

———. *German Nationalism and Religious Conflict: Culture, Ideology, Politics, 1870–1914*. Princeton, NJ: Princeton University Press, 1995.

———, ed. *Protestants, Catholics, and Jews in Germany, 1800–1914*. Oxford: Berg, 2001.

Southard, Robert. *Droysen and the Prussian School of History*. Lexington: University Press of Kentucky, 1995.

Sperber, Jonathan. *The European Revolutions, 1848–1851*. Cambridge: Cambridge University Press, 2005.

———. "Festivals of National Unity in the German Revolution of 1848–1849." *Past and Present*, no. 136 (August 1992): 114–38.

———. *Popular Catholicism in Nineteenth-Century Germany*. Princeton, NJ: Princeton University Press, 1984.

———. *Rhineland Radicals: The Democratic Movement and the Revolution of 1848–1849*. Princeton, NJ: Princeton University Press, 1991.

Spitz, Lewis. "The Augsburg Confession: 450 Years of History." *The Sixteenth Century Journal* 11, no. 3 (June 1980): 3–9.

Stayer, James M. *Martin Luther, German Saviour: German Evangelical Theological Factions and the Interpretation of Luther, 1917–1933.* Montreal: McGill-Queen's University Press, 2000.

Steinhoff, Anthony J. "Christianity and the Creation of Germany." In *The Cambridge History of Christianity: World Christianities, c. 1815–1914*, ed. Sheridan Gilley and Brian Stanley, 282–300. Cambridge: Cambridge University Press, 2006.

Sterling, Elenore O. "Anti-Jewish Riots in Germany in 1819: A Displacement of Social Protest." *Historica Judaica* 12 (October 1950): 105–42.

Stibbe, Matthew. *German Anglophobia and the Great War, 1914–1918.* Cambridge: Cambridge University Press, 2001.

Swidler, Leonard J. *The Ecumenical Vanguard: The History of the Una Sancta Movement.* Pittsburgh: Duquesne University Press, 1966.

Tal, Uriel. *Christians and Jews in Germany: Religion, Politics, and Ideology in the Second Reich, 1870–1914.* Translated by Noah Jonathan Jacobs. Ithaca, NY: Cornell University Press, 1975.

Toews, John Edward. *Hegelianism: The Path toward Dialectical Humanism, 1805–1841.* Cambridge: Cambridge University Press, 1985.

Tracy, James D., ed. *Luther and the Modern State in Germany.* Kirksville, MO: Sixteenth-Century Journal Publishers, 1986.

Tschirn, Gustav. *Zur 60jährigen Geschichte der freireligiösen Bewegung.* Gottesberg, Germany: Hensels, 1904.

Urban, Hans Jörg, and Harald Wagner, eds. *Handbuch der Ökumenik.* Paderborn, Germany: Verlag Bonifatius-Druckerei, 1985.

Vick, Brian E. *Defining Germany: The 1848 Frankfurt Parliamentarians and National Identity.* Cambridge: Cambridge University Press, 2002.

Vierhaus, Rudolf. *Germany in the Age of Absolutism.* Translated by Jonathan B. Knudsen. Cambridge: Cambridge University Press, 1988.

Wallman, Johannes. "The Reception of Luther's Writings on the Jews from the Reformation to the End of the 19th Century." *Lutheran Quarterly* 1 (Spring 1987): 72–97.

Wehler, Hans-Ulrich. *The German Empire 1871–1918.* Translated by Kim Traynor. Oxford: Berg, 1985.

Wiegand, Christian. *Über Friedrich Julius Stahl (1801–1862): Recht, Staat, Kirche.* Paderborn, Germany: Schöningh, 1981.

Williamson, George S. *The Longing for Myth in Germany: Religion and Aesthetic Culture from Herder to Nietzsche*. Chicago: University of Chicago Press, 2004.

———. "A Religious *Sonderweg*? Reflections on the Sacred and the Secular in the Historiography of Modern Germany." *Church History* 75, no. 1 (March 2006): 139–56.

Winckler, Lutz. *Martin Luther als Bürger und Patriot: Das Reformationsjubiläum von 1817 und der politische Protestantismus des Wartburgfestes*. Lübeck, Germany: Mathiesen, 1969.

Windell, George G. *The Catholics and German Unity, 1866–1871*. Minneapolis: University of Minnesota Press, 1954.

Wolter, Hans. "Das Reformations-Jubiläum von 1817 in der Freien Stadt Frankfurt am Main." *Zeitschrift für Kirchengeschichte* 93, no. 1 (1982): 161–76.

Wolter, Maurus. *Der Psalmenfreund: Kurze Betrachtungen zur Morgen: Andacht, vorzuglich fur Mitglieder des "Psalmenbundes" in Auszugen aus den Psalmen-Erklarungen des Erzabts Maurus Wolter, Ord. St. Bened. hrsg. von Julie von Massow*. Augsburg, Germany: M. Huttler, 1916.

Yerushalmi, Yosef Hayim. *Zakhor: Jewish History and Jewish Memory*. Seattle: University of Washington Press, 1982.

Zeeden, E. W. *The Legacy of Luther: Martin Luther and the Reformation in the Estimation of the German Lutherans from Luther's Death to the Beginning of the Age of Goethe*. Translated by Ruth Mary Bethell. London: Hollis and Carter, 1954.

Zilleßen, Horst, ed. *Volk, Nation, Vaterland: Der deutsche Protestantismus und der Nationalismus*. Gütersloh, Germany: G. Mohn, 1970.

INDEX